'As one of our most em   ell
placed to write the definiti   a
thoroughly learned, clear-ey   es

'A considerable achievement [and] a highly readable and thought-
provoking book that deserves to be read by historians,
criminologists and the general public alike' *BBC History magazine*

'A highly readable social history of British policing'
Good Book Guide

'This book, so lively, enjoyable and hugely knowledgeable ...
[that] deserves, and will surely get, a very wide audience indeed'
Times Literary Supplement

'A fascinating history of policing'.   *Guardian*

'Emsley has constructed a fluent narrative from the lives of the
men and women who have served in the police over almost three
hundred years'   *History Book Review*

'In a riveting piece of social history, he traces the evolution of the
police from the watchmen and constables of the 18th century,
right up to the present time, showing the police in their various
guises as figures of fun, hatred, suspicion, admiration and routine
heroism'   *Shotsmag*

The Great British Bobby

A HISTORY OF BRITISH POLICING FROM THE 18th CENTURY TO THE PRESENT

Clive Emsley

Quercus

First published in Great Britain in 2009 by
Quercus
21 Bloomsbury Square
London
WC1A 2NS

First published in paperback in 2010 by Quercus

A CIP catalogue record for this book is available
from the British Library

ISBN 978 1 84916 197 8

Printed and bound in Great Britain by Clays Ltd. St Ives plc
Typeset by Ellipsis Books Limited, Glasgow

Contents

In memory of
Ernest George Emsley (1917–1944)

Acknowledgements

My reason for writing this book will be apparent from the first pages of the introduction. Indeed, perhaps one reason why I have been interested in the history of crime and policing for almost all my academic career is because of a wish to connect with the father that I never knew, except through the stories of my mother and grandparents.

I am indebted to a large number of people for their advice and help over the years that I have trawled through various archives containing material on the police and spoken with former officers, some of whom have allowed me to interview them and use those interviews in my work. As will be seen, those interviews significantly inform the later chapters of what follows. I must also thank Maggie Bird and her colleagues at the Metropolitan Police Historical Collection for giving me a free run of their materials. I have a cluster of excellent colleagues and friends at the Open University or linked with the criminology research centre there, all of whom have always been generous with their time, suggestions, and with sharing their own research. Thanks in this respect to Peter King, Paul Lawrence, Bob Morris, Maureen Scollan, Stef Slater, Terry Waterfield, Jim Whitfield, Chris Williams and John Carter Wood. Paul Lawrence and Bob Morris kindly read the whole of an early draft and provided me with helpful comments. Richard Milbank at Quercus performed a similar onerous task and saved me from a legion of errors and infelicities. Those that remain are mine.

Children – and now grandchildren – never cease to be a distraction and a great opportunity for doing things other than work. I hope that they will enjoy this homage to their grandfather or great-grandfather and those like him who usually have only walk-on parts in history books. Thanks above all to my wife Jenny for her love and support, and for all the times that she has policed the family while I have lurked and shirked in the study.

List of Illustrations

PLATES

Page 6
TOP Cable Street riot, 1936 (Metropolitan Police Historical Collection
BOTTOM Police Group with PC Emsley (Author)

Page 7
TOP LEFT Wartime PC (Metropolitan Police Historical Collection)
TOP RIGHT WPCs in the interwar period (Metropolitan Police Historical
    Collection)
BOTTOM PC Pickering (Author)

Page 8
TOP Brixton Riots, 1981 (Metropolitan Police Historical Collection)
MIDDLE Norwell Roberts newspaper article (Norwell Roberts/*The Sun*)
BOTTOM Police with children (Metropolitan Police Historical Collection)

MAP & TABLES

Introduction

AT NIGHTFALL ON 22 April 1944 Sergeant Air Gunner Ernest 'Ernie' Emsley climbed on board a Lancaster bomber for his first operational raid over occupied Europe. Before him he could expect several hours of cold, dark and certain danger. Ernie was used to long shifts of night-time work. It was only ten months since, with hundreds of his fellows, he had transferred from the Metropolitan Police and joined RAF Bomber Command. Police officers in the 1930s and 1940s, like their forebears for the previous hundred years, had patrolled regular night-time beats in all weathers. The constant roar of a Lancaster's four Rolls-Royce Merlin engines, however, was very different from the usual silence of a night-time beat. And the hours of danger ahead were very different from the occasional adrenalin rush of confronting the violent or the unexpected on a dark London street.

Ernie was born in Battersea in January 1917. His father, a sailor, died in 1919 of wounds received during the First World War; his stepfather, Harry Jordan, was a market policeman in the City of London. Ernie left school aged 14 and for a few years worked as a clerk. He decided to go one better than Harry and on 12 October 1936, three months before his twentieth birthday, he joined the Metropolitan Police. After his initial training in Hendon he was posted to 'P' Division in south-east London. Ernie was never going to rise to the top of the police. He was a bit too much of a Jack-the-Lad. Shortly after joining he was suspended, without pay, for ten days; the reasons for this are not recorded in police orders or on his personnel file, though his wife, whom he married a few years later, always believed that he had been late for parade one morning because his landlady had failed to wake him.

Ernie was said to have known all the dodges. He knew where, while on his beat at night, he might snatch a few hours' sleep in one of the sports pavilions in his division. He knew how to use police connections to get free tickets for West End shows; in particular he loved the Crazy Gang – Flanagan and Allen, Nervo and Knox, Naughton and Gold – well-known for their seaside postcard jokes, slapstick and sentimental songs. He was an able sportsman; he won medals in the Metropolitan Police Divisional Cricket League and with the South East London Thursday Football League. He was a good dancer and he had met his wife Evelyn Ings, the daughter of a City of London carman, at a dance some months before he joined the police. He passed his exams as a Second Class Constable in August 1939 just a few weeks after getting married. In December 1942 he failed the exam for promotion to sergeant, possibly because he was keen to get into the services to do his bit. Or perhaps it was this failure that determined him to volunteer for the RAF as soon as the opportunity arrived.

Ernie's first operational flight ended in disaster. His body was one of two picked up in the North Sea; the other five crewmen of his Lancaster vanished with their aircraft. Three months after his death, his wife gave birth to their only child, a boy. As Ernie had wished, I was named Clive, after Clive Road, West Dulwich, where Ernie and Evelyn had their flat.

The police look after their own. In addition to her pension Evelyn received an allowance for me from the City of London and Metropolitan Police Orphanage. I also received an annual Christmas Box from 'P' Division and regular visits from a local inspector to see how I was doing at school. The visits stopped only when I went to university.

For around thirty years now, as a historian, my research has focused on crime and policing. Perhaps this is the result of a desire to know more of the father that I never met. But then policemen also play an important and prominent role in our society. They deserve a proper understanding of what they have done and what they do now. The British Bobby has been a witness to history and very often at the centre of it. But his collective experience is little known, and while most histories name commissioners, chief constables and occasionally an individual, low-ranking officer who has stood out for some reason, few focus in any detail on the lives of the ordinary Bobby, on his day-to-day duties and experiences. The aim of what follows it to help fill this gap with a kind of collective biography of the ordinary police officer.

The archetypal 'Bobby' remains PC George Dixon, a character created for the 1950 feature film *The Blue Lamp* and resurrected for *Dixon of Dock Green*, a television series which ran from 1955 to 1976. The television Dixon was an avuncular figure who usually persuaded offenders to 'come quietly' and who, at the end of each programme, cheerfully dispensed a simple common-sense moral from the week's story to his prime-time, Saturday-night audience. His enduring appeal was re-emphasized in the summer of 2005 when the BBC adapted some of the early television scripts for a new radio series. But while Dixon remains the model beat Bobby, the modern TV and film drama is fascinated by 'maverick' police officers – tough, cynical rule-breakers who always get their man, but usually after wielding a fist or a gun.

Alongside the contemporary portrayal of the tough, no-nonsense police officer, there are calls by politicians, by the mass media and by members of the public, for more Bobbies on the beat. There is an assumption that the greater presence of this British institution on the streets will reduce both rising crime and a growing disrespect for authority. But when contemporaries call for more policemen on the beat today, the question is rarely posed as to what they suppose Bobbies really did in the past, and what, precisely, they would have them do now, especially in a society that has changed considerably since Jack Warner first wore the uniform of his character, George Dixon.

The name 'Bobby' comes from Sir Robert Peel who, as Home Secretary, oversaw the creation of the Metropolitan Police in 1829. 'Bobby', at times, might also be called a 'Peeler', though that term never became quite as popular in England as in Ireland, where, as Chief Secretary, Peel had earlier been behind the creation of another police institution. Many police forces have slang names – *flic* and *cogne* in France, *Bulle* in Germany, *sbirro* in Italy. Often these are far from complimentary, but then among some sections of the Victorian working class a Bobby was also known as a 'crusher', which might readily be translated as *cogne* or *Bulle*. At the beginning he was also a 'Jenny Darby', a corruption of *gendarme* and an indication of the belief that uniformed policemen were somehow un-English or, worst of all in the wake of the Napoleonic Wars, something French. Other labels were imported, the most notable from the United States, such as 'cop' or 'copper', after the metal badge worn by the first New York officers; and in the 1960s student activists copied their North American counterparts by using 'fuzz' and 'pig' – though the latter seems also to have been used in nineteenth-century England and even earlier. But 'Bobby' fitted best with the way that Victorian, Edwardian and inter-war Britain viewed the men who served in what was often claimed as 'the best police in the world'; and in contemporary Britain 'Bobby' resounds with the appeal of what seems to be a long-lost golden age.

In spite of his position as a national institution and his appeal as a solution to present-day concerns about law and order, the social history of the Bobby has rarely been explored. Yet his story (and since the beginning of the twentieth century it is also *her* story) is as important and significant as that of his military cousin, Tommy Atkins. Bobby served on the front line of what is often characterized as 'the war against crime'. He may rarely have fought in pitched battles and almost never with lethal weapons, but his working life could be hard and dangerous. Up until the last third of the twentieth century he usually patrolled on foot, in all weathers by day and, more often, by night. The drudgery of the foot patrol fostered that other nickname, 'Mr Plod'; something that may, or may not, have passed Enid Blyton by when she chose the name for the policeman of Noddy's Toytown.

In addition to the hard life of patrolling on foot in all weathers, the Victorian Bobby's superiors imposed tough military-style discipline, and he faced regular threats to life and limb from those among whom he worked, particularly in rough, working-class areas. In such districts the men appointed to the beats were often chosen for being as tough as the toughest 'hard men' in the area; these Bobbies earned respect with their fists, often getting their retaliation in first. In some of the most notorious districts during the Victorian period they also patrolled in pairs and were armed with cutlasses. Deployment to rough beats was sometimes used as a punishment for any constable who had committed a serious breach of discipline or offended a senior officer. A man might also be posted to such a beat when it was considered that he was simply not up to the job and in need of some encouragement to resign.

Although, until the late twentieth century, the Bobby was recruited from the unskilled working class, he was expected to behave like the skilled and respectable. He usually joined up as a single man and, in the big cities, he often spent his first years living in a section house, also known as 'barracks' in spite of constant concerns about military traits creeping into the police. When there was no space, or when there was no section house at all, men lived in lodgings. They shared rooms and, sometimes, even beds. Up until the Second World War a Bobby had to get permission to marry and his wife-to-be was vetted for respectability and sobriety just as he had been. His wife was not supposed to take paid work, in case this led to untoward pressures and favouritism. In rural forces where a married man lived in a police house, his wife was also expected to act as his auxiliary. She had to take messages when he was away on patrol and ensure that the building was kept spotless. Like the Bobby, his wife was expected to be a credit to the force and an example to the local working-class community; and a man might be disciplined if his wife ran up debts, created a scandal or otherwise created trouble, since any such behaviour was regarded as besmirching the force. In most working-class families in Victorian and Edwardian Britain it was expected that a wife would also contribute a wage, consequently the restrictions on what a policeman's wife could do usually meant a very tight family budget. However, there were perks: there was the free uniform and the boot allowance which significantly reduced clothing bills; sometimes there was subsidized accommodation or an allowance towards it; sometimes there was help with medical bills; and the police was one of the first working-class occupations to offer some sort of pension. Moreover, if police pay was never high, at least it was regular, unlike much industrial work, and not subject to fluctuations in the economy.

The period covered by this book saw massive economic, social and political change in Britain. The economy had been increasingly capitalist since at least the early seventeenth century. But in the eighteenth century economic change took a sharp new turn with the growth of factory labour and an increasing shift to urban work and urban living. By the middle of the nineteenth century a majority of the population lived in cities and towns, and agriculture had lost its position as the dominant employment sector. Work became regulated by the clock rather than by the seasons. Alongside this came massive technological change. Railways and later motor transport greatly facilitated movement of goods and people, to and from work, up and down the country for business and for pleasure. The time and opportunity for leisure activities changed and expanded. Ordinary people began to make day excursions, and then to take a week's holiday. Many leisure activities also became confined and controlled within strictly limited space such as the football stadium, the music hall and the cinema. There was a gradual growth in democratic politics and, at an even slower rate, recognition of a need to acknowledge gender and ethnic equality. These political developments were sometimes punctuated by violence; and the rough and tumble of the hustings, and of political meetings more generally, continued well into the twentieth century. Police officers were caught up in all of these changes to varying degrees, and the involvement of the Bobby in such developments influenced, sometimes momentarily, sometimes over a much longer period, his relations with the public or at least with certain sections of the public.

A broader, and generally less tangible process in British society over the period has been the shift away from local communities that were, in many respects, flexible, participatory and responsive, to a more centralized, national structure within which participation and response have become regulated through supervised channels. This process has had a considerable impact on the development of policing. The traditional story portrays the Bobby as little more than a citizen in uniform. But the policing institution has shifted gradually, and significantly, from having its primary relationship directly with the local community, to becoming an instrument of the state with, at the beginning of the twenty-first century, targets set and regulated centrally for the good of what politicians and policing professionals consider as the national community.

The concept of a national community within the United Kingdom has become problematic with the embrace of multiculturalism and the appearance of devolved assemblies. Today 'British' is an adjective that refers to national government and institutions but, strictly speaking, there is not, and never has been, a national British police institution. The 'new police' created by Sir Robert Peel in 1829 were restricted to London and they were even excluded from the square mile of the City proper. By the close of the nineteenth century there were over 200 'new police' forces in England and Wales and more than 60 in Scotland, where the police functioned under a different legal structure. The term

'Bobby' was in use in all three countries and there were exchanges in ideas and in personnel between all three. Personnel for these police forces were also drawn from the Royal Irish Constabulary which, in its original form in the early nineteenth century, was closer to the militarized system of the French gendarmerie. While the content of this book strays into Scotland, Wales, Ireland and even parts of the British Empire, the main focus is on Bobbies who have served in English police forces.

Most of the general histories of the English police have tended to be institutional and institutional histories are commonly celebratory and inward-looking. Their authors have generally seen Peel's creation of 1829 as the crucial moment in police history. They have shared an assumption that there was a vision in 1829 of something similar to the modern police and have usually portrayed change as the result of reforms and improvements to solve problems and iron out minor abuses and difficulties on the way to the present. The contemporary institution described in such histories, while not perfect, has been consistently described as fit for purpose and celebrated as among the best, if not the best of its kind. The institutional reforms were explained as the work of sensible politicians and administrators with a clear eye and a clear vision. The arguments of the men who established the police have been taken at face value. Thus Peel's decision to establish the Metropolitan Police in 1829 was a rational reform of an out-of-date system whose old, decrepit, drunken and otherwise useless constables and watchmen were incapable of dealing with new levels of crime and disorder. The more recent arguments of politicians, civil servants and some police reformers that 200 and more local forces were inefficient and less effective than fewer, bigger forces have similarly gone unchallenged.[1]

This book does not ignore institutional change, but such change is not central to the narrative. An appendix provides a timeline of the key legislation and of some of the important moments in the construction of the police institution. The aim of the book is to present a collective biography of the men and women at the sharp end of the institution – who they were, what their day-to-day experiences were, and how they were regarded by the range of individuals and communities that made up the public which they served. The great men of the institutional histories were usually remote from both the ordinary Bobby and the community in which he was based. It was the behaviour of the beat officer's immediate superior and the attitude of the community in which he worked that mattered and that had the most effect on his working life. The focus on the individual officer, moreover, puts a different perspective on the activities of the great men and forces some reappraisal of their actions. Sometimes the reforms and changes effected by politicians and administrators had little impact on events on the ground; sometimes their effects were rather different from those intended. Focus on the Bobby reveals continuities often omitted from the institutional histories. The similarities between the old police and the new, for example; the persistence of violence between police officers and some sections of the working class; the recurrence of complaints that, whatever their modus operandi and whatever the period, police officers could not be found when needed; the instances of corruption. It is unrealistic to expect that officials on relatively low wages will avoid temptation when exposed to wealthy entrepreneurs who are engaged in illicit activities and who are prepared to offer bribes and other incentives to have a blind eye turned. But the persistence of such moral lapses, and the manner in which it seems that such infection can spread, suggests that this is an area that needs rather more than the dismissal of an occasional scapegoat as a 'rotten apple'.

Corruption and suspect behaviour was often a part of the popular image of the policeman, particularly among the working class. The early Bobby was also often portrayed in hot pursuit of female cooks and servant girls. 'What article of dress are Cook's [*sic*] most attracted to?' quizzed *Punch* in 1853, responding with its own answer: 'The Pelisse'.[2] There were jokes among the middle class about the police constable's ignorance and regular use of malapropisms. The old, London-centred histories of the police commonly opened with quotations from Shakespeare, or descriptions of Dogberry and Verges in *Much Ado About Nothing* and Elbow in *Measure for Measure*, as if Shakespeare's comedies were an accurate guide to policing before Peel. But what has been conveniently forgotten in the institutional histories is the extent to which the essence of such comic police characters has endured over the years and been absorbed into descriptions of the Bobby. In 1932, for example, the *Solicitors Journal* had a series of articles ridiculing the pomposity of a police-speak that was similar to Dogberry's misuse of language. 'A constable has been heard to say', chuckled one such article, 'that he saw a man and woman having "intellectual course" together, meaning "sexual intercourse"... One for greater safety spoke of a "foot pedestrian"...'[3] The *Police Review* ran a 'Dogberry column' for many years and stories circulated within individual forces about officers who spoke of police dogs as 'a great detergent towards crime' and ordered their subordinates to 'throw an accordion' round a suspect building.[4] The jokes continue, though now they seem more often directed at senior officers' predilection for management speak.

Today's image of the police officer varies from the nostalgic one of PC George Dixon to the tough, hard-nosed detective, epitomized by Detective Inspector Jack Regan in the 1970s television series *The Sweeney* and his virtual reincarnation in the character of DCI Gene Hunt in the early twenty-first-century series *Life on Mars* and *Ashes to Ashes*. The modern media condemns police officers for not responding immediately to complaints about burglary, sympathises with them for excessive red tape, and praises them for their courage when an officer faces down a violent offender or is killed in the line of duty. It was ever thus.

For rather more than a hundred years police officers largely learned their skills on the job and most appear never to have considered their working life much beyond patrolling the beat. But since the Second World War the public has expected the police to be highly trained and to have access to the latest technology.

Most people are well aware that modern police officers, male and female, sometimes have to deal with truly testing situations, such as the results of transnational crime or international terrorism. But there has never been a time without the fear and threat of crime, and no officer has ever set out on a patrol knowing precisely how his or her shift would end, and what part of their training or resolve might be tested. With or without all the modern advances and technologies, the 140,000 men and women serving today still need many of the old qualities.

The chapters that follow provide a broadly chronological account and seek to construct a kind of composite biography of the Bobby from his immediate predecessors to the present. The focus is primarily on the constables who patrolled the streets, on the detectives who investigated crime, and on those officers who simply kept the traffic moving, picked up the pieces after accidents, and looked after lost children. A few wrote autobiographies; a few others, by accident, have had pocket books and notebooks preserved in various police archives or with their families. Where possible I have traced the service careers of such officers, a task greatly facilitated by the availability of certain records on the Internet, particularly the nineteenth-century census returns, proceedings of the Old Bailey and the British Library's online newspaper collections. At the risk of offending some of the retired police officers who have helped me in my research over the years, and who believe that dirty linen should be kept in the washing basket, or even shredded, the book does not ignore the less savoury side of the police. It shows how the taking and receipt of 'perks' sometimes drifted into corruption, how 'known offenders' and known criminal districts could be stigmatized and hounded, and how the policing of elections, strikes and demonstrations could sometimes turn extremely violent as a direct result of the behaviour of the Bobbies. It describes also the police officer's relations with the public and how different pressures and social changes have influenced them. At the same time, it explores the work and family life of ordinary constables, and contrasts the experiences of police officers in town and country. Throughout, the story of the Bobby is woven into the cultural and political history of Britain from the mid-eighteenth century to the present. This is a history that the Bobby has closely observed, since politicians and monarchs have commonly travelled under his or her watchful eye, and it is a history in which he and she have played a permanent, often unacknowledged but occasionally significant part.

— CHAPTER ONE —

Policing Georgian Liberty

IN EIGHTEENTH-CENTURY England the word 'police' was not much used, and certainly not to describe any institution for preserving the peace, preventing crime and apprehending offenders. Police institutions were regarded with suspicion as the kinds of instruments with which the princes of Continental Europe kept their unfortunate subjects in thrall. The English saw themselves as living in a land of liberty, a Protestant island favoured by Providence.

But if there was no institution called the police in the century before the first Bobbies took to the streets of London, there were men entrusted with tasks that would be understood today as policing. The best known of these officers were constables and watchmen; their roles and responsibilities had begun to be defined in the thirteenth century, but their origins were much older. The watchmen did what their name suggested. Initially they had been householders, performing a civic duty, guarding town gates after dark and patrolling the streets. There were various ranks of constable; the most numerous were the petty constables who served in a rural or urban parish; in some districts, even at the beginning of the nineteenth century, these men were known by the ancient titles of borsholder, headborough or tythingman.

In the reign of Elizabeth I a prominent legal scholar and magistrate, William Lambarde, wrote a guide to *The Duties of Constables, Borsholders, Tythingmen, and Such Other Low Ministers of the Peace*.

He described these duties as threefold: maintaining the peace, preventing offences and using the law to punish offenders. About twenty years later, at the beginning of the seventeenth century, William Shakespeare wrote first *Much Ado About Nothing* and then *Measure for Measure*, both of which contain comic officers: Dogberry, Verges and their watchmen in the former, and Elbow, a constable, in the latter. All of these characters grotesquely misuse the English language for humorous effect. Unfortunately, historian after historian of the English police have grotesquely misused Shakespeare at the beginning of their histories.[1]

The argument has commonly been deployed that Shakespeare's comic characters were portraits of reality. Thus follows the implication that, while there may have been some minor improvements in eighteenth-century London, the system was essentially irredeemable but remained largely unchanged until the creation of the Metropolitan Police in 1829. Yet in 1657, when Oliver Cromwell explained to Parliament the way in which he understood his role as Lord Protector, he chose the analogy of 'a good Constable set to keep the peace of the parish'.[2] If constables were all like Dogberry this is hardly a comparison that Cromwell would have offered. And as this chapter will show, the constables and watchmen of Georgian England showed many of the characteristics, the courage and efficiency that have been associated with the Bobby.

Watchmen and Constables

Eighteenth-century London was a booming metropolis. It burgeoned into the largest city in Europe, the administrative, commercial and financial capital of both a prosperous kingdom and a growing empire. Yet, in many respects, it was a group of distinct and quite separate entities. At the heart was the square mile of the City of London proper, with its formidable financial and commercial institutions, notably the Bank of England and the East India Company, clustered about with small shops and private dwellings. To the west was the separate, largely prosperous City of Westminster, where the nation's Parliament nestled alongside the splendour of Westminster Abbey and where there were fashionable new streets and squares were built, illuminated at night with street lights – tins, filled with cheap fish oil stuffed with a cotton-twist wick. South of the River Thames was Southwark; here land was cheaper and water plentiful, making it home to some of the larger, grubbier manufacturing trades such as brewing, tanning and wood-cutting. On the banks of the Thames east of the City of London was a massive port where crowded wharves and warehouses received the treasures of the world. Narrow, dim streets, the home to sailors and dockworkers, snaked back from the Wapping wharves to Spitalfields, still a centre for weaving. The days of these weavers were numbered, and all around them were the shabby dwellings of poor folk, often newly arrived from rural areas. There was no primitive street lighting here where both hogs and the destitute rooted among the rubbish. But even in such grim districts the local vestrymen, the men responsible for local government and administration within their parish, sought to keep order and protect the law-abiding and their property. From the second quarter of the eighteenth century vestries in all parts of the metropolis had begun to obtain their own private Acts of Parliament that enabled them to establish regular, paid bodies of night watchmen.[3]

Anxieties about crime, particularly property crime, recurred throughout the century. They became especially acute when poor harvests pushed up prices, prompting anxiety that the poor would rob to survive. They were also apparent when the conclusion of one of the century's frequent wars brought rapid demobilization and concerns that men trained in arms, with no jobs and nothing to do, would resort to robbery and pillage. These concerns contributed to the drives to improve the watch. But alongside such fears there was also fierce local pride and a jealousy to preserve or enhance the independence of local institutions and jurisdiction. The City of London zealously guarded its boundaries and privileges. It had its own watchmen organized under regulations promulgated by its Common Council. Other areas of the metropolis were not as grand and rarely as wealthy, but they were equally proud of their own district; the problem was that there were often rivals for the direction of the district. The Westminster Watch Act of 1735 was a private Act of Parliament obtained by the vestrymen of the parishes in the City of Westminster coming together to establish an improved night watch, but also coming together in a power struggle with local magistrates and the city's old Court of Burgesses. Other metropolitan parishes watched the developments and, over the next few years, many followed suit by obtaining their own watch act. The different local government institutions, such as the parish vestries, were run by men motivated by a sense of civic duty rooted in a mixture of religious conviction, local pride and ideas drawn from classical examples. Their service was unpaid, part-time and commonly dedicated and hard-working. They observed each other's experiments with different systems and shifts of watch patrols; they remodelled what seemed to work for their own circumstances and budgets.

The vestrymen generally sought fit ex-soldiers for their watchmen. Some issued their men with firearms and cutlasses; others with staves. The men were also given wooden rattles with which to summon assistance when required; these set up a steady clatter when swung, or 'sprung' in the contemporary parlance. Some men were issued with greatcoats bearing the name of the parish that they served and the number of the beat that they patrolled. The watchmen were instructed in what to look for and, particularly, they were directed to stop and question anyone carrying a bundle after dark. Rather than being ignorant, old and decrepit, or drunken and cowardly, these were men who knew how elements in society worked; and they knew the law and the legal consequences of different actions. In December 1787 John Walker, a watchman in Chiswick, stopped a man driving six ewes; he suspected that the ewes had been stolen since they were not marked as graziers usually marked sheep bound for market, but they did have a butcher's mark. Walker's assumption was correct; and the thief was duly sentenced. A few years earlier Joseph Harris, a watch sergeant in Tottenham, advised one young woman who identified a man as a highway robber: 'be particular in what you are doing, if you swear to him you will take his life away.' Good watchmen treated any individuals out late at night as suspect and challenged them. 'I was in my stand in Hoxton Town, just at the bottom of the prosecutor's garden', John Whitaker told an Old Bailey jury in 1770 during a burglary case. 'I saw these three young chaps go by; I thought they were disorderly by their very looks … I asked them where they were going. They set up a run.' So Whitaker called to another watchman and, together, they pursued and arrested all three.[4] These two instances are taken from the proceedings of trials at the Old Bailey. These proceedings, as well as those of the lower courts, show watchmen acting like Whitaker as a matter of course. They also show watchmen prepared to take on armed opponents and to pursue them at great personal risk.

Robert Grubb patrolled in Brick Lane, a road that ran north from Aldgate to Shoreditch through weavers' Spitalfields. In the early hours of 27 May 1782 he was on his beat as usual when, at about 1.15 a.m., three men passed him and aroused his suspicions. One of the three was carrying a large bundle. Grubb challenged them. Initially they seemed friendly enough, but then one of the three drew a cutlass and slashed Grubb first across the skull and then across the arm. With blood pouring from the gashes in his head and arm Grubb fell to the ground as the three ran off, but his adrenalin was running too. He quickly struggled to his feet, sprung his rattle and set off in pursuit of the man carrying the bundle. Another watchman, alerted by Grubb's rattle, apprehended the man. Grubb himself was taken to hospital where, for two weeks, his life appeared in danger. A second arrest was effected a day or so after the incident and, by 3 July, Grubb was well enough to appear at the Old Bailey as a key witness in the trial for burglary of two men: George Lee, also known as Couch, as Baker and as Baldock; and Job Baker, also known as Filkin. Lee and Baker were convicted and sentenced to death. Their accomplice was never identified.[5]

On 7 August 1782, a month after the trial of Lee and Baker, Richard Hunter, a former soldier, was on his beat in Westminster. Hunter's patrol took him along Margaret Street which ran between Parliament and the Abbey. At around two o'clock in the morning he recognized a maid's voice calling from one of the houses. He ran to the house springing his rattle, but help did not immediately arrive. Pushing open the house door Hunter was confronted by three men armed with cutlasses. He swung his own cutlass at the first man who dodged the blow and stabbed Hunter in the stomach. In spite of his wound Hunter gave chase. Only one of the three offenders was arrested, and he, James Messenger, was tried, convicted and hanged for burglary. Hunter recovered from his wound and continued to serve as a watchman, appearing to give evidence at several other Old Bailey trials.[6]

Just as, on closer investigation, many of the eighteenth-century London watchmen look less and less like the comic stereotypes, so too do the police officials known as constables. The constable was generally one of the lower parish officials who was entitled to claim fees for many of his tasks. His appointment depended upon traditional practice in the locality, and such practices were many and varied. In some parishes, for example, constables were changed annually by house rotation, in others the oldest householder who had not yet served was chosen. A few men embraced the duties with enthusiasm. William Payne, a carpenter in the City of Westminster, was an outstanding example. In 1759 he was selected headborough, or constable, of the Rolls Liberty, a civil parish of Westminster. He served in the post for more than twenty years, until his death in 1782, and he was assiduous in his pursuit of pickpockets, unscrupulous traders and, above all, brothel-keepers and prostitutes. As an ardent low churchman, he also used the law to prosecute Catholic priests and teachers who, he believed, constituted a serious threat to his Protestant homeland and to English liberties. His activities were popular with his neighbours, though they upset some prominent political and legal figures; and his enthusiasm for his policing role also appears to have led him to neglect his carpentry business.[7]

While Payne served in person, many more of his contemporaries preferred either to pay a fine that went towards paying a man to act in their place, or else to hire a substitute themselves who would serve in their stead. Some of the substitutes appear to have served year after year, becoming something of a constable by trade and seeking a living, at least in part, from their fees. One such was James Prior, who was a substitute constable in Bassishaw Ward of the City of London from 1778 to 1807.[8] Parish constables also appear regularly in trial reports and, like many watchmen, they seem often to have acted with courage and determination. In September 1783, for example, Jonathan Redgrave, a constable of St James's Clerkenwell, set off with two other constables in pursuit of three escaped transportees. They tracked them to a house in Onslow Street, Clerkenwell, where they found their entry impeded by two women. Redgrave testified:

[W]e got past them and when we entered the room Matthews [one of the escapees] stepped towards the bedstead with a poker in his hand. The others were armed, one with a large iron fire shovel, and the other with a large knife. I told the prisoner, knowing him perfectly (though I knew all three), that it would be impossible to escape, but they might do us some mischief. Matthews, with the others, made a reply that they would sooner die than be taken. Matthews then struck [constable] Seasons on the head with a poker, which cut his head very much. He did not cut me. Seasons immediately closed on him, and they fell down on the bed together. [Constable] Isaacs and I were engaged with the other two men and two or three women, who fought as well as they could, and as much as the men. We had three cutlasses, and very happy was it for us that we had. The other two wounded me here on the head and cut me in the breast. At the same time one of the women struck me on the back of the head and stunned me. When I came to myself I found the blood running down. They said they were only sorry they had not cutlasses, for if they had we never should have gone away without murder.

Redgrave, Seasons and Isaacs eventually overpowered the three escapees, saw them taken to court and sentenced.[9] The three constables were ordinary parish officers, but by the time of this incident there was a new body of professional constables in London that were attracting the limelight – the Bow Street Runners.

'Runners' and Thief-takers

Bow Street became a centre for police activity in the metropolis in the middle of the eighteenth century. In 1739 Sir Thomas De Veil, a mercer's apprentice who, after a career as a soldier and adventurer, had become a magistrate in Westminster, set up house in Bow Street from where he administered justice. He liked to describe himself as 'the first magistrate of Westminster' and while the term had no official meaning or sanction, it was also used by his successors, the novelist and dramatist Henry Fielding and his younger, blind half-brother John, when they moved into the house and assumed his role. The Fieldings, typical of public officials of the day, were venal. They received money from a variety of clandestine government and administrative sources and they also ran the *Universal Register*, which acted as both a kind of labour exchange and an estate agency. But the money collected by the Fieldings enabled them to administer justice to the poor, charging low fees and even, in some instances, dispensing with fees altogether. Even more significant, however, were their innovations in policing. Around 1763, following the demobilization after the Seven Years' War, Sir John Fielding established a mounted patrol for the main roads in and out of the metropolis. The experiment was short-lived, but it provided a model for regular nightly foot patrols organized by one of the Fieldings' successors, Sir Sampson Wright, in 1790; and the mounted patrol itself was re-established in 1805. These patrols acted across the old jurisdictional boundaries of London's parishes, but did not penetrate the City proper. The most significant of the Fieldings' innovations, however, was the force of constables popularly known as the Bow Street Runners.[10]

The Runners were created at some point in 1748 or 1749. There were usually eight of them, though the number could vary and at one point in 1831 it had risen to eleven. They came from a variety of backgrounds; they were sworn as constables of Westminster but their official title was Principal Officer of Bow Street. The name 'runners' appears to have been used for the first time in a trial at the Old Bailey in September 1755.[11] The men themselves regarded it as demeaning and disparaging. The word 'runner' implied some sort of messenger or a junior member of an organization; the principal officers saw themselves as an elite. They did not run errands; they were invited to investigate offences and detect offenders, and they did this for fees and their expenses. As John Sayer, one of the most successful of them, explained to a parliamentary committee in 1816: 'if the gentleman writes, the gentleman pays'.[12] Sayer was said, probably with some exaggeration, to have accumulated a fortune of £30,000 by the time of his death. John Townsend, another successful officer, was said to have £20,000. Townsend was a great favourite of George III; and when George IV was away from his London residences, Sayer and Townsend accompanied him.[13]

The principal officers appear to have known the hot spots for offences such as pickpocketing, and to have kept a weather eye out for people carrying suspicious packages, for known offenders and receivers. They became well-known in the courts for their thief-taking: Charles Jealous, for example, appeared in 127 trials at the Old Bailey between 1774 and 1794. And they inspired fear among offenders. William Pritchard, with two others, had robbed the Surgeons' Company of some ceremonial silver; he confided to an acquaintance his fear that 'it was all over for him, for the traps were all after him – meaning Sir John Fielding's runners'. Unfortunately for Pritchard and his fellows, on this occasion it was the confidant, who shopped him to Jealous.[14] When a principal officer was called to the provinces, or travelled abroad, to investigate crimes that baffled the locals, he appears to have proceeded in a rational, systematic way. He asked questions. He interviewed people. Sometimes he went underground in disguise to track, for example, gangs of poachers. The officers also used simple but effective forensic techniques. When one of the Runners, Harry Adkins, tracked down the man who robbed and murdered a Staffordshire farmer in 1812, he matched a mark on the bullet taken from the victim with a bullet mould used by the killer.[15]

There were other developments centred on the Bow Street Office, begun by the Fieldings and financed principally by central government through the Home Office. Armed officers, known as 'patrols', walked the main roads in groups from dusk to midnight, and later if necessary. By the end of the century there were sixty-eight patrols organized into thirteen parties, eight on the main roads coming into the metropolis and five in the central districts. In 1805 a mounted unit was added, and a major reorganization in 1822 saw the creation of a small force wearing blue coats and trousers and red waistcoats who patrolled the central districts by day; for obvious reasons they became known as the 'Robin Redbreasts'. But change was not all centred on Bow Street. The Middlesex Justices Act of 1792 established seven Police Offices across the metropolis each staffed by three stipendiary magistrates and up to six, later a dozen, constables. The magistrates were appointed by the Crown and the intention was that their offices be funded from the fees that they charged for services; the fees were to be collected and redistributed by a receiver of police. In the event, however, the fees were insufficient to run the new system and the government picked up the tab. In 1798, in keeping with the self-help practices of the period, a police force was established for the Thames principally by West India merchants who were worried about thefts from their ships, wharves and warehouses. After two years the central government agreed to incorporate the River Police with its other Police Offices. Both the magistrates and constables attached to the London Police Offices performed roles not connected to their legal tasks, but the legislation of the 1790s heralded a further extension of professionalism in policing. John Griffiths, a constable of the Police Office in Lambeth Street, Whitechapel, for example, appeared in cases of burglary, coining, pickpocketing, receiving, robbery and shoplifting heard at the Old Bailey between 1794 and 1804. Similarly John Foy, a constable of the Great Marlborough Street Office, appeared at the Old Bailey on more than two dozen occasions between 1803 and 1810 in cases ranging from arson to shoplifting and from coining to murder.

But there was also a dark side to eighteenth-century policing. The Glorious Revolution of 1688 removed the last Stuart monarch and contributed significantly the eighteenth-century Englishman's notions of liberty and freedom from arbitrary monarchy. But during the following half century or so there were periodic moments of anxiety about crime and immorality that prompted measures to stiffen the law and ensure more convictions. An act of 1699, 'for the better apprehending, prosecuting and punishing of Felons who commit Burglary, House-breaking, or Robbery in Shops, Warehouses, Coach-houses or stables, or steal Horses', introduced a certificate that exempted the person who apprehended such an offender from duty in any parish office in the parish where the offence had been committed. These so-called 'Tyburn tickets' were known to sell in wealthy parishes for up to £30 or more. A statute of 1692 promised £40, together with the offender's arms, horse and money – providing they were not stolen property – for the conviction of a highway robber. This reward was subsequently extended to include first burglary, counterfeiting and shoplifting, and then cow- and sheep-stealing. A particularly horrific murder or other appalling crime encouraged one government after another to offer similar rewards for limited periods.

This 'blood money' system was vulnerable to exploitation by the unscrupulous and also by those who lived on the fringes of legality. Jonathan Wild, the self-styled 'Thief-Taker General of Great Britain and Ireland', made a comfortable living from the system during the reign of George I. The son of a joiner in Wolver-hampton, Wild moved to London early in the 1700s, leaving a wife and child in his home town. After a spell in prison for debt he went to work for Charles Hitchen, an officer in the City of

London who was reputed to be in league with local thieves. In 1714 Wild branched out on his own, establishing a Lost Property Office in the Old Bailey, the street that housed the celebrated court. From here he advertised himself as able to return lost and stolen property for a payment. He also apprehended offenders for the rewards and the blood money. But while this side of his business appeared respectable and public-spirited, Wild also set up various robberies and burglaries. Occasionally too, he offered up a sacrifice for the Tyburn Tree, something that kept his business looking good and kept his scattered, subordinate criminal operatives loyal and up to the mark. Wild's luck ran out in 1725; he was exposed, prosecuted for theft and receiving, found guilty of the second charge and executed.[16]

By the middle of the century there was increasing disquiet over the 'blood money' system, and the disquiet turned to outrage with the exposure of the McDaniel gang in 1754. The thief-taker Stephen McDaniel and his confederates had engineered a highway robbery which, following the successful conviction and execution of the men that they had set up for the offence, would have brought them the sum of £120 in blood-money rewards. McDaniel and his gang were exposed, prosecuted and sentenced to death; but unlike Wild, McDaniel appears to have escaped execution.[17] And these events occurred just as Henry Fielding was seeking to make the thief-taker a respectable individual pursuing a respectable trade: 'if to do Good to Society be laudable, so is the Office of a Thief-catcher; and if to do Good at the extreme Hazard of your Life be honourable, then is this Office honourable.'[18] In the end Fielding's efforts, and those of his brother, met with success. William Garrow, who made his name as a barrister at the Old Bailey in the last two decades of the eighteenth century, was scathing about common thief-takers, criticizing them publicly for their pursuit of blood money. But while he vigorously interrogated constables from Bow Street and the post-1792 Police Offices, he also acknowledged them as genuine officers of justice and the law, and hence as different from the old thief-takers.[19]

Even after the exposure of McDaniel – and in spite of the increasingly formidable reputation of the men of Bow Street – there remained opportunities for the unscrupulous; and the unscrupulous were to be found in both Bow Street and the new Police Offices. In 1812 George Vaughan described himself as a 'broker' living in Gray's Inn Lane with his mother. Between 15 January 1812 and 18 September 1816 Vaughan made twenty-five appearances at the Old Bailey. At his fifth appearance, on 16 February 1814, and thereafter he was identified as a Bow Street Officer; in fact he belonged to one of the patrols. Vaughan appeared in a variety of cases: burglary, coining, pickpocketing and shoplifting. In some instances he was simply the arresting officer called in by someone else; on other occasions he claimed to have acted on information received or to have observed the culprits committing the offence. A passionate plea by defence counsel in December 1815, that a pickpocketing case had been 'got up', led to the acquittal of the accused. In May 1815 nineteen-year-old John Cole, charged with shoplifting, protested: 'That officer [Vaughan] wants to swear my life away. I went up the gate way to make water.' A year later 48-year-old William Soames, charged with two others for picking pockets, claimed: 'I wish to say Mr Vaughan has declared he would send me out of the country for life if he could: and tis a very hard case to be sent for this case for I know nothing of it.' Soames was found guilty and, as he had feared, was transported for life. Of course, these protests might have been fabricated to win the sympathy of the court. What gives them an additional dimension, and an aura of truth, is the fact that in September 1816, in his last appearance at the Old Bailey, Vaughan, still only twenty-four, was in the dock himself, prosecuted and convicted of being an accessory to burglary before and after the fact. As with McDaniel and other earlier thief-takers, Vaughan had been organizing offences for the rewards. He was one of four London police officers charged with this kind of offence in 1816; and a counterfeiting case that he was involved with earlier in 1816 suggests that he may also have been involved in this case for the blood money[20]

In the year following the conviction of Vaughan a parliamentary select committee investigating the policing of the metropolis recommended that the system of rewards be abolished. In 1818 an Act of Parliament replaced both the statutory rewards and Tyburn Tickets with expenses that were to be decided by the judge trying a case. The intention was to ensure that victims came forward to prosecute in serious criminal cases without fear of losing money and that efficient, entrepreneurial police officers continuing to pursue offenders received generous expenses in the place of the blood-money system and the temptation that it encouraged.

Beyond the Metropolis

Policing in eighteenth-century London is well documented and is being increasingly well researched. Evidence suggests that elsewhere in the country there were also growing numbers of long-serving, active and competent police officers. The social status of the rural parish constable may have declined during the eighteenth century He was increasingly regarded as the lowliest of the parish officers and was appointed from among the poorer artisans and even labourers. Yet this did not mean that the men were ineffectual. They were generally literate and often served for several years rather than stepping down after one; longevity in the post gave them experience. On occasions, rather than using the full authority of the law to settle matters – even criminal matters – they sought reconciliation between offenders and victims. From time to time, too, they may have abused their discretion. Much of their time as constable was taken up with the safe-keeping of prisoners after capture, or assisting in obtaining and executing warrants. They were reactive police. They served as constables alongside their other employment, appreciating the fees and other emoluments of the post as a useful supplement to the family budget. But the lure of fees and rewards occasionally prompted significant feats of detection and pursuit. A constable in the small North Yorkshire town of Guisborough, for example, read a newspaper advertisement for a watch stolen in Whalton, Northumberland. He recognized the watch in the possession of a man passing through the town, and tracked him twenty miles to Whitby where, in order to claim his reward, he made his arrest and recovered the property.[21]

Towns, boroughs and cities also witnessed significant developments in their policing in the late eighteenth and early nineteenth centuries. The ancient cathedral city of York, two hundred miles north of London, offers one example. In the early 1700s it was a centre of commerce and leisure for the local gentry, though its prosperity began to decline towards the end of the century as it was bypassed by the burgeoning industrial districts of the West Riding of Yorkshire. The parish constables, some of whom were substantial citizens, appear to have taken their policing duties seriously but, as the century wore on and the city's population increased without an increase in the number of such constables, they began to look for recompense similar to other civic law officers. Watches appear to have been established for short periods as and when a parish, or the city as a whole, considered it necessary. A permanent city-wide night watch had to await the passage of the York Improvement Act of 1825. But significant developments occurred in the city through the development of the post of Common Informer. The post, which was not unique to York, originated in the need to supervise economic regulations particularly in a town or city market. The post had been established in York during the seventeenth century; the Informer received an annual stipend and was recognized by his official green coat.

In the early eighteenth century the title of the post was changed to Inspector of Markets and eleven men held it between 1722 and 1825. Socially they were similar to the constables; indeed six of the eleven served as constables and most had the freedom of the city or a trade. In the middle of the century the Inspector took on the additional duties of supervising some of the constables' duties. Thomas Robson, who served for twenty years from 1776 and who combined this role with being the constable of the parish of St Mary Castlegate, also began to take on the role of thief-taker.

27

He appeared regularly as a witness in felonies and received money from the court in addition to his expenses. The magistrates employed him to convey prisoners and paid him for arresting vagrants.

Joseph Pardoe, a hornbreaker, took over the post in 1798; he combined it with the role of constable in his parish for only one year (1800) but, like Robson, he acted as a thief-taker and was commonly described in the press as a 'police officer' or the 'corporation constable'. Pardoe's salary increased exponentially from just over £10 a year when he began, to £25 in 1805 and to £40 in 1814. His sons, William and James, assisted him as thief-takers and in 1821 William, the eldest, became the city's 'sole principal police officer' with £80 a year and the allowance of reasonable expenses. When the Municipal Corporations Act of 1835 required boroughs to appoint watch committees and police institutions, Pardoe became the first superintendent of the city's police force.[22]

York was not alone in such developments. The efficiency and effectiveness of such provincial police officers were tested, and well-rewarded, by the Bank of England in its struggle with banknote forgers. In February 1797 the financial stress of the war against Revolutionary France and anxiety about a French invasion threat provoked a run on the banks and led to the Bank of England suspending cash payments. Over the next quarter of a century, as a result of the issue of a large number of £1 and £2 notes, the Bank was faced with a major forgery problem. The Bank's solicitors built up an informal police network across the country drawing on provincial solicitors as local co-ordinators and using men from the London Police Offices and various semi-professional constables in the cities and towns as investigators and arresting officers. Birmingham was acknowledged as a centre for the production of forged notes and William Payne, a prominent constable in the town, was regularly rewarded for his efforts in helping bring forgers to book. Similarly active and well-rewarded were Joseph Nadin, the Deputy Chief Constable of Manchester, John Miller, Chief Constable of Liverpool, and a variety of constables in smaller places.

But the policing of forgery, while it was effective, highlighted the blood-money issue once again. These constables might have been competent in investigation and detection, but they were not much interested in the prevention of crime and they focused their attention on matters that would bring them financial reward.[23]

Radicals and Rioters

Eighteenth-century English policing did not just involve the pursuit of thieves and the protection of property. There were also problems of national security and public order. Sometimes magistrates, particularly those of the London Police Offices appointed at the close of the eighteenth century, also conducted sensitive inquiries. During the wars against Revolutionary and Napoleonic France this could involve intelligence work for a government fearful of French Jacobins fomenting insurrection among British Jacobins and their sympathizers.

In the winter of 1791–2 popular radical societies began to spring up across the country in which artisans and journeymen rubbed shoulders with shopkeepers, liberal-minded attorneys, dissenting ministers and others, to call for parliamentary reform. The societies were enthused by the French Revolution; many of their members feared that the French would soon surpass the liberties of which Britons had boasted since the overthrow of James II in 1688. The societies drew on the idea of the Freeborn Englishman, who was popularly conceived as a man as good as his king and his king's ministers; a man who had the right of trial by jury and who, unlike his unfortunate Continental neighbours, had his freedom from arbitrary arrest guaranteed by the Habeas Corpus Act. They also built on a long tradition of open political discussion and of debating clubs that had often and regularly met in pubs. Recapturing the spirit of these meetings requires imagination beyond the surviving, fragmentary written record. The pub rooms were candle-lit and smoky. The men – few women appear to have participated – gathered after their long day's work and drank a beer or two. They probably assembled with some initial chatter about the day's news; eighteenth-century English artisans often surprised foreigners with their interest in the political news carried in the press. Their discussions were tinged by their perceptions of an Englishman's liberty and by the success of radical ideas in France where, at least until the summer of 1792, it appeared to many that the French were developing a new and enlightened form of constitutional monarchy. The meeting was probably called to order with appropriate seriousness but, as the formal discussions and debates got under way, the men with a reputation – or seeking a reputation – for oratory would take the floor. They sought the approbation of their mates for their logical arguments, often developed from the publishing sensation of 1791 and 1792, Tom Paine's *Rights of Man*. The best of them employed a fine wit and played to the gallery: 'Mr Thewall took a pot of porter and blowing off the head, said – "This is the way I would serve Kings".[24] And it was popular to invoke the personal courage and the glories of the men who had fought against arbitrary monarchy and for the common weal in the seventeenth century. The problem for the government came in assessing how far such radicals were prepared to go to achieve their political aspirations, especially when the French Revolution took a radical lurch following war against the principal powers of the Continent and when, following the execution of the French king in January 1793, the French also declared war on Britain.[25]

The Home Office at the end of the eighteenth century consisted of less than two dozen individuals ranging from the secretary of state at the top to the delightfully named 'necessary woman' who cleaned and tidied. There were two under secretaries, one 'permanent' the other 'parliamentary', and a dozen or so clerks, most of whom sat round a table and copied out correspondence. An Aliens Office was established in 1793 ostensibly to supervise foreigners in the country but, under the management of William Wickham, one of the new stipendiary magistrates, it rapidly became a clearing house for the reports of many spies and informers.

It is never easy to be sure of the motives of men who gave information on political radicals. Some of the government's informants appear to have acted out of their perception of civic duty. George Lynam, for example, was an ironmonger with a warehouse in Walbrook in the centre of the City. He took business commissions from the button and buckle manufacturing centre of Birmingham and the cutlery centre of Sheffield, and had big plans for developing his business in the East Indies. In October 1792 he visited a meeting of one of the divisions of the London Corresponding Society (LCS), the principal popular radical association in the metropolis. Lynam claimed to have been shocked by some of the sentiments that he heard and promptly offered his services as an informant to Sir Evan Nepean, permanent under secretary at the Home Office. Nepean wrote to John Brook, a magistrate in Birmingham, asking for information on Lynam. Brook knew nothing of him. Nepean may have made other inquiries and from at least the beginning of 1793 Lynam began to send regular, sober reports on meetings of the LCS. He was chosen to be the president of one of the society's divisions and this meant that he regularly attended the general committee, where he took notes that formed the basis of the reports that he gave to both his division and the Home Office. Some of his radical compatriots suspected him and he was twice tried as a spy by the society. Each time he was triumphantly acquitted. At the end of 1794, however, he appeared at the Old Bailey as one of the principal witnesses in the trial for treason of Thomas Hardy, a Scottish shoemaker who had acted as secretary of the LCS. Hardy's defence counsel was able to undermine some of the government's other agents by finding flaws in their character or behaviour, but Lynam appeared to be nothing more than he claimed: a man genuinely concerned by the radical sentiments that he had heard expressed. The jury, however, was not convinced of the charge of treason. Hardy and two others that stood trial were acquitted, and the government released its other suspects.

The problem for Lynam and the other informers was that, once they had given evidence before the Privy Council and then appeared as witnesses in court, they were no longer useful to the government. Some of them may have faced difficulty in the communities where they lived and with clients and customers when they were exposed, especially when the men accused were acquitted. They could look like the blood-money thief-takers. What happened to them after their exposure is largely unknown, though in Lynam's case Home Office correspondence provides a bitter-sweet postscript. In the spring of 1803 Lynam's brother, Francis, contacted the government explaining that, following his appearance at Hardy's trial, George's

> reputation and character were destroyed and his business then in the East India line which netted him seven hundred per annum annihilated and he never after such exposure received an order of any description . . . [He] was deserted by his friends and relations and frequently insulted in the streets which so preyed upon his mind that both he and his wife's days were thereby shortened.

Both George and his wife died in 1796, leaving Francis, who lived in Sheffield, to bring up their eighteen-month-old son. In the summer of 1803, and after due inquiry, the Home Office agreed to pay Francis £30 a year towards bringing up the boy.[26]

But if Lynam was an honest informant, motivated by what he understood as his civic and patriotic duty, others appear to have been far less savoury. Some informants accused men of radicalism and sought to have them prosecuted out of revenge or spite. It is, for example, difficult to know whether Thomas Upton, the principal informant about a plot to assassinate George III, was acting to revenge himself on a group of radicals who had accused him of being a spy, or whether he was simply an agent provocateur. 'Oliver the Spy', who gave information on the sorry group of Derbyshire labourers that attempted to start a revolution by marching on Nottingham in 1817, appears to have trodden a line very close to being a provocateur; but his reports also emphasized the misery of the labourers.

Three years later a more serious group of conspirators was confronted by Bow Street officers supported by soldiers in a stable in Cato Street just off the Marylebone Road. The conspirators were planning to break in on Lord Liverpool's cabinet at dinner and assassinate them. In the event the only fatality was Richard Smithers, a Bow Street officer. The Cato Street conspiracy resulted in the last five decapitations for treason in England. The most disquieting element in the affair, however, was that George Edwards, whose information led to the exposure of the plot, without doubt was a key figure in fomenting it in the first place.[27] The disgust at the use of such agents combined the old revulsion about the blood-money thief-taker with concerns that the employment of such informers subverted the constitution. The use of surveillance in the supposed attempt to preserve all that was good about 'the land of liberty' was seen as decidedly un-English behaviour.

Another component of the eighteenth-century belief that England was a land of liberty was the limited size of the standing army and the underlying hostility to things military. This was based on a memory of Cromwell's major generals and the Catholic James II's attempts to create an army that would enforce his will. It meant that, while eighteenth-century English observers admired the apparent efficiency of French policing, they recoiled not only from the apparent intrusive behaviour of plain-clothes police spies but also from the military structure of the national force that patrolled the principal rural roads, the *Maréchaussée*.

The problem for the authorities at both the national and the local level, however, was that when large crowds demonstrated on the streets, no matter how professional the constables and the watch were becoming, they were usually insufficient, and certainly untrained for crowd control and the suppression of riot. In such instances magistrates could call upon special constables. In some districts such constables were nominated annually by the magistrates but, more often, they were sworn in to deal with a specific emergency. The problem was that special constables, sworn in ad hoc, were no more use against determined protesters than the beleaguered parish constables that they were required to assist.

The force that could be relied upon to stand firm against a crowd under a barrage of abuse and missiles, and that could be depended upon to clear a street, square or field when ordered, was the army. The eighteenth-century British redcoat was not trained in riot control, though his officers began to develop tactics that would lessen the likelihood of fatalities. Infantrymen trying to control a riot were directed to fire warning shots, to fire high, or to fire individually or in pairs rather than directing a volley at a crowd. Cavalry might try to push a crowd back with their horses, without drawing, let alone using, their sabres.

But policing deployments to deal with riots or the threat of riots were never popular with soldiers. Two years before he found glory, and death, at Quebec, Lieutenant Colonel James Wolfe found himself stationed in the West Country where clothiers, hit by depressed wages and the high cost of food, were threatening riot. 'What kind of duty do you think I am engaged on and what enemy am I opposed to?' he asked in a letter to a friend.

Hungry weavers! A dishonour to our arms; and they have had the impudence to make assaults, and commit riots *à ma barbe* – but as the poor devils are half starved, and as their masters have agreed to mend their wages, I have hopes they will return to work, rather than proceed to hostilities.[28]

Such duty was especially unpopular with the working men that joined the volunteer corps to protect their homes and communities during the wars at the end of the century.

If anyone was killed by military action during a riot the soldiers were, legally, not to blame. Rioting was a felony and felonies were punishable by death. The 1715 Riot Act also gave magistrates the authority to order crowds to disperse even if they were not yet in a state of riot. The act concluded with a proclamation that the magistrate could read in such circumstances; and persons remaining assembled one hour after the reading were deemed to be in a state of riot and, in consequence, could be dispersed by force. But the theoretical clarity of the law prevented neither heated debates on the topic, nor the occasional charge of murder being levelled against soldiers and even magistrates when someone was killed in a police action.

John Wilkes was a popular hero with the plebeian crowds of London during the 1760s. In his scurrilous political journal *The North Briton* he had lampooned the king's ministers who, suitably infuriated, set out to get him and his publishers. Following a serious wound in a duel Wilkes went into voluntary European exile while the courts passed a sentence of outlawry. In the spring of 1768, after four years on the Continent, he returned home, his popularity undimmed. He successfully fought for a parliamentary seat in Middlesex, surrendered himself to the authorities and was sentenced to a year in the King's Bench Prison on the south side of the Thames in Southwark. As Wilkes began his sentence, there was serious industrial unrest in London involving the Spitalfields weavers, coal-heavers from the Thames docks and various other trades. The King's Bench Prison bordered the open space of St George's Fields where speculative builders sought to profit from new roads running south from the bridges at Westminster and Blackfriars. From the beginning of Wilkes's confinement crowds had begun to assemble regularly outside the prison walls to cheer 'Wilkes and Liberty!' Early in May the magistrates in Surrey thought the situation sufficiently serious to request a permanent military guard around the prison. Parliament was due to open on 10 May and a troop of horse together with a hundred men from the Third Foot Guards were ordered to the prison.

Trouble around the King's Bench Prison began shortly before noon on 10 May. A junior officer and three guardsmen set off in pursuit of a young man who appears to have been particularly offensive towards them. The soldiers lost sight of their quarry, but thought they had found him again in the cow house of a nearby pub. William Allen, the publican's son, was almost certainly not the man they had chased, but was shot dead by one of the soldiers. A little later, back on St George's Fields, local magistrate Samuel Gillam, eager to avoid trouble, read the Riot Act proclamation for a second time and begged the crowd to disperse. He was promptly struck on the head with a stone and, apparently with some reluctance, gave the troops the order to fire. Perhaps as many as eleven were killed and more wounded, but the evidence of what actually happened is conflicting. Some witnesses spoke of the troops firing directly into the crowd, though by other accounts and by the position of those who were shot, it appears more likely that the troops fired in pairs into the air until the crowd dispersed. The people with bullet wounds were all some way from the trouble and seem to have been hit by bullets that were fired over the heads of the angry crowd.

The murder charge against the Guards officer and two of the soldiers involved in the death of young William Allen was dropped. Guardsman Donald McLane, however, was tried for the murder at the Surrey Assizes; he was acquitted. The unfortunate Samuel Gillam was also tried for murder at the Old Bailey. He too was acquitted, but the trial left a legacy of nervousness. Arguably it contributed to the failure of the London magistrates to nip in the bud the terrible, week-long Gordon Riots of 1780 which sacked the property and churches of Catholics, left prisons aflame, distilleries ransacked and, allegedly, saw drunken crowds trying to lap flaming gin from the gutters. It also contributed to continuing concerns about when and how troops might be used to deal with public disorder and other armed confrontations. On several occasions there was an exchange of letters between the Customs House and the Home Office requesting a Royal Warrant respiting any sentence passed on a soldier or sailor charged with assaulting or killing a smuggler 'as it is doubtful what a jury may do on such an occasion'.[29]

The system of policing in eighteenth- and early nineteenth-century Britain was far from perfect. There were some reluctant constables;

there were also men who took the job seriously and were turning it into a trade. There were inefficient watchmen; but many, perhaps even the majority were not the decrepit old drunks subsequently condemned by police reformers and some police historians. The army was not the best means for dealing with popular disorder; there was nervousness about what the law allowed, and individual officers sought to develop tactics that did not require the use of lethal force as the only resort. As will be shown in later chapters, the problems of popular disorder and political unrest, as well as of the difficulties of dealing with day-to-day criminal behaviour, were not much better handled when the new police began to be deployed. Moreover, the courage of watchmen like Robert Grubb and the detective abilities of men like Harry Adkins would have been a credit to the men of the institution that first appeared in 1829 just as they were to its police antecedents that had evolved over the previous century.

The problem with policing, as perceived at the beginning of the nineteenth century, was not that constables were reluctant and that watchmen were old and decrepit. It was rather that policing depended upon where the money was. The entrepreneurial constables of Bow Street and beyond were relatively competent at detecting crime, but they applied themselves primarily for rewards. Many parishes recruited watchmen, but the wealthier parishes paid better wages, recruited more men and gave them better equipment. A further factor is rather more difficult to pin down to precise dates and sudden change. It is possible to detect over the eighteenth and early nineteenth centuries a changing sensibility to order and decorum. In respectable society – from artisans and journeymen to shopkeepers and to gentry – a man's social worth was increasingly dependent upon his good works and probity, rather than on his physical presence and strength. Coupled with this was a growing belief that elegant streets and urban vistas should not be cluttered and encumbered with rude behaviour, with loiterers, itinerant street sellers, the refuse of butchers' shops and other rubbish. There was a growing perception too that criminality was the work of an incorrigible criminal class that lurked in the rougher parts of towns. The fury of the Gordon Riots fuelled such a perception, as did the reports, a decade later, of horrific violence and massacre in revolutionary Paris and other French towns. Organization by the politically unenfranchised to demand the vote served only to aggravate such anxieties.

In late August 1829, almost exactly one month before the new police took to the streets of London, Francis Haley was brought before Bow Street Magistrates' Court charged with being riotous, drunk and disorderly, and assaulting a gentleman. He was, it was alleged, 'so exceedingly drunk that he scarcely knew a man from a woman'. Haley, an Irishman, claimed that he had never been drunk before, though the keeper of the local watch-house claimed that he, personally, had known him drunk twenty times. And the watch-house keeper must have known, since Haley was employed as a watchman. Thus far the story has one of the major accusations levelled against the watchmen that patrolled the streets before the new police. But here the affair takes a twist. On being arrested by two members of the Bow Street Patrol, Haley turned on them. According to a contemporary newspaper, 'he called them ———— vagabonds, and told them that he should be their equal in a day or two, as he was appointed to the New Police, and should obtain his clothes, for which he had been measured, next week'.[30]

— CHAPTER TWO —

The First Bobbies, 1829–1860

FRANCIS HALEY'S DRUNKEN antics were sufficient to ensure that he never donned the uniform for which he had been measured. At 6.00 p m. on the evening of Tuesday, 29 September 1829, however, dressed in top hats and tightly buttoned blue tunics with high, stiff collars, the first constables of the Metropolitan Police stepped out on to the streets of London to begin their beat patrols. Many perhaps felt self-conscious; some probably wondered how they would be received; and some may have tended to arrogance, believing that they had considerable licence to lord it over ordinary civilians on the streets.

Over the next few months many of the first recruits turned their back on the job and many more were dismissed. Their replacements fared little better. Some men loathed the work and the discipline used to enforce it. Some may have been shaken by the violence that they occasionally confronted, and the violence itself forced some men out.

By May 1830 the force had increased from its initial 1,000 to about 3,300. A centrally controlled, uniformed body of men patrolling the streets was something quite new for London. Yet there were also continuities, not least in personnel. The new police continued and developed many of the changes that had been formulated or that had evolved over the previous hundred years and more; and for some time the new police continued to exist alongside the old.

'A military body employed in civil duties'?

While Sir Robert Peel stressed an increase in the statistics of crime when making the case to Parliament for the new police – crime statistics that he might well have recognized as suspect – it appears that he was more concerned to bring a degree of sense and order to the fragmented system of local watches and constables. Probably also he wanted to create a force that would obviate the need for the military in dealing with disorder, and a body that, centrally directed, could enforce the new thresholds of public decency and decorum on the streets. The Metropolitan Police has often been described as a completely new departure. It was, in so far as within a few months there was a centralized body of over 3,000 uniformed men on the streets. It was also novel in that the force's commanders, initially the two Commissioners of Police and a receiver who was responsible for financial matters, were appointed by and answerable to the home secretary and, ultimately, to Parliament. The two men chosen as Commissioners suggest something of Peel's thinking behind their selection. Colonel Charles Rowan was a veteran of the Peninsular and Waterloo campaigns who was capable of inculcating the necessary discipline. Richard Mayne, a Dublin-born lawyer, possessed the legal expertise.

The new institution declared the prevention of crime to be its principal object. Yet what has commonly been ignored is the way that it built upon and formalized into precise instructions the kinds of behaviour that men like Robert Grubb had followed half a century before. Unlike the old watchmen the new police were not to call the hour, but they were to patrol designated beats and they were supposed to get to know everyone who lived on those beats. The initial instructions specified that a constable should be able to cover the whole of his beat in ten to fifteen minutes. This was feasible in the teeming central areas of the Metropolitan Police District where the acreage of the police divisions was relatively small. It was, however, quite impossible in the outer divisions where beats were long and often stretched through open countryside (opposite).

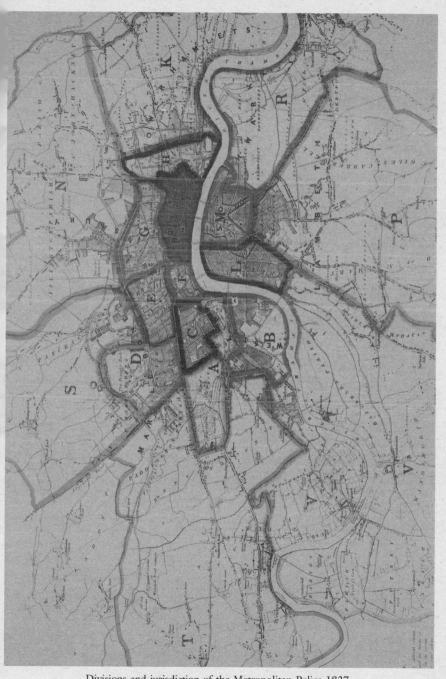

Divisions and jurisdiction of the Metropolitan Police 1837.

Initially half of the new force was directed to patrol at night; within a generation, however, around two-thirds of the constables were patrolling after dark. Again, like the old watchmen, the new police constables were authorized to stop and question anyone carrying a bundle or suspected stolen goods 'after sunset, and before sun-rising'. They could arrest anyone they considered 'about to commit a felony'. But they 'were to be civil and obliging to all people, of every rank and class . . . and cautious not to interfere unnecessarily, in order to make a display of authority'. The instructions prepared for the police outlining the duties of each rank and the respectful manner in which they were to behave towards the public were considered of sufficient importance to be printed, in full, over four-and-a-half columns of *The Times* four days before the first men began their patrols.[1]

The new police had unimpeachable overt aims, but it struggled for acceptance. Ratepayers objected to having to pay for a body of men that, unlike the old watchmen, were not under their control. Those in the wealthier parishes complained that there were now fewer men patrolling their streets than there had been when they ran their own watches. The poor objected to the ways in which the new constables interfered with their behaviour on the streets or moved on costermongers from whom they bought goods. If a costermonger objected to a police constable's claim that he was blocking a street, he knew that he could probably count on local support to intimidate or even physically resist the constable. The Commissioners struggled hard to ensure that their men behaved on their beats as instructed; they also set strict regulations for the manner in which constables were required to perform their duties, and these were enforced with rigid discipline. Some of the former watchmen wore coats with their parish and their beat painted on the back; every member of the new police had the letter of his division and a personal number on his collar which made him readily identifiable to any member of the public. Unlike the former watchmen the new police were required to patrol their beats at a measured steady pace, initially set at three miles an hour and later reduced to two-and-a-half. Also unlike the watchmen the new police were forbidden to talk to each other or gossip with members of the public. Work during the eighteenth and early nineteenth centuries was regularly punctuated with drinking a glass of beer, but the Bobbies were not allowed to drink, or even enter a pub, while on duty. The discipline appeared to be too militaristic to many outside the force, and many police recruits had difficulty in adjusting to something that was so alien to the practices of most early nineteenth-century civilian labour. In 1834 the Commissioners admitted to a parliamentary select committee that many men resigned after only two or three days, that drunkenness was a problem and the cause of most dismissals, and that of the 2,800 constables serving in May 1830 only 562 remained in the force.[2] The list of dismissals from one day in May 1830 is illustrative of the problems (and the reference to men serving in 'companies', rather than divisions, is illustrative of the military nature of the force at the time):

William Showger, 1 Compy. For talking to a female when on duty in Whitehall Gardens at ½ past 11 p.m.

James Rogers, 2d Compy. For being drunk and fighting with a woman in Tufton Street and abusing PC 125 Jos. Clark and pulling off his coat to fight him.

Wm. Kendall, 3d Compy. For being drunk and very disorderly in the Station House at one o'clock in the morning.

Thomas Tapp, 7 Compy. Brought to the Station House yesterday drunk.

Charles Cooper, 4 Company [sic]. For being in a Public House with a female when on duty at one o'clock in the morning.

Thomas Vaughan, 7 Compy. Not attending Worship Street Office with a prisoner, afterwards, drunk on duty.

Jos. Lyall, 8 Compy. For being absent from his beat three quarters of an hour and when found was in liquor.

George Mears, 11 Compy. Highly improper as a Police Constable in getting into debt at his lodgings and assaulting the landlord.

Michael Svollard, 14 Compy. For being in liquor when off duty in the streets, and making use of abusive language, and unfit for duty at 12 o'clock.[3]

The constables listed above broke the rules and they paid for it. They could be shown no leniency as the Commissioners sought to crack down on behaviour that might damage the good image and reputation of the police.

Unfortunately, when the Tory government that included Peel was replaced by a reforming Whig ministry, a delicate relationship emerged between the Commissioners, the Home Office and, particularly, the senior magistrate at Bow Street, Sir Frederick Roe. Undoubtedly some officers had promising careers ended by getting caught up in these sensitive political issues. Inspector Squire Wovenden was a case in point. In June 1834 Ruth Morris was arrested in 'D', the Marylebone Division, for being drunk and attempting to bilk a cabman. She was detained overnight in a police cell and the following morning she accused Inspector Wovenden of rape. Wovenden had been one of the first recruits to the police. He was a veteran of Wellington's Peninsular army, a sergeant-major recommended for a commission that was not granted only because of the end of the war. He was the father of seven children, one of whom was a constable in the force. The local superintendent would have none of the woman's complaint and refused to take action, but the ever-sensitive Commissioners insisted that the accusation go before a magistrate. At this point the woman refused to proceed with the charge but Roe, hearing of the case, took it before Lord Duncannon, the Home Secretary. Duncannon had one of the shortest ever tenures in that portfolio and, given that his abilities seem to have been better suited to backstage party-management, that was probably no bad thing. He authorized Roe to have Wovenden arrested and a case was prepared. Wovenden never faced trial; the grand jury threw out the indictment. Nevertheless, Duncannon insisted that both Wovenden and his superintendent be dismissed; the public, he insisted, had to rest assured that police behaviour was above reproach. Rowan and Mayne reluctantly agreed to the instruction, and failed to get Duncannon's successor to change it.[4]

The Commissioners worked hard to maintain the public's good opinion of the men in their charge. The press was scoured for stories about the police; an explanation was demanded of the appropriate divisional superintendent when a critical newspaper report was printed, and further details were sought in other, not necessarily eye-catching cases.[5] As well as the dismissals and punishments, the Commissioners' daily Police Orders abounded with concerns that the constables were not behaving as they should. Talking with servant girls was a particular bugbear of the Commissioners, and a regular subject for lampoons in the popular media.

> I'm one of the new police, egad,
>> The servant maids declare,
> There's not a chap in all the force,
>> Can start with such an air;
> My gloves of white, my coat of blue,
>> My dignity increase,
> And every gesture shows to you,
>> That I'm one of the new police.
>
> I'm partial to an outside beat,
>> For there I feel secure,
> Then with the servant maids I romp,
>> And play at some back door;
> I love to loll in kitchens too,
>> Some mutton joints to fleece,

I'm never in the want of prog,
    'Cause I'm one of the new police.

More seriously the Commissioners were concerned also about reports of constables seeking to conceal their personal numbers from the public, becoming angry or officious, and 'using their truncheons in any manner that may cause annoyance or irritation except when absolutely necessary'.[6] Another humorous ballad of the period picked up on this behaviour, suggesting in addition that, as well as being free with their batons and their authority, the constables might seek bribes from street sellers.

Of the boys, I'd be a terror mind,
The fruit stalls, too, I sell 'em,
And disturbance of every kind,
I with my staff would quell 'em.
A 'charge' would be as good as pelf [money],
My pleasures 'twould increase man,
For I'd make the 'charges' up myself,
When I'm a new Policeman.[7]

'Police Soldiers' and Popular Disorder

Some among the public, particularly those that espoused radical politics, felt threatened by this new, uniformed police force. The top hat and blue swallow-tail coat of the first Bobbies was designed to look civilian rather than military, but it was still a uniform and that, together with the hierarchical discipline of the police ranks, was enough to raise concerns. As the pro-parliamentary reform *Weekly Dispatch* put it before the force was a month old: 'The New Police is a military body employed in civil duties ... it is a powerful engine in the hands of Government, and may be employed for the suppression of public freedom.' The *Dispatch* became a regular critic, commonly referring to constables as 'police soldiers'.[8]

Hostility to the use of troops for controlling riot and disorder continued, and had been given a new edge following the massacre of Peterloo in August 1819 when cavalry, ordered to arrest radicals addressing a mass meeting in Manchester, killed at least eleven of the crowd and wounded many more. The new police did not carry lethal weapons, though they were sometimes issued with cutlasses if it was feared that they would have to confront a large, hostile crowd. It took the police time to develop tactics for crowd management and control that commanded the respect of the populace without the hallmarks of a military operation.

One of the first major confrontations with a political crowd in London aggravated concerns that the police were some kind of military body. This episode, which came to be known as the Calthorpe Street affray, had tragic consequences for one constable.

Robert Culley was one of the first recruits to the Metropolitan Police, joining on 21 September 1829 when he was twenty-three years old. He was posted to 'C' Division and his career looked promising; by early 1833 he had been allowed gratuities on four occasions. He had married in 1831 and lived in Litchfield Street, just north of Leicester Square and within the bounds of his police division. On 13 May 1833 he was one of a group from 'C' division ordered to assist in the dispersal of a meeting of the National Union of the Working Classes (NUWC) in Coldbath Fields. The NUWC was one of the small radical groups that had appeared during the agitation that concluded with the passage of the Great Reform Act in 1832. It had opposed the act on the grounds that it did not go far enough; it wanted all adult males to be given the vote and had called the meeting in Coldbath Fields as the first step towards a National Convention aimed at securing 'the Rights of the People'. Lord Melbourne, the Home Secretary, wanted to prevent the meeting. The Commissioners of the police, however, were concerned that there was no justification in law for banning the gathering in advance. In the aftermath of an unsatisfactory meeting between the Home Secretary and the Commissioners the former issued a poster warning people not to attend the event and the

Commissioners, fearing that there would be trouble, made plans that they hoped would not only prevent a riot but also placate Melbourne.[9]

Coldbath Fields was an open space in Clerkenwell. To the west it was bounded by Gray's Inn Lane and to the east by Bagnigge Wells Road. On the south-east edge was Coldbath Fields Prison; on the south-west edge were two short streets: Wells Street and Calthorpe Street. A pub, the Calthorpe Arms, was on the corner of Wells Street and Gray's Inn Lane. The police plan was to send seventy men from 'A' Division easterly along Calthorpe Street to arrest the NUWC leaders, confiscate banners and force the meeting to disperse north and eastwards across Cold Bath Fields. 'A' Division was the elite of the Metropolitan Police, based in and around Whitehall and commanded by Superintendent John May, a former sergeant major of the Grenadier Guards. May's contingent was to be augmented by men from 'D' Division proceeding northerly along Gough Street to the corner where Calthorpe Street became a foot-path running along the edge of Coldbath Fields to Bagnigge Wells Road. Men from 'C' and 'F' Divisions were to act as reserves in case the meeting did not disperse rapidly and in an orderly manner.

The plan did not work as intended. From the top of a wagon the speakers had urged their more enthusiastic supporters to roll up their banners and remove the heads from any pikes before they saw the police approach. When they saw 'A' Division marching along Calthorpe Street they got down from their platform and withdrew, but their enthusiastic supporters were not prepared to be so easily dispersed. The police were met with stones then, as they came face to face with the crowd, the crowd began swinging whatever weapons came to hand and the police began swinging their batons. 'A' Division fought their way through on to Cold Bath Fields and began clearing the small groups that hung around and making occasional arrests. But crowds remained in Calthorpe Street as 'C' Division came up in support and linked with the men from 'D' Division at the junction of Gough Street. Here the hand-to-hand fighting was brief but ferocious.

Police Sergeant John Brooks, like Superintendent May, had served for twenty-five years in the Grenadier Guards and had fought at Waterloo; he appears to have moved straight from the Guards to the police and had been a policeman for only about a year before the Calthorpe Street affray. Brooks insisted that he had not ordered his men to draw their batons and he was unsure to what extent the fighting had been joined when he saw a man carrying what appeared to be an American flag. As Brooks grabbed at it the flag-bearer, George Fursey, thrust at him with a brass-handled dagger. The point grated on Brooks's sixth rib otherwise, a surgeon feared, it would have pierced his heart. Constable Henry Chance Redwood heard his sergeant cry out, but did not realize that he had been stabbed. Redwood, in turn, grabbed the flagstaff and tried to wrench it away. He saw the dagger, raised his left arm to defend himself and received a thrust through the forearm. Redwood responded by bringing his baton down on his assailant's head and then passed the bloodied and dazed Fursey into the custody of two other constables. Pressing on up the road with Brooks, Redwood and the rest of the men from 'C' Division were constables Samuel A'Court, Robert Culley, Tom Flack and James McReath. As stones flew towards them McReath recalled Culley saying: 'Now for it.' The four officers were then engulfed in a tangle of cursing, sweating men lashing out at each other with whatever came to hand. Briefly Flack and A'Court saw Culley clutching his chest and saying he had been stabbed, but then they lost sight of him as they battled forward. Culley, blood soaking through his uniform, staggered back down the street into the Calthorpe Arms pub. In the pub he begged assistance; a barmaid endeavoured to comfort him, and he died with his head in her lap.

The aftermath of Culley's death highlighted the Freeborn Englishman's continuing sensitivity to the handling of demonstrations, the depth of hostility among sections of the population to the new police, and a new antipathy among some previous supporters. People had been able to watch the proceedings from windows and balconies, and some had been out on Calthorpe Street unaware of the meeting and of the Home Secretary's warning. A few commended the police, but others were highly critical. Local baker Samuel Clark, for example, thought that the men who patrolled the beats around Calthorpe Street generally did their duty well. But while he had always been a supporter of the police he was shocked by what he thought to be 'misconduct' leading up to and during the affray. It had 'made [his] blood run cold'.

A coroner's jury of seventeen local tradesmen was appointed to look into the circumstances of Culley's death. These men were not radicals. They were cheesemongers, grocers, ironmongers, pawn-brokers. Their foreman, a baker called Samuel Stockton, was to become a highly respected vestryman and secretary of the St Pancras Benevolent Institution. As the inquest progressed there were increasingly heated exchanges between the jurors and the coroner that climaxed when the jury brought in a verdict of justifiable homicide on the grounds that

> no Riot Act was read, nor any proclamation advising the people to disperse; that the Government did not take the proper precautions to prevent the meeting from assembling; and that the conduct of the police was ferocious, brutal and unprovoked by the people; and we moreover, express our anxious hope that the Government will, in future, take better precautions to prevent the recurrence of such disgraceful transactions in the Metropolis.

The jury went on to express its conviction that the one witness, a girl, who claimed to have seen Culley stabbed, had been 'tutored' by the police. Culley was buried immediately after the inquest and some of the onlookers jeered the 200 or so police who paraded at his funeral. A subscription was started for Culley's pregnant wife which reached £188.2s.6d, and the government paid her £200. These were considerable sums, bearing in mind that a constable's pay was £50 a year. The Court of King's Bench overturned the verdict of the coroner's jury, but stepped back from calling a new inquest. The jurors were feted across the metropolis; they were given dinners, cups and inscribed silver pens on which Culley was described, in the phrase of the *Weekly Dispatch*, as a 'police soldier'. A little over a month later George Fursey stood trial at the Old Bailey for assaulting Sergeant Brooks. Following the pattern set by the coroner's jury, the Old Bailey jury found him 'not guilty'.

Fursey's acquittal was not the last occasion that a jury manifested its concerns about police behaviour. John Peacock Wood, a 32-year-old Thames waterman, was taken into police custody in Shadwell High Street on 11 July 1833. There was dispute over the precise circumstances of his arrest, whether or not he was drunk, whether or not he had been involved in a fight. He was held overnight in police cells, and died a few hours after his release. Rumours circulated that he had been brutally beaten by the police; and there was some evidence that he had no injuries until after his arrest. The coroner's inquest attracted a considerable crowd, and once again there was tension between the jury and the coroner. Once again the jury was composed of a group of local worthies including a butcher, a mathematical instruments maker, a tailor and draper, and one man styled as a 'gentleman'. The jurors were unhappy about police officers in plain clothes seated in the court. They saw such policemen as 'spies'. They were also concerned that money might have been removed from Wood's pockets when he was in police custody, and not returned. As the inquest drew to a close, the jury foreman explained that he did not object to the police as a whole: 'The old system was defective, but the new might be most materially improved.' Moreover, picking up on the popular complaint of the time, he insisted that ratepayers should have control over the police. The jury returned a verdict of 'wilful murder by a policeman of K Division of the Metropolitan Police'.[10]

The Battle of the Bull Ring and a Model Bobby

In spite of criticism of the police for its conduct in the Culley affair and for other instances of violent behaviour, the Metropolitan Police provided the government with an alternative to sending troops to deal with provincial disorder. The New Poor Law of 1834, with its harsher discipline and grim workhouses, created considerable unrest; on average, some 300 officers were dispatched to the provinces every year during the 1830s largely to restore order or to maintain the peace in areas protesting against the new restrictions on poor relief and the workhouses, labelled by the poor as the English 'bastilles'. In 1838 the number of London policemen sent into the provinces reached a peak of 764.[11] The following year witnessed the first wave of Chartist agitation for political reform, and this brought new demands both in the capital and in the provinces. It was also notable for perhaps the most significant incident involving the Metropolitan Police as a kind of national riot squad when ninety officers were sent to Birmingham to deal with Chartist demonstrations.

In 1839 Birmingham was a thriving industrial town specializing in a variety of metal and brass ware, in jewellery and in gun barrels and locks. It did not have the kind of bleak, grimy, smoky atmosphere usually associated with the burgeoning industrial centres of the early nineteenth century. Indeed, thanks to the efforts of its street commissioners during the 1820s it had become known for the good roads – clean, drained and gaslit at night – that radiated out from an open space in the centre, known as the Bull Ring. The population had increased two-and-a-half times, to around 183,000, since the beginning of the century. Many lived in buildings clustered around courtyards; there were 2,000 courts in the town in the 1830s. There were also large gardens and open land in the city centre. There were factories, notably the great Soho engineering works at Handsworth, but most production was carried out in small workshops, often converted dwellings concentrated in the centre. This meant that there was little social distinction between master and man; moreover, given the nature of the Birmingham trades, a very high percentage of the workforce was skilled. The railway provided a new and promising transport link; a line to Liverpool had opened in 1837 and one to London in 1838. Also in 1838 the town received a Charter of Incorporation allowing it to appoint its own mayor and council. But while economically and socially it appeared successful, in July 1839 Birmingham had become a centre of Chartism and was seething with political unrest.

Birmingham's Chartists believed not only in the basic demands for suffrage and annual parliaments, but also in the power of numbers. More seriously for the authorities, an alliance of middle-class reformers and working-class radicals had broken down and it was in Birmingham that the firebrand Chartist orator Feargus O'Connor had made his first public statements about physical force, arming, drilling and, if necessary, fighting. In the first days of July 1839 the Chartists commandeered the Bull Ring for evening meetings. The local magistrates had infantry and cavalry on hand but were reluctant to deploy them; the meetings were, after all, perfectly peaceful in spite of the occasional blast of violent rhetoric. At the magistrates' request, the Home Office agreed to send a detachment of the Metropolitan Police. On the evening of 4 July the Chartists assembled as usual at about eight o'clock, but their meeting had scarcely commenced when the police, straight off the London train, marched, allegedly with batons drawn, into the Bull Ring and proceeded to disperse the meeting, arrest speakers and pull down banners. At first the crowds were stunned and gave way, but the more spirited Chartists rapidly recognized their numerical superiority and began a violent resistance. Within minutes the police were on the defensive; they were driven out of the Bull Ring and several were so badly beaten that, in the initial reports, it was suggested that some of them had fatal injuries. The magistrates now felt compelled to call on the army and a detachment of the Rifle Brigade and troopers from the 4th Royal Irish Dragoons rescued the police and secured the Bull Ring. Four days later the Metropolitan Police, now increased to ninety men, restored their pride when they dispersed another Chartist crowd in the Bull Ring without the aid of troops.

On 12 July Parliament overwhelmingly rejected the petition presented in the name of Chartists from all over the country. The rejection prompted more unrest and once again anger flared in

Birmingham. On 12 July there was serious rioting in the town and buildings were set on fire. Once again, their numbers reduced to forty men, the Metropolitan policemen, armed with cutlasses and backed by soldiers from the start, waded in, broke heads, but broke up the crowds.

No one was killed in the sporadic disorder and fighting in Birmingham that July, but the material damage was considerable. The events provided more ammunition for critics of the police. The Chartists' weekly, *The Charter*, described them as a 'Bludgeon Army' and an 'unconstitutional novelty'; and it had not forgotten the verdicts of the coroners' juries in 1833.[12]

Among the battered, bruised and bloodied Bobbies that struggled with the crowds was Police Sergeant William Edwin Fairbrass. Fairbrass was a former soldier, but the hand-to-hand fighting in and around the Bull Ring was the only serious battle that he ever fought. Born in Whitstable, Kent, in 1806, Fairbrass had enlisted in the 7th Foot in 1825. But there were no conventional European wars for the British army to fight in the aftermath of Waterloo and Fairbrass had spent seven years with his regiment on Corfu which, in the aftermath of the Napoleonic Wars, was the seat of the British High Commission for administering the Ionian Islands. Early in 1832 his service with the army expired, he embarked on the transport ship *William Henry* and returned to England for his discharge. On 10 August that year, aged twenty-six, he joined the Metropolitan Police.

Fairbrass was one of the success stories among the early recruits to the Metropolitan Police. He was not the only member of his family to join the force; two brothers, Alfred James and Edward Augustus, joined shortly after him but both lasted just six months before resigning. William's career, in contrast, was long and followed the kind of pattern that Peel, Rowan and Mayne had hoped for from the men. He lived for most of his twenty-two years' service in police stations or police accommodation close to a station. In January 1835 he married Mary Ann Davis who, over the next fourteen years, bore six, possibly seven children. Two of the children, and perhaps a third, died before their tenth birthdays and several of the others were packed off while still children to grow up and work in their mother's native Wales. Fairbrass was promoted to sergeant in May 1839 and to inspector four years later. As an inspector in 'A', or the Whitehall Division, during the Chartist agitation of 1848, he became involved in another confrontation with radical politicians, though on this occasion his role was rather different from that in Birmingham.

Charles Cochrane, a gentleman radical who had run for election in Westminster in 1847, sought to win Chartist acclamation and recognition by staging mass demonstrations against unpopular legislation. In March 1848 he organized a meeting in the unfinished Trafalgar Square to protest against income tax. The following month he called a second meeting; this time the target was the hated Poor Law. Fairbrass was not on duty during the second demonstration but he noticed that Cochrane's carriage wheels had become caught up with those of a cab. What happened next is unclear. Some of the police appear to have thought the obstruction deliberate and waded in with their batons. Fairbrass seems to have attempted to take control of the situation, but was accused of assaulting George White, a messenger for the Poor Man's Guardian Society who was working as Cochrane's driver, and was summonsed to appear at Bow Street Magistrates' Court. The magistrate concluded that the police were only doing their duty, that Fairbrass had no case to answer, and discharged him. In a curious twist Cochrane subsequently rewarded the inspector with an elegant box full of sovereigns; presumably Cochrane accepted Fairbrass's insistence to the Commissioners that, rather than striking White himself, he had, in fact, rescued him from the assaults of one of the respectable gentlemen sworn in as special constables to assist the police.

Three years after the last great Chartist manifestation and after revolution had once again run amok through Continental Europe, Victorian Britain celebrated its economic success and, to a less obvious extent, its constitutional satisfaction by hosting the Great Exhibition of 1851. As Joseph Paxton's elegant Crystal Palace took shape in Hyde Park, Inspector Fairbrass was given the task of drilling and equipping the 1,000 new men recruited by the Metropolitan Police to ensure order and decorum at this cele-bration of the Victorian gospels of work and progress. The success of the exhibition, with excursion crowds coming from all parts of Britain as well as from across the English Channel, was seen by many as a demonstration of the superiority of London's new police. It seemed nothing short of a miracle that such crowds, drawn from all classes, could gather, mingle and circulate without trouble. An article in the *Edinburgh Review* explained how, each day, nearly 400 police patrolled inside the Crystal Palace with another 250 outside; and there were, it boasted (probably wrongly), only eight cases of pickpocketing and ten of pilfering – and all of the stolen property was recovered. How far Fairbrass's role in such success was ever acknowledged by his superiors is unclear though, together with several other officers, he was awarded a gratuity of £5 at the beginning of 1852.

Two years later, noted as 'worn out', he retired with an annual pension of £67. He lived on, however, for more than twenty years, finding a new wife after Mary Ann had died and moving to North Yorkshire, where he died, following a stroke, in November 1876.[13]

Spies and Detectives

Like their predecessors in the London Corresponding Society, the radicals of the 1830s met in public houses to discuss politics and debate contemporary issues. The Home Office and the Commissioners of the new police recognized that they had to tread carefully in the investigation of radicals. The Bobbies were already criticized in radical circles for resembling a military force like the French Gendarmerie. There were also suspicions, voiced in the Wood inquest of 1833, that they would adopt another attribute of the French police system, one that had already caused disgust and disquiet in recent British history: the role of 'spy', and worse still of agent provocateur. Unfortunately for the Metropolitan Police, the affair of Police Sergeant William Popay, which virtually co-incided with the Calthorpe Street affray and the inquest on Wood, exposed a police officer apparently acting in precisely this fashion. For the ex-soldier and idiosyncratic radical William Cobbett, who looked back to a mythic England through bucolic spectacles, the Popay affair demonstrated just how 'French' the new Metropolitan Police was: 'I hate it because it really tears up the government; that good natured government, that gentle, that confiding, that neigh-bourly and friendly government, under which I was born, and under which my forefathers lived.'[14]

Popay had joined the police in August 1831. Aged about thirty-three he had travelled down from Norfolk where he had been a schoolmaster and where he also acted as a coal meter in Yarmouth. There were thirty-two coal meters in the town whose job was to check and weigh cauldrons of coal brought into the port. The post was something of a sinecure in the gift of the Yarmouth Corporation; Popay had a deputy to keep the job going for him and he continued to enjoy the profits of the post after he had moved to London, receiving about £23 or £24 a year from it. He served as a Metropolitan Police constable for a few weeks in South London, first in Brixton and then in Streatham. His wife was employed doing ornamental needlework for ladies in Streatham, while the eldest of his eight children went into service with a London alderman. Popay's health deteriorated in the early months of his police career and, on the recommendation of his inspector, he moved to the police station in Walworth where he took on clerical duties. His superintendent at Walworth, Andrew McLean, requested that he attend meetings of the radical National Political Union (NPU) and report on its proceedings. Over several months Popay sent in fifty-one reports of the political debates and meetings that he attended in the same kinds of pubs and assembly rooms that George Lynam had attended forty years before. But, unlike Lynam, Popay appears to have done rather more than just send in reports. He also began to play an active role in the Union, a role that encouraged the more extreme forms of radicalism. It came as a considerable shock to James Burrell Brown, a bootmaker of East Street, Walworth, and a member of the NPU when, returning from chapel one Sunday morning, he saw Popay sitting in the local police station. He made inquiries and discovered that one of his mates had a brother in the force, Police Sergeant Thomas Dean, who confirmed that Popay was indeed a police officer, now newly promoted to sergeant.

The repercussions were serious. Members of the National Political Union made a formal protest about the police being deployed as spies and a select committee of Parliament met to investigate. The Commissioners, Superintendent McLean and Popay himself were all called to give evidence. Popay was censured and was dismissed from the force. The committee also probed the Commissioners on what had happened to Police Sergeant Dean. It turned out that he too had been dismissed. Dean had been in the police for two years but appears to have shared the popular understanding of the Freeborn Englishman and his brother's commitment to political radicalism. Commissioners Rowan and Mayne considered his behaviour to have been close to insanity. Following the Calthorpe Street affray he had abused the police, applauded the coroner's jury, criticized Lord Melbourne as 'a damned fool' and, when ordered to appear before the Commissioners, replied that he 'would appear damned well armed'.

The concerns about Popay were particularly focused on the fact that he had attended political meetings in plain clothes and had done rather more than simply report what he saw and heard. But the questions of the select committee also yielded information on the extent to which other members of the new police were also taking to the streets in plain clothes to deal with the more conventional problem of crime. Superintendent McLean explained that 'a man in uniform will hardly ever take a thief'. The Commissioners explained that to guard against 'the most difficult sort of robberies', specifically those in which skeleton keys were used after dark, they had sent men in plain clothes into a division other than their own to watch for offenders. They had also deployed men in plain clothes to watch for pickpockets when processions were held in the streets.[15]

A few years after the Popay affair the problems of trusting certain men to act in plain clothes were again exposed, but – probably because the context was criminal rather than political – the affairs were more muted and at least one was kept from the public. PC Jesse Jeapes joined the Metropolitan Police in 1840. Several times in over fifteen years' service he was described in the press as an 'active officer' and he seemed to have an exemplary record. He appeared frequently as a witness or as the arresting officer in magistrates' courts and at the Old Bailey. He used his initiative and discretion to stop and question people in the street. Knowing of a reception at the Duke of Wellington's house he suspected John Thomas Hunter of taking an overcoat belonging to one of the guests' coach drivers. Hunter had a good character and was acquitted but when, a few years later, Jeapes stopped nineteen-year-old Benjamin Moore carrying a small bundle, it turned out that Moore had just stolen goods from a dyer's shop. A similar stop and search of twenty-year-old John Dismond early one April morning in 1850 resulted in a successful prosecution for burglary. Not only did Jeapes find various goods under Dismond's hat and in his clothing, he also found a screwdriver which he was able to match to marks on a door that had been forced. Jeapes was authorized to work in plain clothes and, alongside William Ballard, a veteran of the old Bow Street Police Office, he investigated and made the arrest in a fraud case that collapsed only when a bank representative failed to attend the Old Bailey to give evidence. But Jeapes was not all that he appeared. In 1853 his sergeant accused him of selling stolen watches. An internal inquiry exonerated Jeapes and censured the sergeant, who was moved to another division. But the rumours of Jeapes's corruption continued. He was, allegedly, known to his criminal confederates as 'Juicy Lips' and, while there seems to have been insufficient evidence to bring a criminal prosecution against him, in 1855 he was dismissed from the force.[16]

PC Charles King did not cover his tracks as well as Jeapes. King had also appeared to be a good officer and was frequently entrusted to work in plain clothes. But suspicions about his behaviour led to his dismissal towards the end of 1854. Early in the following year he was arrested and questioned by the magistrates in Bow Street about corruption and links with criminal offenders. *The Times* ran a story about a witness being threatened and reported letters about the King case 'received from all parts of the country, and disclosures . . . which, if to be relied on, tend to implicate other officers of the metropolitan police in practices more or less reprehensible'. The result was that the Commissioners issued an order forbidding superintendents from allowing any of their constables to work in plain clothes. In April 1855 King stood trial for theft at the Old Bailey. Although he was prosecuted for only a single offence, it appeared that he had been running a gang of young pickpockets. He was found guilty and sentenced to fourteen years' transportation.[17]

It is tempting to think of King taking his inspiration from Fagin; Charles Dickens's *Oliver Twist* had, after all, appeared in both serial and book form in several versions since the late 1830s. Dickens himself developed a fascination for the detectives of the Metropolitan Police and produced three articles about them in *Household Words*. Most dramatically he went on patrol into the slum, or 'rookery', of St Giles with Inspector Charles Frederick Field and wrote an evocative account of the experience.

Saint Giles's church strikes half-past ten. We stoop low, and creep down a precipitous flight of steps into a dark close cellar. There is a fire. There is a long deal table. There are benches. The cellar is full of company, chiefly very young men in various conditions of dirt and raggedness. Some are eating supper. There are no girls or women present. Welcome to Rats' Castle, gentlemen, and to this company of noted thieves!

'Well, my lads! How are you, my lads? What have you been doing today? Here's some company to see you, my lads!' . . .

Inspector Field is the Bustling speaker. Inspector Field's eye is the roving eye that searches every corner of the cellar as he talks. Inspector Field's hand is the well-known hand that has collared half the people here, and motioned their brothers, sisters, fathers, mothers, male and female friends, inexorably to New South Wales. Yet Inspector Field stands in this den, the Sultan of the place. Every thief here cowers before him, like a schoolboy before his schoolmaster. All watch him, all answer when addressed, all laugh at his jokes, all seek to propitiate him. This company alone – to say nothing of the crowd surrounding the entrance from the street above, and making the steps shine with eyes – is strong enough to murder us all, and willing enough to do it; but let Inspector Field have a mind to pick out one thief here, and take him; let him produce that ghostly truncheon from his pocket, and say, with his business-air, 'My lad, I want you!' and all Rats' Castle shall be stricken with paralysis, and not a finger move against him, as he fits the handcuffs on![18]

Dickens's experience of Rats' Castle and other dingy haunts where Field showed off his authority fed into the underworld scenes of *The Mystery of Edwin Drood* (1870). Field himself has often been taken as the model for Inspector Bucket in *Bleak House* (1851–3). Dickens's praise for Field was probably a contributory factor in the overall improvement in the image of the police in the middle decades of the century. Nor was Dickens alone in presenting an attractive picture of the new police detectives. The journalist William Russell, writing as a police detective under the name 'Waters', produced a series of short stories for *Chambers Journal* between 1849 and 1853; in 1856 these were collected together and published as a popular book, *Recollections of a Detective Police-Officer*. In 1860 there was another mock memoir, *Tom Fox: Or, the Revelations of a Detective*, which described the detective as far better educated and much more intelligent than 'the common peeler'. Tom Taylor's popular play *The Ticket-of-Leave Man* was first performed in 1863; one of the central characters, the honest, upright master of disguise Jack Hawkshaw, was a police detective. Five years later in *The Moonstone*, often described as the first English detective novel, Wilkie Collins presented his readers with the sympathetic but unyielding Sergeant Cuff.

For the first ten years of the Metropolitan Police, much detective work remained in the hands of constables still based in the old magistrates' Police Offices like Bow Street. On occasions there was rivalry and as noted earlier, Sir Frederick Roe, the chief magistrate of Bow Street, was decidedly hostile to the new police. The rivalry could inhibit some police work. When an elderly clerk was found bludgeoned to death in December 1832 the investigation was initially pursued by a constable from the old office in Hatton Garden. His inquiries yielded little and Superintendent Dixon of 'G' Division of the Metropolitan Police took over. Dixon convinced himself that he had identified the murderers and two known offenders were arrested. But the waters were muddied further when an experienced constable from the old Lambeth office, investigating a burglary, closed in on one of the men arrested on Dixon's orders and released new evidence to the press without consulting Dixon. Even so, there were still insufficient grounds for any prosecution. Dixon's suspects were released, and the case remained unsolved.

But rivalry between members of the old and new police was by no means universal. Some members of the former transferred to the latter. Joseph Sadler Thomas, for example, had been a constable of the parish of St Paul's, Covent Garden before he was appointed as the Superintendent of 'G' Division, which covered part of his old patch. Three others of the first seventeen superintendents had held similar positions – the other thirteen were former warrant officers in the army. Inspector Nicholas Pearce of 'A' Division, who was regularly employed on 'special detective duties', was a former member of the Bow Street Patrol. Perhaps more interesting and more surprising, some members of the new police transferred to the old: Henry Fall, Abraham Fletcher and Joseph Shackell all went from the Metropolitan Police to be Principal Officers at Bow Street between 1832 and 1836. Individual constables from the new and old police appear to have worked out a live-and-let-live arrangement on the streets, even assisting each other when necessary, until, in 1839, the old system of principal officers and constables in Bow Street and the other magistrates' offices was finally disbanded.[19]

The Metropolitan Police still boasted of being a force for preventing crime by watching; the detection of crime was considered as secondary. Rowan and Mayne, the first two Commissioners, had high hopes for the concept of prevention. A uniformed man, it was hoped, would drive offenders off the streets, while the number on his collar made him readily accountable to everyone. But, in spite of the efforts of popular literary figures like Dickens and Collins, some of the old English concerns about the very idea of a policeman persisted, especially an unidentifiable detective officer wearing plain clothes; and these concerns were even in the minds of the two Commissioners, especially that of Mayne. The detective policeman smacked of things French, of the sinister, snooping practices of Napoleon's police minister Joseph Fouché, and this fostered the public's fear of the undercover men among the Bobbies. Moreover, a very public failure could provoke a wave of public criticism. The murder of a three-year-old boy, Saville Kent, at Road Hill House near Trowbridge on the night of 29–30 June 1860 was the most notorious such instance.

Inspector Jack Whicher was one of the Metropolitan Police's leading detectives. He had been lionized by Dickens alongside his then superior, Inspector Field, and had a string of successful arrests and prosecutions behind him when, after nearly two weeks, the Wiltshire magistrates asked Mayne to send a detective to sort out the local force's stalled murder investigation. For nearly another two weeks Whicher searched and questioned. He concluded that the little boy had been killed by his stepsister Constance, the daughter of his father's first marriage. Whicher's conclusion was correct, but it led to no action. Constance Kent confessed five years later, but by that time Whicher had resigned from the police. Some of his colleagues thought him a broken man; the doctors said he had 'congestion of the brain', which may have been anxiety brought about by his denigration by the press.

Whicher, like other Metropolitan Police officers, was recruited from the working class; born in 1814, he was the son of a gardener in Camberwell, then a rural area a few miles south of the city. The press and respectable society were quite content for Whicher and his comrades to plunge fearlessly into the rookeries in pursuit of what was increasingly referred to as 'the criminal class'. But it was quite another thing when the same policemen began to ferret into the homes and lives of the respectable middle class and to accuse their daughters of heinous offences. Everyone had their own theory about who had murdered poor Saville; few agreed with Whicher. Even Dickens told friends that he had lost faith in the detective police, and some newspapers began to make hints about detectives being motivated by greed, resurrecting fears of the blood-money scandals of the previous century.[20]

Blood-money accusations were unfair and unjust, but after the abolition of the constables of the old Police Offices some of their daily practices, and sometimes their slightly dubious ones, were continued by the new police. A good example was presented in 1844 when former Bow Street officer Francis Keys told a parliamentary inquiry into the problem of the theft of expensive dogs in the metropolis how he had negotiated with thieves for the return of such dogs. Joseph Shackell, who had transferred back from being a Principal Officer at Bow Street to being an inspector in the Metropolitan Police in 1839, gave a similar account of speaking with such offenders, including 'an organised gang', over the previous fifteen years.[21] Shackell had acted with the permission of magistrates and had taken no personal reward, but other officers, as evidenced by the cases of Jeapes and King, appear to have become involved with criminal offenders. And in the same way that the new police worked alongside the constables of the old Police Offices, so too, on the fringes of their jurisdiction and for an even longer period, they worked alongside traditional parish constables. The men holding the post of parish constable were not necessarily overawed by the new police or by their social superiors, and they continued to manifest the old notions of the Freeborn Englishman and duty to their community.

Policing Aristocratic Duellists

Historians have recently pointed to a growing refinement in manners apparent at least from the early eighteenth century. This led to increasing limitations on male aggression, particularly among those social groups that considered themselves respectable. The development was largely encouraged by peer-group attitude and approval, but sometimes it was even enforced by the courts. One of the clearest manifestations of the development was the way in which duelling was increasingly frowned upon in early nineteenth-century England. Even so, there continued to be men, particularly in the military, who responded to a perceived slight against their honour with a challenge. Wimbledon Common, which abutted 'V' Division of the Metropolitan Police District, was a popular place for such confrontations. Towards the end of the 1830s the local magistrates were sufficiently concerned about the number of duels on the Common to seek a new parish constable for Wimbledon. They found their man in Thomas Hunt Dann, a local miller who lived with his family in the windmill that overlooked a site popular with duellists. In the late afternoon of 12 September 1840 Thomas Brudenell, 7th Earl of Cardigan, and Captain Harvey Tuckett faced each other on the Common twelve paces apart. The first shots of both men missed their targets. Tuckett fired a second time, and missed again. Cardigan took his second shot; the ball ripped its way under Tuckett's ribs, exiting his body by his spine. The duellists and their seconds were not aware of being observed. Constable Dann, standing 20 feet up on the stage of his mill, had seen their coaches arrive and, as the scene began to unfold, he suspected their intentions. He called to his wife to keep watch on the proceedings as he rushed into the mill and down the stairs. He ran outside, but turned back to get his constable's tipstaff: 'I did not like to go without my authority.' He ran the 220 yards to the scene, arriving moments after Cardigan's second shot. He arrested Cardigan, took Tuckett's card and ordered a surgeon to take him home and see to the wound – a wound which Tuckett was fortunate to survive. It says much for Dann's courage, his commitment to his office and his faith in the standing of that office, that he was prepared to confront and arrest a man who was clearly his social superior and who was among a cluster of other men who were also his social superiors. Moreover, while the notoriously prickly Cardigan and his entourage may, in private, subsequently have mocked Dann as a local Dogberry, they bowed to the authority of his office. Cardigan and his second, Captain John Douglas, got into a post-chaise with Dann and were escorted by him to the nearest Metropolitan Police station at Wandsworth, where Dann handed over his charges to Inspector John Busain.

It was not the first time that Dann had been involved in prosecuting duellists; and he claimed that he had even managed to prevent some confrontations. But the Cardigan duel was exceptional in that the earl stood trial before his peers. Dann, his wife and their fourteen-year-old son gave evidence at the Home Office, before the Grand Jury and then in Cardigan's trial in the House of Lords. The earl was acquitted on the charges of intent to murder, and intent to maim and inflict grievous bodily harm, largely on a technicality. Cardigan went on to lead the Light Brigade into the Valley of Death at Balaclava. Dann went back to his mill and probably remembered, with advantages, that particular feat on Wimbledon Common and its aftermath.

In the metropolis proper Police Sergeant William Fairbrass, the cuts and bruises from the violent confrontation of the Birmingham Bull Ring now healed, settled to supervising his squad of Bobbies as they patrolled their various beats at the steady, regulation two-and-a-half miles an hour. Out in the provinces the country cousins of Dann and Fairbrass were beginning a police relationship of their own as more new police began to be established alongside the old.[22]

— CHAPTER 3 —

Country Cousins: Policing outside London, 1839–1860

CHANGES TO POLICING outside London gathered pace during the 1830s and 1840s. The new Metropolitan Police provided one example for men in the provinces to follow, but advocates of revising and reforming the old system could still mount a convincing case and still had influence. The Metropolitan Police provided a cadre from which the leaders of police in the provinces could be recruited, but since it was neither the only model available nor universally applauded, its ranks did not constitute the only pool from which senior officers might be drawn.

As in London, the police in the provinces provided opportunities. The life was tough, but so were many other working-class jobs in Victorian England and any man able and prepared to stick with it might enjoy a good career, with a pension, and even some social advancement. Also, as in London, the new forces often had to struggle for acceptance, and it mattered not whether they were situated in a district with a traditional, rural way of life or in one of the burgeoning industrial areas.

New Police for the Counties

By the second quarter of the nineteenth century Britain could boast proudly of being the 'workshop of the world'. The products of her new industries outclassed and outsold every competitor, and her insistence on free trade helped to boost her economic dominance. But while large areas of Britain became used to living under the sooty clouds produced by the chimneys of new factories, vast swathes of the country remained rural, if not necessarily agricultural.

Some fifty miles due north of London was Woburn Abbey, the seat of the Russell family, the Dukes of Bedford. During the early years of the nineteenth century the family extended and consolidated its estates. The population of the small village of Woburn itself was tied closely to the massive stately home and to the work offered within it and on the surrounding estate. An old turnpike ran north out of the village over a heath and close by the open quarries where, for several hundred years, fuller's earth had been mined for cleaning sheep's wool before it was carded and spun. After two miles or so the turnpike ran through the hamlet of Hogsty End where some inhabitants already preferred the more salubrious name of Woburn Sands. Over a small hill and scarcely a mile to the east of Hogsty End was the ancient village of Aspley Guise. Aspley Guise was not tied to any estate; according to the *Bedfordshire Commercial Directory of 1847* it was a village 'large and handsome and noted for its respectability and pleasantness of situation'. Its 800 inhabitants ranged from genteel householders and artisans, who provided some work in service and cottage industry, to farm workers.

William Pepler had a beer house in Aspley Guise. He was said to keep it open after hours. On 26 May 1840, after closing time, a man entered Pepler's house and asked for a beer. Indeed, some witnesses claimed that he begged for a drink. As the man was being served a woman came running into the house and shouted a warning to Pepler's wife: 'Sally, that's a trap for you, here's the policeman!' At this point William Clough, Police Constable 40 of the new Bedfordshire Constabulary, entered the house and announced that he intended to take proceedings against Pepler. The case came before the magistrates at Woburn Petty Sessions. Clough declared that he had only sent his colleague ahead in plain clothes to see if anyone was in the house, for fear that, as policemen, they might be assaulted. The magistrates appeared to accept his story but the case was dropped on Pepler paying costs.[1]

Most internal migration during the nineteenth century was into the cities, but PC William Knight Clough had moved in the opposite direction. He was born in 1815 in the East London district of Shadwell; his wife, Mary Ann, about a year later in neighbouring Limehouse. Clough had served for a year in the City of London Police when he decided to move to Bedfordshire and sign on as the fortieth recruit to the new Bedfordshire county force which began its duties officially on 23 March 1840. He was posted to the village of Hockliffe, just north of Leighton Buzzard and close to the border with the county of Buckinghamshire. Hockliffe was overwhelmingly agricultural, with a population of 1,100. The ratio of one policeman to a population of about 1,000 became the rule of thumb for officialdom in Victorian England though, in reality, the ratio broadly averaged out to roughly one officer for 700 inhabitants in the boroughs and one to 1,500 in rural areas.

While rural Hockliffe was a far cry from the bustle of Thames-side Shadwell and the City of London, Clough and his wife appear to have enjoyed the new life. In April 1840 he was reprimanded for absenting himself from duty without leave, but after that he appears never again to have blotted his copybook. He was promoted to sergeant in 1850, inspector in 1856, and superintendent in 1857, whereupon he moved, with his growing family, into the small market town of Leighton Buzzard itself. Leighton Buzzard had become the centre of a new petty sessions division three years earlier, but it was still very different from the East End of Clough's birth. There was a population of around 6,000 when he moved. Aside from its market the town was known, like much of Bedfordshire, for its straw plait; there were a few basket-makers and watch-makers, and some sand merchants. The town was also popular with some London sportsmen who kept horses there and travelled up to hunt with the Whaddon Chase. Clough retired in Leighton Buzzard in April 1875, after thirty-five years' service in the Bedfordshire force. Mary Ann, who had born him at least ten children, died a few months later but William, remarrying a woman some ten years younger, lived on in the town until his death in 1903, a few weeks short of his eighty-eighth birthday.

Thomas Woollaston was another man who moved from town to country police and who, like William Clough, grew into the job, stuck with it and made a career for himself. Unlike most of his contemporaries, Woollaston left a memoir of his thirty-eight years' service in Staffordshire. Although published as a book in 1884, Woollaston's memoir is essentially a series of disconnected narratives, each chapter signed off at the end with his name. Woollaston was born in Albrighton, near Shrewsbury, around 1816, although other details of his early life are a mystery. In December 1840 he was one of the earliest recruits to the Stafford Borough Police; two years later, when the borough force amalgamated with the new county constabulary, Woollaston transferred along with it. He continued to serve in Stafford until the close of the 1840s; his daughter and son were both born there. But he then moved to Stone, from there to Leek, and he finished his service as the superintendent in command of the West Bromwich division, where he retired, in 1879, on an annual pension of £110–12 shillings.[2]

Clough's Bedfordshire was virtually untouched by industrialization but Wollaston's Staffordshire was quite different. The southeast of the county, that area contiguous with Birmingham, was pock-marked with mines furnishing coal and iron. The north of the county had similar rich deposits that had been exploited from the eighteenth century; and it was also home to the Potteries where artisans produced the fine china ware of the Wedgwoods and the Mintons. Woollaston had, perhaps not surprisingly, little to say in his memoir about the local economy. Similarly, he made little mention of the mundane, day-to-day aspects of the beat patrol, preferring to jump from one exciting or notable event to another. He described a life of 'remarkable' pursuits and arrests. Among his most notable achievements was the investigation leading to the arrest of Lewis Ansell, a cordwainer charged in 1846 with the rape of a six-year-old girl. Woollaston had the unpleasant task of taking Ansell to the victim's bedside for identification and then escorting him back to the lock-up through an angry crowd showing 'much anxiety to get at him, groaning and yelling fearfully, the female portion using strong imprecations'. He also described the pursuit of a variety of thieves and robbers; on one occasion the suspect was an Irishman, thought to have stolen a watch, who set off from Stafford on the Uttoxeter Road.

> I called at a cottage and obtained the loan of a countryman's coat and straw hat. Divesting myself of Police uniform and donning these . . . I then pursued hotly, occasionally across fields to avoid being noticed. My reason for this was, if the man had noticed me hurrying after him, he may have suspected, and hurled the watch (if he had it) away.

Woollaston had little time for Chartists, which may have been because of his own, deferential political opinions. But it may also have been because he was serving in Stafford in 1842 during the national disorders when physical-force Chartism appeared to link with major economic unrest. In Staffordshire the disorder was particularly serious: the miners in the north of the county came out on strike, the Potteries were hit by the economic depression, and the loathed workhouses were bursting at the seams with new inmates. Chartists chased the county elite from the Shire Hall when they gathered to draft congratulations to the young Queen Victoria on escaping an attempted assassination and, as the situation slid from bad to worse, widespread rioting saw local police stations sacked and looted. Troops had to be called in to restore order.

Woollaston's move from Stafford to Stone in 1849 may have been due, in part, to a confrontation with a local gentleman who accused him of failing to organize his men sufficiently to suppress a disorder in the district where the complainant lived. Woollaston, then an inspector, was particularly annoyed not only that the gentleman made a formal complaint before the Stafford Town Council, but also that he was never 'called into the Council Room to hear or reply so that [the complaints] were made, listened to and observed upon in my absence, and his *exparte* statements afterwards published in the *Staffordshire Advertiser*, without an answer'.

At two of the stations where he served, Woollaston, like many other policemen at the time, also fulfilled the role of an assistant Poor Law relieving officer. He recalled being instructed that officers should 'be firm in their refusal to dispense charity, by issuing relief tickets, and to do so only in the cases of persons positively and actually destitute'. But in Woollaston's experience such instructions were not particularly helpful; he and his colleagues felt that they had 'to grope their way in the dark' to sort out genuine cases of want. He claimed that he was sympathetic to the real mendicant, but since he considered 'vagrancy [to be] very nearly allied to crime' it seems unlikely that many poor wayfarers would have benefited from a confrontation with Woollaston.

Finally, while many contemporaries lionized London's Metropolitan Police, Woollaston did not think much of their behaviour when, in June 1858, men from the elite 'A' Division came to assist at the opening of Aston Hall and Park during Victoria and Albert's royal progress through Warwickshire. The Metropolitan Police commander sought to ease the crowd pressure on police ranks by using a heavy ornamental walking stick to knock off people's hats. He claimed that this was a usual tactic in London and, for a few moments each time he did it, the stratagem had the intended effect; the front ranks of the crowd turned and pressed back looking for their hats. But, as the hat-seekers jostled and pushed the crowd rather than the police, much annoyance began to develop and the local police feared trouble. 'The dilemma was met by using kind words and persuasion, and thus by keeping the assemblage in good humour matters passed off better than anticipated. The London Police, however, were decried and unfavourably spoken of.'

Woollaston took pride in his work and in his force, and he relished the responsibility that was given him. But he confessed that one duty, entrusted to him in 1853, was 'disagreeable'; this involved checking the expense claims of fellow officers. Before the creation of the new police most criminal prosecutions in England were brought by private individuals. Such individuals had to pay for the preparation of an indictment as well as any other expenses incurred by themselves, by their witnesses and by any counsel that they employed. Legislation in the mid-eighteenth century permitted some expenses for the poorest prosecutors and this was significantly extended in the 1820s. In some areas the new police appear to have taken over the role of public prosecutors from their inception, mainly for the many 'victimless' offences like drunkenness, but also when the victims were poor or female and hence, given the separate gender spheres of Victorian England, largely omitted from the public arena. Solicitors disliked the police having such a role; and, given the hierarchical nature of nineteenth-century society, many expressed their concerns in terms of class. 'One knows perfectly well the class of men from whom policemen are selected,' declared the Attorney General, Sir Alexander Cockburn, to a parliamentary committee in 1854.

> When you get a policeman, you get a minister, though a very subordinate minister, of justice, and you look upon him as a person on whom you may therefore rely; and I own it was not until I became a criminal judge that I saw the necessity of extreme watchfulness over them, without importing undue motives to them. I see that they take such an interest in the prosecution, by getting credit for the intelligence, and energy, and skill which they show while getting the witnesses together and bringing them to the court, and in bringing the prosecution to a successful issue, that I have become very sensibly alive to the necessity of watching their evidence carefully.

In the mid-century there were accusations of police constables engineering malicious or trivial prosecutions in order to supplement their wages out of the costs awarded by the courts, and sometimes sharing such costs with disreputable solicitors.[3] Woollaston did not mention such corruption in his memoir but, given when he was ordered to examine police officers' expenditure, it seems likely that the County Finance Committee may have had such concerns in mind as well as the overall cost of the criminal justice system in the county.

New Life for the Old System

The Bedfordshire and the Staffordshire Police, in which Clough and Woollaston served, were among the first of the new county forces to be established following the Royal Commission on a Rural Constabulary that met from 1836 to 1839, the County Police Act of 1839 and the amending act of 1840. The legislation was far less comprehensive than the Royal Commission had recommended. It was enabling rather than obligatory and authorized county magistrates to establish police for the whole or for a part of their county if they so wished. Indeed, the Staffordshire force was initially established only for the Hundred of Offlow in the south of the county where there was both a large mining population and concerns about 'gangs of depredators' from neighbouring Birmingham pillaging the area. But even though the men in Beds and Staffs, and in the other forces established under this legislation, commonly wore blue uniforms and top hats similar to those of the Metropolitan Police, and even though a few of the men, like William Clough, had police experience in London, there was no single model for the new forces to follow. There had been discussions about and experiments with different forms of county policing since the beginning of the century, and while there was a broad consensus that policing could and should be improved, by the 1830s and 1840s there was no general acceptance that creating a hierarchical organization of nothing but full-time, paid officers was the best way to proceed.

George Burgess was a constable in Macclesfield. At the end of the 1820s, he was sufficiently well regarded for the Cheshire magistrates to seek to appoint him as a special constable who would be paid to superintend his fellows. Unfortunately the magistrates found that, as the law stood, while they could pay Burgess various allowances and fees, they could not pay him a regular salary for his new post. The upshot of this was that the county bench petitioned for a private Act of Parliament. The Cheshire Constabulary Act of 1829 pre-dated the Metropolitan Police Act by a few weeks; it enabled the appointment of the first regular and paid constabulary for an English county. The new Cheshire Constabulary was never particularly large; at its peak it appears to have consisted of no more than three special high constables and about two dozen assistant constables. It was centred on the industrial districts, rather than spread across the county as a whole, since it was here that the magistrates felt there was most need for a significant new police presence.

The Cheshire force became a model for other counties even after the enabling legislation of 1839 and 1840 and a series of Acts of Parliament, driven by magistrates at the opposite end of the country in Kent, gave an alternative path for reform. These magistrates sought to develop the old system mainly by providing for professional, superintending constables to direct and supervise the existing parish constables.[4] Parsimony was probably a major spur to this legislation; a few superintending constables were much cheaper than a regular, hierarchical force. In some instances, however, the system seems often to have been undermined by the cadre from which magistrates selected their superintending constables. The magistrates wanted men with experience of policing to oversee their parish constables and increasingly these men were to be found in the new, hierarchical police forces. Thus the men appointed as superintending constables appear often to have been like John Dunne, William Hamilton and Alfred Hughes, who all gave evidence before the parliamentary select committee inquiring into policing in 1853. Dunne had served for a year as a constable in Manchester, seven years as a constable, and then an inspector in Essex and two years as an inspector in Bath, before becoming a superintending constable in Kent. He was in Kent for thirteen months before going to Norwich as Head Constable. Hamilton had been in the Irish Constabulary and both the Lancashire and Essex county forces before becoming a superintending constable in Buckinghamshire. Hughes had served in the Metropolitan Police, the Surrey County Police, as a superintending constable in Northumberland, and had then moved on to be the chief of police in Bath. All three were highly critical of the superintending constable system and did not hesitate to say as much.[5] But while the old system of parish con-stables was far from perfect, and while the attempts at superintending them had many drawbacks and problems, it is probably true to say that the more ardent police reformers, and those with a background in the new police forces, were always going to find it difficult to see any virtues in, or to adapt to the old system. They wanted clear lines of authority and full-time men under them who obeyed their orders, rather than men who were integrated with the communities in which they lived and commonly worked at a trade in addition to that of constable.

Even in those counties where the new police were established, the break with old systems and practices was not total. Most counties sought their chief constables from among gentlemen with some experience as military officers or as officers in the Irish Constabulary Northamptonshire, however, opted for an old-style London professional with a formidable reputation as a detective. Henry Goddard was a fishmonger by trade but in 1824 had joined the Robin Redbreasts. He had moved quickly to become one of the constables in the Great Marlborough Street Police Office, and by 1834 he was back in Bow Street as one of the Principal Officers. When the Bow Street establishment was disbanded in 1839 he had become a private detective before applying for the Northamptonshire post when it was first advertised.[6]

Goddard was an exceptional appointment for a county police, but at the beat level in many, perhaps most county forces, there appears to have been co-existence between the old-style parish constables and the new police constables. In some instances the old and the new co-existed relatively amicably and the parish constables undertook tasks that were not yet part of the policeman's duties. Even in Essex, noted for having an exemplary force commanded by John Bunch Bonnemaison McHardy, a former naval officer and inspecting commander of the Coast Guard who was an enthusiast for the new police, it was intended from the outset that the old would continue alongside the new. Indeed, some of the old police continued to be very active. Benjamin Carrington, for example, the High Constable for the Essex Hundred of Tendring, remained active in day-to-day policing and made regular arrests for drunkenness, obstruction and vagrancy. In 1843 it was a parish constable in the Chelmsford division that did the lion's share of the work in a rape case before handing the suspect over to his local, professional colleague in the county force. In some instances, however, given their local connections, the parish constables might side with the community against the police. Eaton Bray was a village in south Bedfordshire; in the mid-1840s its thousand or so inhabitants made their living principally from arable farming. When PC Thomas Sinfield charged eight men with assaulting him and rescuing a prisoner from his custody, the chairman of the local petty sessions felt compelled to comment on the 'irregular conduct' of the parish constables who had stood bail for one of the accused. Thomas Woollaston had a rather similar experience. On his second day as a policeman he was assaulted when endeavouring to break up a fight, and his assailant received the backing of those who opposed the new police in Stafford, including one of the old parish constables.[7]

New Police for the Towns

Just as the counties debated and experimented with policing systems, so too did the towns. Sometimes men like the Pardoes in York, whose policing dynasty was described above and began at the close of the eighteenth century, increasingly acquired the attributes and responsibilities of professional policemen; sometimes professionals were sought and recruited from elsewhere. In March 1821, for example, Stephen Lavender, formerly one of the Principal Officers at Bow Street, moved to Manchester to take up the appointment of Deputy Constable. Lavender served in the expanding industrial town until his death twelve years later, and he kept in touch with his former colleagues and superiors in Bow Street throughout this period.[8] Leicester also looked to the new London system and, after consultation with the Metropolitan Police Commissioners, Frederick Goodyer, an inspector in 'A' Division, was appointed to command the new borough force in January 1836. Goodyer's career followed a novel trajectory when, nearly four years later, he transferred to take command of the new Leicestershire county police.[9]

Incorporated boroughs like Leicester and York had powers of local government which enabled them to develop some measure of policing as they wished. Even so, the Municipal Corporations Act of 1835 established a degree of uniformity in the governance of such boroughs and required each of the new, elected town councils to appoint a watch committee that would take responsibility for policing within the limits of its jurisdiction. The industrial conurbations that had mushroomed from small towns and hamlets in the eighteenth century, as well as the small towns that remained, had always been able to apply for a private Act of Parliament to enable them to establish improvement commissioners who could levy a rate for lighting, watching and cleansing the streets. The Lighting and Watching Act of 1833 obviated the need for private legislation and enabled unincorporated towns and country parishes to levy a local rate that would pay for a local police. The small town of Horncastle in Lincolnshire was one of the many that took advantage of the act, holding a public meeting in October 1838 at which sixty-one ratepayers appointed an executive committee of seven (three merchants, two doctors and a grocer) to establish and run a police force of two. The committee went on to appoint Frank Ackrill, a local man, the son of a shoemaker and apparently known for his toughness, and William Gapp, a former member of the Metropolitan Police who had experience of patrolling the St Giles rookery.[10]

While there was debate, a Royal Commission and legislation concerned with police and policing in the 1830s and 1840s, the changes on the ground were often gradual. In the incorporated towns, following the Municipal Corporations Act, it was quite common for the old police to continue under the new regulations. In Portsmouth, for example, it appears that about half of the new police were former beadles, constables or watchmen; and in the Essex boroughs men slipped easily from one system to the other. In York, while advice was sought from the Metropolitan Police, the leadership of the watch committee's new force remained in the hands of William Pardoe, now named Superintendent of Police.[11]

Yet the old and new police were increasingly different in the way that their work practices and relationships were defined and understood. These differences were highlighted in the career of George Bakewell and in the pamphlets that he wrote on policing. Bakewell was born in Dereham, Norfolk, around 1807. He was one of ten children and seems to have grown up in Derby and Stafford. His father was a small businessman who was twice made bankrupt and who also appears to have escaped more financial troubles when a fire at a London warehouse was followed by a convenient insurance payout. Staying one step ahead of creditors seems to have been a way of life for the Bakewell family. George's elder brother James, a bone disposer and glue manufacturer, was bankrupted three times, and George himself got into financial difficulties while a farmer. These difficulties led him to write his first pamphlet, *Observations on the bill now before Parliament for the abolition of imprisonment for debt*, published in Manchester in 1836, which implies that he had himself been imprisoned for debt, and which set his life's pattern of bursting into print whenever he considered himself wronged. In a subsequent pamphlet Bakewell claimed that, while he was a farmer, he had served as a parish constable. In the summer of 1840, possibly having just been released from debtors' prison, Bakewell found himself in need of a job and, looking back perhaps to his time as a constable, he joined the new Birmingham City Police.[12]

The Birmingham City Police was one of three forces that, in their first years, were very similar to the London model. In the aftermath of the rioting in Birmingham in July 1839 and the rejection of the Chartists' National Petition, Whigs and Tories in Parliament concluded that they were living in desperate times and that these needed determined measures. Party divisions were largely set aside; Parliament resolved to ignore local sensibilities and passed three acts creating government-controlled police for, respectively, Birmingham, Bolton and Manchester. The bills, together with that which enabled county magistrates to create county constabularies, were rushed through in the last four weeks of the parliamentary session. Former army officers were appointed by the Home Secretary to command each of the three new urban forces. The Chief Constable in Birmingham was Captain Francis Burgess, who had fought at Waterloo and who, after the war, had become a barrister in Northamptonshire. Burgess thus combined, in his own person, the military and legal attributes of Rowan and Mayne in London.[13]

Burgess was an enthusiast for the Metropolitan Police model. His Police Instruction Book repeated the mantra that the 'principal object' of the new police was the prevention of crime. He required his men to patrol at the regulation two-and-a-half miles an hour while their supervising sergeants checked up on them, walking themselves at three miles an hour. But Burgess also put a greater emphasis on detection than the London commissioners. His force established a significant detective department in advance of London; his detectives enjoyed considerable success, particularly against coiners, who remained a problem in Birmingham among men who transferred their skills in the local button and buckle trades into the fabrication of false money. A hierarchical and military element appears to have been strong in the Birmingham force, and the fear of Chartist disorder occupied much of Burgess's time. But Burgess also tried conciliation and tact, and made strenuous efforts to ensure that his men appeared politically impartial.[14]

The city worthies of Birmingham were outraged by the government and Parliament imposing a centrally directed police force upon them, but much of the initial criticism was disarmed by Burgess's tact in dealing with the radicals and the significant number of arrests for crimes and petty offences. George Bakewell, however, had his own ideas about policing and he considered that the Birmingham force that he had joined did not measure up to them. His ideal was the old-style constable. He intensely disliked the military hierarchy, the discipline and the rigid beat system. The new police were too regulated; the discretion and skill of the constable was destroyed by the mechanical, repetitious beat and the insistence that men stick to it. In *Observations on the Construction of the New Police Force*, published in 1842, he speculated on what would happen to a young man who, down on his luck, joined the new police.

> I consider that no greater punishment could overtake him, than his being compelled to earn his bread by Police servitude, the storm and tempests of Heaven, the severity of frost, and the scorching heat of summer, to all of which he is exposed, are no hardships compared to the insults which an unpromoted Policeman must daily submit to, from men who are only his superiors by courtesy. . . I did feel both astonishment and regret, to witness a class of persons filling what has always been regarded as a responsible office, treated as if they where [sic] slaves, instead of servants of the Country and Crown.

The pamphlet stressed abuses in the Birmingham force and the inefficiencies and incompetence of many of the men. Some of this had a basis in fact; in Birmingham, as elsewhere, there was an enormous turnover of men in the early years. Though Bakewell insisted that he had resigned with honour in December 1841, there is other evidence to suggest that he was dismissed two months earlier for being drunk and disorderly. Either way, the Birmingham Police gave him a certificate of good conduct and he moved on.

Bakewell claimed that, briefly, he joined the Manchester Police, though since like that of Birmingham, the Manchester force was under Home Office control between 1839 and 1842 with a former soldier, Sir Charles Shaw, as Commissioner, it is difficult to know why. In 1846, however, Bakewell was in Sheffield and here, once again, he enrolled in the police.

Policing was different again in the great cutlery centre of Sheffield. An Act of Parliament in 1818 had established a body of improvement commissioners for the town and watching had always been the largest single component of their budget. In order to avoid being policed by a county force under the direction of the magistrates of the West Riding, the town worthies arranged to be incorporated as a borough in 1843. In accordance with the regulations for boroughs under the Municipal Corporations Act, the new town council appointed a watch committee with responsibility for policing. There was much continuity. The senior officer was retained and five of the fifteen active members of the watch committee were former improvement commissioners. The new police subscribed to the idea of prevention, but the differentiation between day police and night watchmen was maintained, at least in theory, into the 1850s. The day police were given a complete uniform; the night police were given only hats and greatcoats until the mid-1850s. The Sheffield Police appear to have been less military and less subject to harsh discipline than those in Birmingham, but Bakewell's career in the Sheffield force was no more auspicious, and ended with him penning new pamphlets of self-justification as well as being drawn into a radical political critique of policing in the town.

Bakewell lived in lodgings run by William Richardson and his wife Elizabeth. William Richardson was a fellow member of the night watch. On 15 May 1847 Bakewell accused Elizabeth of stealing a pair of his trousers and he threatened to arrest her. The police chief, Superintendent Thomas Raynor, attempted to calm matters and, on hearing the evidence, concluded that Bakewell's accusation was groundless. But Bakewell was determined on revenge and let other watchmen know of his intentions. The situation was such that when Inspector Matthews found Bakewell off his beat in the early hours of Sunday 16 May, he marched him to the Town Hall where the senior inspector, named Wakefield, ordered him to surrender his hat, coat and truncheon. Bakewell flew into a rage, threatened Wakefield with the weapon, and had to be overpowered and put in the cells. Over the next few days Raynor again, together with the mayor, attempted to settle the matter. Bakewell's trousers were found at a neighbour's where, it was alleged, he himself had left them. Elizabeth Richardson was advised to take out a warrant against Bakewell, and the mayor suggested that Bakewell enter into sureties for good behaviour towards her. Bakewell claimed that he had no money, but offered to leave the town. The offer was accepted; the mayor gave him a pound for his journey and Raynor gave him ten shillings. But then Bakewell refused to leave, insisting that the mayor and Raynor had no right to judge him, since that was the responsibility of the watch committee, and threw in his lot with a local radical grouping, the Sheffield Democrats, the leaders of which took up his case.

Bakewell's pamphlets on his Sheffield misfortunes returned to the issues that he had raised in Birmingham. Inspectors and sergeants of the new police were brow-beating the men 'as if they were slaves', and the men of the new police were generally a militarized force separated from the communities in which they made their mechanical patrols.

> The old and excellent constables the country once had, have, in great measure, been turned adrift, *without remuneration*, simply because they were sinking into the vale of years, or that they would not submit to be *drilled, and harassed, and tormented* by the chief of a police establishment, and their situations have been filled up, generally speaking, by young men, *some of whom have grossly abused the powers with which they have been entrusted*.

Bakewell continued to press for justice for himself during the summer of 1847; he even appeared before the watch committee to demand a reference. He had, after all, obtained a reference when he left Birmingham and, by this time, appears to have considered himself a professional policeman with all necessary attributes and understanding for the job. The watch committee refused his demand. For at least a year, Bakewell remained in Sheffield publishing pamphlets on the abolition of the death penalty and on the state of the poor and the iniquitous poor law; what happened to him after that remains a mystery. For a few years also the Sheffield Democrats, without any apparent involvement by Bakewell, developed their own critique of policing and the law and urged an end to the new form of bureaucratic policing and a restoration of an old style of local law enforcement rooted within the community.[15]

Triumphs, Trials and Tribulations

The 1830s and 1840s saw a significant growth in the opportunities for men who sought to follow the trade of police officer. The life was not easy, but then many working-class jobs involved long hours of often tedious and occasionally dangerous work, if not necessarily the fierce discipline of the new police. Unskilled, semi-skilled or even skilled men whose immediate job prospects were poor, by joining a police force and sticking with the trade, had the opportunity to pull themselves a few rungs upward on the ladder of the Victorian social hierarchy. A few, like Clough and Woollaston, did this by remaining loyally with one force for thirty years or more. Others watched for openings and applied for jobs often far away from where they were born or had begun or improved their police careers. Men like Stephen Lavender, Frederick Goodyer, Henry Goddard and John Dunne were among those who climbed the highest. Goddard went from Chief Constable of Northamptonshire to continue his career as both a private detective and as one of the three principal door keepers of the House of Lords – a job that appears to have been largely a sinecure with £300 a year. John Dunne climbed even higher. After his appearance before the select committee in 1853 he left Norwich to be head constable of Newcastle upon Tyne; from here he became Chief Constable of Cumberland and Westmoreland combined where, seemingly drawing a veil over both his humble origins and his age, he acquired a wealthy wife from the gentry and a knighthood. He retired in 1902 when he must have been well over 80 years of age. In addition to these nomadic, social-climbing professionals, some of the other men who joined the new provincial police forces following the legislation of the 1830s and 1840s had some experience of the policing role and tasks. A few had served in the old incorporated boroughs and simply changed their job title from watchman to police constable. But the majority of the recruits to these forces in the middle third of the century probably had little idea of what to expect in the new job.

As in the Metropolitan Police, a high percentage of recruits resigned or were dismissed within a matter of months, weeks or even days. They absented themselves from their beats, got drunk, consorted with prostitutes, tipped off friends and acquaintances about police actions, abused their superiors. Some disliked the boredom and loneliness of the beat patrol and the occasional vicious violence. Members of the new police were often abused by members of the working class as 'blue drones' and 'blue locusts'. Words may not hurt physically, but the abuse was often accompanied with sticks, stones, fists, boots and clogs as Bobbies sought to enforce licensing hours, for example, or to break up street brawls or a boisterous, rough entertainment such as a boxing match. There could be violence during political demonstrations and industrial unrest, and in one or two cities the police sometimes found themselves confronting sectarian crowds. Nineteenth-century Liverpool, for instance, was notorious for clashes between Irish Catholics and Orangemen and the two groups regularly set out to antagonize each other with their marches on, respectively, St Patrick's Day and 12 July – the anniversary of the battle of the Boyne in 1689 when Protestant King Billy beat Catholic King James.

Country workers were no different from working-class towns-people when it came to dislike of and occasional violence towards the police. A few weeks after William Clough's summons of the Aspley Guise beer house owner, the man who enrolled immedi-ately before him, PC 39 William Burns, was so badly beaten after attempting to clear a pub that he was unable to leave his house for a week. Burns resigned from the force soon afterwards. On 30 July 1844, in rural West Suffolk, PC James McFadden confronted three men who were breaking into a barn at Gisleham near Lowestoft. The three offenders were well-known locally; their leader was William Howell, who commonly wore a policeman's hat, a trophy from an earlier clash with the law. Howell shot McFadden in the thigh and the policeman was kicked as he lay bleeding on the ground. McFadden died of his wounds, but not before he had named his assailants; William Howell was executed and his abet-tors were transported. The Chief Constable considered the arson, animal maiming, poaching and robbery in rural Suffolk sufficiently serious to request firearms for his men. The Home Office refused but henceforth Suffolk constables routinely patrolled at night armed with cutlasses and they do not appear to have been reticent when it came to drawing and using them. In September 1863, for example, two Suffolk policemen claimed to have seen Samuel Branch attempting to steal fowls in Wherstead. Branch was a strong man and resisted arrest until PC William Balls struck him three times over the head with his cutlass. Branch's injuries were so severe that he was unable to appear in court. His counsel protested that Balls's use of his cutlass was the kind of conduct that he considered 'would never be permitted in England'. The magis-trates exonerated the constables on the grounds that Branch was strong and that Balls had lost his truncheon, but, on the grounds that his injuries were part punishment, they sentenced Branch to two weeks' imprisonment only, instead of the three months that they could have awarded. The regional HM Inspector of Constabulary and the Home Office were less than happy with this use of cutlasses. Major General Cartwright, the Inspector, did not consider East Suffolk had sufficient of a 'rough and disorderly population' to justify the regular issue of cutlasses. Officials in the Home Office considered that such an issue was not in accordance with the legislation regarding county police. But while these critical comments were sent to the county, there is no evidence that the Chief Constable and the magistrates ever discussed the matter or immediately issued orders changing the situation.[16]

The Home Secretary had little direct control over the provincial police. His approval was required before the appointment of a chief constable in a county, but even in the largest boroughs the watch committees had a completely free hand. The Home Secretary and his civil servants recognized that cutlasses and even pistols might sometimes be necessary for police officers, but they strongly resisted some of the more grandiose schemes that would have allowed military training and full-scale arming of the police. There was a cluster of such proposals following a plot to assassinate Napoleon III in 1858 that was hatched by Italian refugees in England and involved the use of bombs made in Birmingham. The proposals grew out of a fear that the French would overreact to the plot, especially in light of the improvements they had been making to their fleet and to the naval base at Cherbourg. The militia was found to be wanting; a Volunteer Force and a National Rifle Association were created in 1859 and, at the close of the year and the beginning of 1860, the Home Office received letters from the chairman of the Cheshire Police Committee, the Chief Constable of Cumberland and Westmoreland and the Chief Constable of Kent proposing that the police be trained in the use of rifles. The Home Secretary, Sir George Lewis, scrawled on the back of the letter from Captain John Hay Ruxton, the Chief Constable of Kent: 'This gentleman has very grand ideas. I wish these constables would think more of their staves and less of rifles.' In the following summer Chief Constable McHardy of Essex, who had now risen automatically to Rear Admiral on the Navy List, sent in his plan 'for rendering the National Constabulary numerically efficient, and a powerful auxiliary defensive Artillery Rocket and Rifle Corps, capable of being at least doubled, in 24 hours, by enrolling and training one Volunteer for each member of the Constabulary'. McHardy's plan, which included equipping the police with breech-loading rifles and putting field pieces in police stations, never got beyond his dreams.[17]

As in the metropolis, provincial Bobbies often had to struggle for acceptance. Thomas Hall, a Liverpudlian would-be Charles Dickens, encapsulated much of the criticism directed at the provincial police in the heavy-handed satirical speech that he wrote for a magistrate in his novel *The Life, Adventures, and Opinions of a Liverpool Policeman*. The magistrate began by explaining that the Liverpool Police, 'the most efficient police in Europe', could not be expected to deal with much serious crime or with the various forms of corruption and duplicity practised by a few supposedly respectable gentlemen. That fact established, he went on to praise the police for prosecuting journeymen who sought to profit from perks at their workplace so that they could frequent low theatres and pubs. In addition, he pointed out, the police preserved order and security by prosecuting tradesmen, and others,

for leaving out handcarts, steps and ladders, in the way of foot passengers, stopping roads by means of throwing down rubbish, not paling off new buildings, shaking carpets, chimneys being set on fire, firing squibs on the 5th of November, not sweeping away snow, boys flying kites, manure men for not pursuing their avocation at the right hours. See how many girls have been brought up here for threatening gentlemen . . . unless they satisfied their rapacious exactions. See how many boys have been brought up here for sleeping in brick kilns and under gentlemen's porticos . . . gentlemen brought here for safety, being found frequently, returning from political dinners, or church association ones, in a state of helpless drunkenness, and would, but for our very active police, would, I say, be found either in a state of decomposition, through going off in spontaneous combustion, or rendered useless to their wives, and the glorious cause they have *espoused*, by their fingers and toes being bitten off by the frost. And yet I am sorry to add here, that, though these gentlemen have received so much attention from the police's hands, they have not unfrequently complained (with shameful ingratitude) that the very men who had rendered them assistance, had robbed them.

He scoffed at the idea that the police were in the pay of pawnbrokers. 'The police have to a man declared their innocence in any participation.' He similarly pooh-poohed the idea that the police expected drink, tobacco and food from publicans and made up charges against those who did not offer such. 'I perceive the reporters are busily engaged in taking down my remarks: it perhaps is as well, as the rate-paying portion of the Liverpool inhabitants may see to what excellent uses their money is put.'[18]

In their early years the new provincial police faced considerable ratepayer hostility. Resentment was expressed at the escalating costs of crime-fighting especially when, as some complainants protested, for all their rates, they never saw a policeman. Others were annoyed by the way in which the new police seemed to spend their time enforcing pettifogging regulations. In 1842, in the midst of a wave of Chartist activity that was closely linked with the serious industrial unrest of the Plug Plot – so called from the activity of strikers moving from factory to factory and drawing the plugs from the boilers that drove the machinery – there was a major petitioning campaign directed at different county quarter sessions for the abolition, or at least for a considerable reduction in the 'expensive' and 'ineffective' new police. In Lancashire this led to the county force being cut from 502 men to 355; the Chief Constable lamented that the cut left him with insufficient men to deal with the Plug Plot.[19]

But the Bobbies also had strong advocates and these had as good a case as those ratepayers who protested about the expense of the new system. Supporters of the new police stressed that the prevention of, and protection from, crime was a benefit for all social classes. In addition, for all their advocacy of laissez-faire economics and politics and their celebration of a complex, unwritten constitution with its attendant vagaries, Victorian politicians also liked the idea of establishing uniformity within certain instruments of the state. Neither a single national police nor an armed police was in keeping with their reading of the constitution and their understanding of liberty but, by the middle of the century, leading politicians of both Liberal and Conservative hue were increasingly keen on a relatively uniform system of police for the country as a whole. This brought a clash with local government in the early 1850s and a government climb-down over legislation that would have spelt the end of many of the smallest police forces. In 1856, however, the County and Borough Police Act was passed, making the creation of a police force obligatory on counties and boroughs. The compulsion was mitigated by the promise of a Treasury grant of one quarter of the cost of pay and clothing for forces deemed to be efficient. The sting in the tail for the local authorities was that their local police had to be inspected every year, and assessed for 'efficiency', by one of the new HM Inspectors of Constabulary. These inspectors, recruited from senior military officers, presented annual reports to Parliament with their findings and recommendations.

By the end of the 1850s the new police were firmly established outside of London and the system of annual inspections began, very gradually, to establish a degree of uniformity among the provincial police. But Victorian Britain did not just look inward. At mid-century Victoria's realm was the centre of a vast and expanding empire. Imperial possessions also required policing, but for many the Bobby did not seem the ideal candidate for the task.

— CHAPTER 4 —

Further Afield: A United Kingdom, an Empire and Two Models

Victorian London was not just the home of the British government and the bustling financial centre of the national economy, it was also an imperial city and the heart of a vast empire – an empire so extensive that its apologists boasted, probably expressing the hope for eternity, that the sun never set upon it. As described in the previous chapter, London's new Metropolitan Police provided one of several models available to English county magistrates and borough watch committees during the 1830s and 1840s. It also provided a blueprint for some of those claiming to take policing, as one of civilization's benefits, to subject peoples overseas. But at the same time that the metropolitan exemplar appeared attractive to many, an alternative was also perceived in the new Irish Constabulary. For the imperial administrator and governors, and perhaps also for colonial settlers isolated in vast tracts of territory and surrounded by thinly spread, but potentially hostile indigenous people, the paramilitary Irish model offered greater peace of mind.

The two models were never tightly defined and both colonial administrators and senior police officers cherry-picked to suit their circumstances. Moreover, it was always useful if a practice or form of behaviour could be given legitimacy by a successful precedent in the motherland, even if there was elasticity in the extent to which the exemplar was copied. As in the English provinces, bringing models also meant bringing men to show how things should be done. For some individuals, serving as a police officer beyond Great Britain became a means of social mobility, a way to start a new life on a new continent with new opportunities. For a few, social mobility was achieved outside England, but still within the compass of the British Isles.

Over the Border

Alfred John List had a Hungarian father, who had anglicised his name by removing a 'z', and a Welsh mother who, it was said, spoke only Welsh. His father ran a sugar-refining business in London but it is not clear that Alfred was intended to continue in the business. In any case, in September 1829 he opted to be one of the first recruits to the Metropolitan Police, and within nine months had been promoted to inspector. Two years later, and newly married, Alfred received an offer he felt he could not refuse that turned out to be an even greater turning point in his life. The Commissioners of Supply for the Scottish county of Haddingtonshire (also known as East Lothian) were concerned about the numbers of vagrants and the levels of crime within their jurisdiction. Akin to the county magistrates in England, though without their authority in criminal matters, the Scottish Commissioners of Supply were responsible for county administration and government. On behalf of the Haddingtonshire commissioners the Marquis of Tweeddale approached his old friend and former army comrade, Colonel Charles Rowan, for the name of a Metropolitan police officer who might be invited to command a new Haddingtonshire Police. Rowan recommended List; List promptly accepted and went on to become the most influential police officer of mid-nineteenth-century Scotland.[1]

The Scottish Borders of the 1830s were a world away from the London of List's youth and early police career. Three-quarters of a century of agricultural rationalization was drawing to a close; thousands of people had been driven from the land to be replaced by sheep and cash crops. A few had continued to find work as wage labourers in agriculture; others had set up as linen weavers or fishermen, or had moved to work in new woollen mills and even further afield to the heavy industry developing in central Scotland and elsewhere. The rationalized agricultural system required the periodic use of seasonal labour supplied by itinerant gangs from the Highlands and from Ireland. In spite of their importance to the agricultural economy, these gangs were often stigmatized as criminal vagrants and, no doubt because of the precariousness of their lives, at least a few did commit the occasional offence. How far List came to Scotland with ideas that equated the vagrant and the criminal, and how far this impression developed and was strengthened through his discussions with the Commissioners of Supply and other police reformers, and by his experience of the kinds of offender that his men brought in, must remain an open question. But he soon fused his old experiences in the London police with his new ones in Scotland to develop a policing system that spread across the Scottish Borders.

Initially List's police structure in Haddingtonshire was similar to the superintending constable system that had been established in Cheshire and was deployed for a time elsewhere in England. There were full-time paid district constables assisted by part-time parish constables who received a retainer. List appears to have developed this system independently and as a result of the financial constraints imposed upon him by his political masters. In 1839 the Commissioners of Supply for Forfar announced a competition for the best essay outlining a system of police for their county; this police force was to suppress the problem of vagrancy, but its expense was not to exceed £500 a year. List entered the competition and won with an essay that, when published as a pamphlet (*A Practical Treatise on Rural Police*), was to become a key text for the development of Scottish policing. In many respects the pamphlet was self-congratulatory, emphasizing the success of his Haddingtonshire force. It revealed how closely his ideas matched those of other early nineteenth-century police reformers, notably

Edwin Chadwick, to whom List had given evidence for the 1836 Royal Commission on a Rural Constabulary in England. In the pamphlet List outlined the principal objectives of the police as the prevention of crime, which reflected his London experience and the Metropolitan Police instructions, and the suppression of vagrancy, which reflected the fears in the Scottish Borders. As other rural forces were formed in Scotland, List's ideas were taken up as the model either through the *Practical Treatise* or, as in the case of Berwickshire, through the commissioning of List's advice. In 1840 List moved from Haddingtonshire to become Chief Constable of the Midlothian Constabulary, a post that he held until his retirement in 1877. The command of the Haddingtonshire Police passed to his brother, George Henry List, who served until 1893.

There is no evidence that George Henry List had been in London's Metropolitan Police, though he had been the head of the Musselburgh borough force that was amalgamated with Haddingtonshire in 1840. But other London officers did follow Alfred's move north of the border. In 1840 two Metropolitan Police sergeants, William Cleaver and Stephen Underhill, were appointed as the first chief constables of Roxburghshire and of Berwickshire respectively. Two years later the Superintendent of the Edinburgh Police asked the Commissioners in London for an officer to assist in the reorganization of the city's force and W.F.N. Smith was transferred from Greenwich in 'R' Division.[2] These appointments demonstrate the impact of the creation of the Metropolitan Police, but they also obscure the long tradition of police in Scotland. The word 'police' had been much more common in eighteenth-century Scotland than in England, though it had been understood in the broader European sense of the maintenance of public well-being, generally in a city or town, and had stressed street cleaning, lighting and paving rather than crime detection or prevention.

Scotland had been united with England in 1707. Her parliament had been abolished and henceforth she had sent members to Westminster. She had kept her own legal system, which was largely based upon Roman Law and closer to that in many Continental countries rather than to the English system of Common Law. In many respects, however, eighteenth-century Scottish policing looked similar to that in England. There were parish constables appointed by local justices and increasingly they served for longer than a single year. Indeed in Edinburgh, in the second half of the century, the appointment was formalized as triennial, with a third of the men standing down each year; but by the turn of the century there were men serving for longer than three years. Again, as in England, the post appears to have lacked social prestige; even so, the men seem to have been responsive to their neighbours' problems and to have acted commonly with alacrity and courage. In addition to the parish constables there were town officers, rather like the Pardoes in York, who developed expertise in tackling crime. In some instances new posts were created, often for short periods when there was a particular problem or fear. Thus in 1787 Hugh Muir was tasked with detecting thieves and vagabonds in Edinburgh. Glasgow had created a similar post for a short period in 1779; and in 1788 it appointed an Intendant of Police who was to be supported by 'police officers', not to exceed eight in number. The 1788 appointment was made against a backdrop of industrial unrest and concerns that there were no officials able to shoulder the burden of criminal investigation which was perceived to be expanding along with the enormous growth in Glasgow's cotton industry and its population.

Few Scottish burghs went to the effort and expense of a private Act of Parliament to establish a permanent, paid night watch. It was only the fast-expanding commercial ports of Greenock, Port Glasgow and Dumfries that took this step in the last quarter of the eighteenth century. Elsewhere the old system of watch and ward remained the rule; by this system householders were required to serve as watchmen for a fixed period. As the century drew to a close, however, it was increasingly common for householders to turn to paid substitutes to carry out their watching duties. In booming Glasgow in 1790, the magistrates decided to manage the appointment of substitutes themselves rather than leaving it to householders to find their own; effectively this transformed the watch into a full-time, paid force. In Edinburgh there was a City Guard that was very different from anything found in an English city. The Edinburgh City Guard had been established at the end of the seventeenth century. It was an openly military force; the men had muskets and bayonets available to them, though they generally made their patrols armed with Lochaber axes or halberds. At the beginning of the nineteenth century, and shortly before it began to be reduced in favour of a more conventional night watch, the force consisted of three companies each having a lieutenant, a sergeant, a drummer and twenty-five men. The guards wore cocked hats, uniforms of a muddy red and appear to have been recruited principally from men discharged from the Highland regiments.[3]

As in England there were reformers who criticized the Scottish police system for ineffectiveness and inefficiency, and this was picked up by the first historians of Scottish policing. These historians also liked to point to a cluster of private police acts relating to individual burghs that were passed by Parliament during the early nineteenth century, and they generally concluded from these that Scotland established modern police before England.[4] But these police acts, of which the most celebrated was that passed for Glasgow in 1800, were as much rooted in wider aspirations for urban improvement and renewal as in concerns about crime and disorder. In this respect they were not greatly dissimilar from their English counterparts such as, for example, the Sheffield Improvement Act of 1818. On occasions the new police acts passed for individual Scottish burghs did not contain provisions for the creation of watchmen but continued to look to the old practice of 'watch and ward'. And there were even instances where the local worthies charged with administering the acts chose to ignore such watch provisions as there were, considering a full-time paid body as too expensive and unnecessary.

The main responsibilities of the urban watchmen in the Scottish burghs were maintaining order and decorum on the streets by arresting drunks, prostitutes and vagrants. There were the usual stories about old, decrepit, drunken or otherwise useless watchmen, and the additional criticism of Highlanders, new to the burghs, who took the job but who could not communicate in the English language. But, equally, there were reports of watchmen acting courageously when called upon.

Some of the other police officials that appeared in the burghs during the late eighteenth and early nineteenth centuries showed an aptitude for and interest in detection. One such was James Frederick Denovan, who was appointed Intendant of Police in Leith in 1808, and who developed close links with London's Bow Street Office to their mutual advantage. Mathew Legat, the 'senior criminal officer' in Glasgow, was singled out for praise by the local magistrates for his 'valuable and important services' during an attempted insurrection by radical weavers in 1820. Indeed, there were many local worthies prepared to express satisfaction with the whole way that the system of crime and order policing was developing. Following a major new reform in 1812, for example, the Edinburgh police commissioners, a body composed of senior legal and administrative officers in the city together with men elected from the city's wards on a property franchise, boasted that 'where offenders afraid of the vigilance of the Watchmen have attempted depradation [sic] beyond the bounds of [the City] Police the advantages of the system have been no less experienced by the almost instantaneous apprehension of the delinquents'. They also regularly recorded their annoyance at the ways in which stories of robberies, assaults and even one murder appeared to be fabricated by individuals seeking to cover up losses or injuries that it was otherwise inconvenient to explain.[5]

Changes in policing in Scotland, like those in England, showed as much continuity as sudden change. They do not suggest that contemporaries were creating police institutions in response to any single problem, though the concerns about vagrants in the Borders were a clear spur to action in the 1830s. Yet in spite of the tradition of police and policing, the appointment of men like List and Smith reveals the impact of developments in London. The new

Metropolitan Police provided a model and a cadre of new experts that burgh and county administrators in Scotland could draw upon. Scotland was perceived as a pacified country. Periodically the industrial working class gave cause for concern, but no more so than that in England. The martial Highlanders were seen romantically to have redirected their warrior traditions into the service of the Crown; and if, in reality, they suffered eviction and famine, and opted for serious resistance in the 1880s and for emigration most of the time, they were never considered to present a threat like the peasants of John Bull's other island. Consequently, Scotland did not require a police institution like that created for Ireland.

Across the Irish Sea

The Act of Union between England and Ireland had been passed in 1800, and had come into effect the following year. Before this, Ireland had possessed English laws and institutions but her political, religious and social structure meant that they worked very differently on the two sides of the Irish Sea. Eighteenth-century Ireland had an executive appointed by the King of England and established in Dublin Castle; but there was a parliament in Dublin that was jealous of its own authority. Indeed, when the American colonists declared their independence in 1776, there were concerns that Ireland might go the same way. But while there were fierce political arguments between the Irish gentry and the English government, the social and economic structure of the country created the potential for much greater trouble. Many of the Irish gentry were Protestant and a large number of the wealthiest landowners were often resident in England, but the majority of the tenant farmers and labourers were Catholic. There was little in the way of urban and industrial expansion to provide for those that could not make a living on the land, and there was no system of poor relief as in England. There were sporadic outbreaks of rural disorder that grew more serious as the eighteenth century gave way to the nineteenth. In the northern province of Ulster where there was some industry, there was also a significant plebeian population that was largely Presbyterian. Here rural disorder acquired a savage sectarian twist as Catholic 'Defenders' lined up against Protestant 'Peep o' Day Boys'.

In England, until the early nineteenth century, Catholics and Protestant dissenters were technically barred from public office, but there were ways around this, particularly for dissenters. In eighteenth-century Ireland, in contrast, the law was rigorously enforced. In Dublin the twenty-one Protestant Church of Ireland parishes appointed their own watch. Protestant magistrates and Protestant Grand Juries appointed Protestant constables across the country. But the turbulence of rural Catholic Ireland and of divided Ulster easily exposed the ineffectiveness of scattered Protestant constables. As the disorder increased during the 1780s, the British-directed government intervened to create an armed force controlled from the seat of its Irish administration, Dublin Castle. To assist magistrates in the unruly countryside there were various attempts to create police in the subdivisions known as baronies. The presence of the baronial police on the ground, however, was patchy. They had some success in the mid-1790s in some of the most troublesome counties, but the United Irishmen's rebellion necessitated the use of troops across the whole country.

The military defeat of the rebels in 1798 and in the smaller rising of 1801 had little impact on the agrarian disorders that plagued the country. In the government's eyes the rebellions served principally to aggravate concerns about Ireland. Political activists who condemned 'Saxon oppression' were perceived as lurking behind violent peasants. In 1814 these fears led the 26-year-old chief secretary for Ireland, Robert Peel, to establish his first police institution – the Peace Preservation Force. These 'Peelers', as they were known, were a mobile paramilitary force largely recruited from former soldiers. They were centrally directed from Dublin Castle and were available to be dispatched to any part of the country which the local lord lieutenant had 'proclaimed'. They began as a force of thirty-two officers and men deployed in the Tipperary barony of Middlethird. By 1822 they had grown to a body of 2,326 men under the direction of fifteen special magistrates. The central direction infuriated local gentlemen and magistrates who considered it a slight on their independence – even though procla- mation by the lord lieutenant in itself was an announcement of their failure to maintain order. Local gentlemen and magistrates also objected to being required to pay the cost of having men from the Peace Preservation Force quartered in their district.

By 1822 it had become apparent that the Peace Preservation Force was not best suited to solving the problem of rural unrest in Ireland. The British government's answer was a new body, perma- nently situated in every part of the country – the County Constabulary. Jointly funded by Irish taxpayers and the British government, the constabulary was organized on a county level with a significant input from the local magistrates who appointed constables and had a say in the actions of their local force. But the constabulary resembled the French National Gendarmerie inasmuch as the men were armed like soldiers and stationed in squads of about half-a-dozen, living in and working from small barracks across the length and breadth of the country. When the bill to establish the force was first brought before Parliament disquiet was expressed about the French nature of the force. Nevertheless, concerns about the internal peace of Ireland and the voting strength available to the government ensured that the bill became law with few amend- ments. Thereafter the French comparison was largely forgotten even though, in 1836, the similarities became more marked as the constabulary was centralized. In that year the force was renamed the Irish Constabulary and was put under the direction of the authorities in Dublin Castle. At the same time many of the men still serving as members of the Peace Preservation Force were recruited into it.[6]

In many ways the constabulary reflected the social structure of Ireland. Recruits for the rank and file were largely Catholic; they were the sons, especially the younger sons, of small farmers from the south, the west and the midlands of the country. They joined up at around the age of twenty years, opting for the regular wage and employment of the policeman as opposed to the uncertain life on the land or the big step of emigration. Unlike in England where all ranks, save for that of commissioner in London or chief constable in most counties and the biggest cities, were open to the working-class recruit, the Irish Constabulary had an officer class. The officers were recruited from young gentlemen who lacked financial resources but who were almost entirely Protestant.

For the first thirty years of its existence the Irish Constabulary spent a disproportionate amount of its time dealing with popular disorder and enforcing the law at bayonet point. On 14 December 1831, at Carrickshock in south Kilkenny, thirty-eight armed constables escorted a process server who was delivering summonses to local Catholics who had not paid tithes to the (Protestant) Church of Ireland parson. The constables were attacked in a narrow lane by a furious crowd throwing stones and wielding knives and agricultural implements. *A New Song Called the Battle of Carrickshock* exemplified the triumphal and vengeful tone of contemporary ballads dedicated to the event:

> Then Peelers did fall, without murmur or bawl,
> Then their guns and their bayonets were shattered
> How sad was their case, when their eyes, nose and face,
> When their lives and firelocks were battered.

Captain James Gibbons, a Waterloo veteran and commander of the constables, was killed together with a dozen of his men and the process server. Carrickshock demonstrates the hostility that the constabulary could provoke, but the outcome here was exceptional. In almost every other incident the firepower, discipline and organization of the constabulary meant that they were the winners in confrontations. After the appalling, decimating famine of 1845–50, however, and the damp squib that was Ireland's participation in the European Revolutions of 1848, the constabulary's role became more like that of the English police. The Royal Irish Constabulary (RIC), as it became known from 1867, remained a militarized, centralized force of some 8,000 to 10,000 men situated in 1,400 barracks across the country, but its patrols became less like forays into hostile territory. And, but for occasional periods of unrest, most notably the Land War of 1879–82, the RIC had little need to show its fire-power and was increasingly integrated into the communities that it policed.[7]

In 1836, at the same time that the Irish Constabulary was reorganized as a centralized body for the policing of rural and small-town Ireland, an Act of Parliament established a government-controlled police institution for the Irish capital – the Dublin Metropolitan Police (DMP), though the first patrols of this body did not take to the streets until January 1838. In many respects the DMP was a copy of the London force. There were two commissioners: one a barrister, the other a former army officer. Superintendent James Johnston was sent from London to advise; more than half of the original superintendents and inspectors for the new force came from London, as did a number of the lower ranks. The DMP patrolled regular beats and, as in London, the constables were armed only with a wooden truncheon. As with the boroughs in England and Scotland, two other large towns in Ireland – Belfast and Londonderry – maintained their own police until 1865 and 1870 respectively, when they were incorporated into the juris-diction of the Royal Irish Constabulary. In Belfast at least the force evolved gradually out of the old watch, but by the middle of the century its rule book closely resembled that of the London police.[8]

English Magistrates Follow Ireland's Example

The traffic in police ideas and police officers was not all one way across the Irish Sea in the 1830s and 1840s. Just as London offered a model for the authorities in Dublin, there were English county magistrates who, looking for ideas, were not deterred by the para-military aspects of the Irish Constabulary. When, in 1839, the magistrates of Gloucestershire sought a chief constable for their new police they looked to Ireland and selected Anthony Lefroy, a former commander of the constabulary in County Wicklow. Lefroy brought a cadre of a dozen Irish Constabulary men with him and he commanded his new force with a rigid discipline. The men were expected to live in barracks and only the barrack commander was permitted to have a wife and family with him. Furthermore the other men were restricted in their visits to home and family. It was a similar story in Staffordshire three years later when the magistrates decided to extend the small force that they had created in the south to the whole of the county. Here the magistrates chose John Hayes Hatton who, like Lefroy, had served for sixteen years in the Irish Constabulary. Hatton, who had also served as Chief Constable in East Suffolk for two years, likewise brought Irish constables with him: thirteen of his new force came from the constabulary, thirteen more from the Dublin Metropolitan Police, and just over a quarter of the first recruits in Staffordshire (56 out of 210 men) were Irish. Hatton did not establish a deployment in barracks and neither of these forces patrolled with firearms, but the Irish ethos remained strong for many years.[9]

There was one region on the eastern edge of the Irish Sea where, during the 1830s and 1840s, an Irish-style constabulary might have seemed valuable but where the option appears to have been totally ignored. In 1831 the ironstone miners and skilled puddlers of Merthyr Tydfil seized the town and held it against soldiers for four days. Eight years later miners from the South Wales coalfields marched on Newport, leading to the most serious armed clash of the Chartist disturbances. Over the following years the mythical heroine Rebecca led her children in a wave of protests against toll gates and toll houses, the New Poor Law, tithe commutation, trade restrictions and parliamentary representation. One home secretary expressed concerns that Wales was becoming 'a second Ireland'. Moreover, the vagrancy problem in Wales was often attributed to Irish people. These vagrants spoke Irish; and the Welsh peasant generally spoke only Welsh and may not have possessed even a rudimentary knowledge of English, the language of law and authority. Yet the Welsh magistracy looked to England for their policing models. Indeed, probably for parsimonious reasons, they initially sought to rely largely on police sent from London supported by troops.[10]

Beyond the Oceans

The year that Chief Constable Alfred List moved from Haddingtonshire to Midlothian, two other exporters of new British policing methods were given appointments in places far more distant. William Augustus Miles was appointed as Commissioner of Police for the city of Sydney in New South Wales; Benjamin Woods landed in the even younger colony of New Zealand, where he took up a far less exalted police rank but, ultimately, had the greater impact. Miles and Woods could not have been more different in their origins or in their application of police ideas. Miles was an ideologue who believed in the excellence of the London model. Woods came from the Irish experience, but also showed himself a pragmatist who shaped his police methods according to the circumstances.

William Augustus Miles appears always to have believed that he was never given the recognition that his birth, and his abilities, merited. He had never served as a police officer, but he could claim a detailed investigative knowledge of crime, of criminals and of the new and old systems of English policing. He had close links with the leading advocates of police and penal reform, such as the 5th Duke of Richmond and the indefatigable utilitarian Edwin Chadwick. He had conducted inquiries for the Select Committee on Gaols in 1835, published a pamphlet on the need for a centrally organized, national police in 1836, and had served as an assistant commissioner for the Royal Commission on a Rural Constabulary between 1836 and 1837. After his work for the commission Miles had found himself with little to do and began looking for an appointment significantly elevated to match his high birth. The point here was that, while he appears never to have named a royal father, Miles encouraged the belief, for which there seems some validity, that he was the illegitimate child of a profligate Hanoverian prince. He hoped for the command of the Manchester Police following the 1839 act that made it a Home Office force. When the post of Superintendent of Police in Sydney became available the following year Miles still hoped for something better, though it seems also likely that those whom he continued to press for an appointment saw this job as an opportunity for sending him a very, very long way away.

When Miles stepped ashore in Sydney in August 1841 he entered a world where the respectable sought to follow what they remembered or imagined were the social niceties of the mother country and tried to distance themselves from their colony's convict origins. Sydney was growing rapidly: the population soared from about 25,000 to 40,000 during the 1840s. It was largely insulated from the depredations of bushrangers and runaway convicts and from the 'collisions' with Aboriginal peoples; these were problems of the hinterland and entrusted to a mounted police recruited from the military stationed in the colony. But within the broad city limits, where there was far less pressure for land than in the towns and cities of the mother country, buildings were much more spread out and this was to create some difficulties for Miles in his attempt to impose a London model of policing.

The Sydney police were already looking to London for ideas when Miles arrived. He appears to have hoped that a rigorous imposition of the London system would have raised the standing and efficiency of the force. He began by successfully negotiating a change in his own title from 'superintendent' to 'commissioner'. He ordered that convicts and emancipists (ex-convicts) no longer be employed as police officers, reorganized the force into divisions and ordered new uniforms, identical to those worn in London, for his men. As many pointed out, however, the heavy top hat and thick, tightly buttoned tunic were inappropriate for the Sydney climate, especially the summer's heat. The extensive layout of the city meant that the beat system, designed for the courts and narrow streets of central London, needed a much larger force per head of the population to provide equivalent protection; Miles was much criticized when he told a special committee of the city council in 1843 that, because the houses were so scattered, he believed that his men had to function as 'a *detective* rather than a *protective* force'. Try as he might, Miles could get neither the numbers nor the pay of his police increased; and he never succeeded in overcoming the prejudice that he was an outsider in the colony. Moreover, London's police reform had happened in a moment of political harmony between the city's local parish vestries and the central government; in Sydney, the city and the colonial authorities were at loggerheads, and the police force was one of the issues over which they argued. In 1847 a Sydney journal chose to criticize Miles and his police in the language of English radicals that even separated him from his roots:

> The system of *espionage* and *centralisation* which Mr. Miles was so anxious to introduce into New South Wales, are so un-English in theory, and mischievous in practice, that we cannot but rejoice at the vehement opposition he has hitherto met in carrying out his plans . . .
> May the day be far distant when the conventional ethics on which the social system of France is so insecurely founded shall be introduced into an English colony!

The following year, after an investigation into claims that he had misappropriated police funds and accusations of drunkenness, Miles was discreetly moved sideways to the post of stipendiary magistrate; the money for this position was removed in 1850. Miles died in Sydney in 1851 of a mixture of heart disease and a liver enlarged by heavy drinking; he was still trying to use his claimed royal parentage to win government patronage for employment.[11]

Benjamin Woods was from much humbler stock. He was the fifth of six children born to a Protestant shopkeeper in King's

County, Ireland, in 1793. He had served briefly in the army during the war against Napoleon and, returning to Ireland in 1815, had joined Peel's recently established Peace Preservation Force. Woods had worked his way up to be a District Head Constable in the Irish force, and had then transferred to a clerical post. He had left Ireland in 1839, initially travelling to Sydney. In March the following year, however, as an experienced police officer, he was appointed to the post of Chief Constable (confusingly here this was a non-commissioned rank, also referred to as inspector, sub-inspector and head constable) across the Tasman Sea in New Zealand. He was to become, in the words of the historian of early policing in New Zealand, 'the most prominent policeman in the north island in the colony's first decade and beyond'. But the form of policing that Woods developed for the new colony depended as much on his Irish experience as on any model established in London. In the early years of the colony in New Zealand there were fast-growing towns with a disproportionate number of people from those social groups labelled as 'the dangerous classes' in Britain. Beyond the towns were the Maori who grew increasingly hostile the more aware they became of the implications of the Pakehas' presence. Thus in the towns Woods established practices that were similar to those of the London Bobby which he had witnessed deployed in Sydney. He also arranged for some sergeants to be brought over from the Australian city as advisers and examples. For the hinterland, however, where he believed that more overt coercion might be necessary, he deployed men in the fashion that had been established for Ireland.[12]

While Miles was wedded to the London system and Woods selected according to circumstances, the Australian colony of Victoria provided a singular example of the London and Irish models being recognized as distinct and, in some measure, transported side-by-side. In July 1851 the largely pastoral settlers in Victoria separated from the older colony of New South Wales. Almost immediately afterwards came the proclamation of the discovery of gold. The announcement immediately generated anxieties about disreputable and undesirable men pouring into the colony seeking gold and creating violent mayhem. Indeed, within twelve months the population had doubled to 160,000 and the colony's tiny, ill-equipped police forces haemorrhaged officers as they resigned in droves, invariably driven by the hope of making their own fortunes in the gold fields. Early in 1852 a group of leading figures in the colony approached the Secretary of State for the Colonies in London for the loan of fifty men from the Irish Constabulary. They were told that Irish police could not be spared but fifty men were recruited from the Metropolitan Police to travel to Victoria and assist in solving the problems. A few months later, in July 1852, a member of the colonial legislative council, Peter Snodgrass, established a committee to look into police reform and reorganization.

The Snodgrass Committee identified the two models of policing and expressed a preference for the London version; police legislation was introduced early in the following year. In May 1853 the 'London Fifty' arrived and were deployed to bolster the recruits to the new Victoria Police. There were, in fact, fifty-four Metropolitan officers: fifty constables and three sergeants commanded by Inspector Samuel Freeman, a veteran with fourteen years' service. It is difficult to know exactly what the London officers were expecting in Melbourne, but they became rapidly disillusioned with their new conditions. Their contract on arrival did not appear to be the one they had agreed before their departure; they complained about the standards in their 'barracks' and protested that they were expected to do menial tasks and to perform the role of soldiers rather than policemen. Freeman, however, had a major impact. As police superintendent in Melbourne he extolled the London principles, established the London beat system and more prosaically, recognizing the major problem of drunkenness in the city, he introduced special handcarts in watch-houses so that constables might wheel the drunk and incapable to the lock-up rather than having to drag or carry them.

Sadly Freeman's promising colonial career came to a tragic end when a new Chief Commissioner of Police was appointed for the colony. Frederick Standish, the wastrel son of a wealthy Lancashire family, had served as a captain in the Royal Artillery and on the staff of the Lord Lieutenant of Ireland. He left for Australia at the news of gold, and to escape his gambling debts. In 1858, after a series of minor government posts, he landed the job of commissioner and, keen to surround himself with his hedonistic cronies, he replaced Freeman with a renowned breeder of fighting cocks. The old London man was packed off round Port Phillip Bay to the town of Geelong. For Freeman the move from the colonial capital to another town, admittedly not much smaller, must have appeared like a move from the Hyde Park Police Station of the prestigious 'A' Division to the wilds of, for example, 'K' Division's Barking. In London such a move might be ordered as a punishment or some kind of demotion. Alone, away from the home that he had made in Melbourne and without his family who stayed in the city, Freeman cut his throat with his razor.[13]

London-style policing may have worked for urban areas like Melbourne and Geelong but, apart from them, there was little else in the way of large, settled towns in the Australian colonies. During the gold rush the mining districts, with their boom towns of shacks and tents, were heavily policed. The police in the goldfields became extremely unpopular with the gold diggers. They took bribes from illicit grog sellers, but vigorously enforced the requirement that 'diggers' have a licence; part of the fine for not having the appropriate licence went into the policeman's pocket. The situation deteriorated so much that, at the beginning of December 1854, the diggers assembled at the Eureka Stockade in Ballarat where a few spoke of a republic. It took a combined force of 276 policemen and soldiers to storm the stockade. The attack left some thirty diggers dead, and a long legacy of suspicion and hostility towards the police.

Such easy pickings as there were in the early goldfields gave way to deep shaft mining by the end of the 1850s. The prospectors drifted away and left the hinterland to the sheep and a growing number of wheat farmers. Beat policing was irrelevant to a colony of around 88,000 square miles with a population of less than a quarter of a million people and something in the region of six million sheep. For the police supervision of rural Victoria the advocates of a mounted, paramilitary-style police modelled on the Irish Constabulary came into their own. But the economic and social friction between established 'Squatters' and the new, generally poor 'Selectors' who sought to carve a new life for themselves in the bush led to a police identification with the wealthy that had all the worst elements of the Irish Constabulary in the first half of the century. The most celebrated and bloody moment in this relationship came with the violent career of the Kelly gang between 1878 and 1880. But it was not just the style of policing that appeared Irish; a disproportionate number of the policemen themselves were veterans of the RIC.

Ned Kelly is the iconic Irish-Australian rebel and in many ways typifies the popular image of the Australian's devil-may-care lack of deference. In Kelly's colourful words the police were 'a parcel of big ugly fat-necked wombat headed big bellied magpie legged narrow hipped splay-footed sons of Irish bailiffs or English landlords'. To the extent that he identified them as 'Irish sons', Kelly was right. In the mid-1870s 82 per cent of the Victoria police were Irish born and of these, 46 per cent had served in the RIC. The leader of the four-man police patrol gunned down by the Australian-born Kelly among the gum trees of Stringybark Creek on 25 October 1878 was 36-year-old Sergeant Michael Kennedy, a Catholic born in Westmeath. RIC men were to be found in large numbers elsewhere in Australia. In Queensland, in the mid-1860s, 44 per cent of the police had served in the RIC and, later in the century, the definition of a policeman provided by a newspaper in Western Australia was 'A man with a uniform, a brogue and a big free thirst.'[14] Quite why so many men who had opted for the RIC as an alternative to emigration subsequently resigned and emigrated must remain an open question, but probably stories filtered back of better pay, more freedom and independence in less regimented police stations, and greater opportunities to marry and raise a family either in the police or, eventually, on their own land.

Mounties and the Irish

Just as Irish policemen played a role in policing Australia, so fourteen former members of the Royal Irish Constabulary rode with the North West Mounted Police on their Great March West in 1874. Irishmen, and former Irish policemen, were not to play a great role in the history of the Mounties; most of the recruits were Canadian-born and were drawn from skilled workers and clerks apparently seeking adventure in the west.[15] But more important than Irish personnel in the creation of the Mounties was a perception of the Irish model of policing. Sir John A. Macdonald, the first premier of the dominion of Canada, wanted an organization to establish Canadian authority over the vast prairies running west from Manitoba to the Rocky Mountains. In 1869 the dominion had just acquired an enormous expanse of territory which had formerly been part of the land granted by charter to the Hudson's Bay Company. Macdonald was keen that the area should be policed by a body acting under civil law rather than by soldiers. Nevertheless, the members of his North West Mounted Police were to be 'trained to act as cavalry, but also instructed in the Rifle exercises. They should also be instructed, as certain of the Line are, in the use of artillery, this body should not be expressly Military but should be styled *Police*, and have the military bearing of the Irish Constabulary'

Macdonald telegraphed London for information on the RIC and eventually appointed as first commissioner Lieutenant Colonel George Arthur French of the Royal Artillery, an Irishman who also had experience of the RIC. Some four years after Macdonald made his initial plans, just over 200 Mounties set off on their 800-mile expedition from Dufferin, Manitoba, across the wide and empty prairies of Saskatchewan, to what is now southern Alberta to bring the Queen's law to the Plains Indians and to a mixture of hardy trappers and rough adventurers.[16]

While the constables of the RIC became branded as traitors to their fellow Irishmen in the mythology that was constructed around them following the creation of the Irish Free State, a very different image grew up around the Mountie. In popular Canadian history the Mountie, who always got his man, became the key figure in the development of the Canadian west. Whereas the American west was characterized by murder, gun-slinging lawmen, Indian massacres and the blue-coated cavalry, the Canadian west was perceived to have been settled with the minimum violence. And in the place of the cavalry fort was the tiny post of the sometimes solitary Mountie who, while the English Bobby measured his beat by a thousand inhabitants, measured his jurisdiction by the thousand square miles. Across the empire, where men were required to police vast distances with thinly spread populations often suspicious of white men or of imperial motives, it was the so-called Irish model, with its paramilitary element, that particularly appealed. In 1907 it became a requirement that all officers destined to command colonial police forces in the British Empire should undergo instruction at the RIC Depot in Dublin.

Home and Away: Two Models for Overseas Policing

But there were contradictions. Even after the two models had been identified as distinct and great play had been made about the non-military, unarmed tradition in London, officers from the RIC, the colonial police and the army continued to be appointed to command the biggest and best-known English forces. Thus Sir William Nott-Bowyer moved from the junior commissioned ranks of the army to five years in the RIC, after which he went on to command the forces of Leeds (1878–81), Liverpool (1881–1902) and the City of London (1902–25); Sir Charles H. Rafter served in the RIC for sixteen years before becoming Chief Constable of Birmingham from 1899 to 1935. Sir Edward Bradford enjoyed a career that could have originated in one of the ripping yarns presented to Victorian boys. He began as a cavalry officer in the Indian army and lost his left arm to the quarry during a tiger hunt. His police experience when appointed Commissioner of the Metropolitan Police in 1890 consisted of directing operations against Thugs and Dacoits during the mid-1870s and acting as secretary to the Secret and Political Department of the India Office. Bradford's successor as Commissioner of the Metropolitan Police, Sir Edward Henry, had risen through the ranks of the Indian Civil Service to become Inspector General of Police for Lower Bengal. The style and practice of policing in India was always very different even from the roughest areas of London, but the differences in the policing task and police procedures can easily be overestimated. By the time that he became Commissioner Bradford had long ceased to be a soldier and had successfully morphed into a very senior, politically adroit civil servant and administrator – precisely what the post required (and, some would say, still requires). Interestingly, however, in contrast to other English forces and in contrast to these, and other, ex-Indian police officers, no officer from the RIC ever found his way into the senior ranks of London's Metropolitan Police.

While contemporaries identified the different models of London and Irish policing, and while subsequent historians have often followed their lead, it needs to be stressed that there were rarely attempts simply to impose one or other of the models. Indeed, it was always possible to construct a police system to meet contingencies without reference to any template, as appears to have been the case in New South Wales in the 1820s when attacks by Aborigines and bushrangers prompted the creation of a paramilitary Mounted Police to patrol the vast scrubby expanses beyond Sydney and the smaller towns.[17]

The London and Irish models were also difficult to define precisely. The argument was that the London model was unarmed and non-political, and in essence this was the case. Yet in emergencies London Bobbies were given edged weapons and even, as will be described below, occasional authorization to patrol with revolvers. And while they were non-political in the sense of not being used to maintain a particular political group or elite in power, the argument can be made that the role of the police is to maintain an unequal division of property and a particular form of social order. The RIC, in contrast, was considered as a military body, centrally controlled and living in barracks.[18] Again, in essence this was true, though while borough and county police in England and Scotland were subject to significant local control, London's Metropolitan Police was a national force whose police authority was the home secretary and, again as will be discussed below, many of the younger members of English police forces lived in barracks.

The declaration that a colony was deploying a particular model of policing was pragmatic and often largely rhetorical. Men took stock of their policing needs and drew from the models what seemed best suited to their circumstances. In urban districts with a large, white settler community the authorities were relatively content to establish something that resembled London's Metropolitan Police. But the beat patrol, even the equivalent of that found in English rural counties, did not suit vast areas of bush, prairie, mountain or tundra. Nor was it felt to suit those areas where the Victorians considered the indigenous populations to be at best uncivilized and at worst dangerous and hostile. The London model scarcely appeared in African or Asian colonies. In India and Ceylon there were periodic statements about the need for the police to be unarmed and in 1840 a sergeant from the Metropolitan Police, John Colepeper, was recruited to reorganize the police in Ceylon. Nevertheless, most British imperial policing on the subcontinent drew its inspiration from the Irish Constabulary.[19] The policemen brought their own English or Irish experience and understanding to their jobs and they organized and policed their new communities with echoes of what they knew and what they had done before.

The idea of two models of policing became popular with contemporaries since it suited well their image of Britain and her civilizing mission. The claim that the Metropolitan Police was civilian, unarmed and accepted by the community had an element of truth. But it also enabled a separate categorization to be made for the more military style of police forces in those parts of the empire where, in the eyes of Victorian imperial culture, the indigenous populations did not yet acknowledge or understand the values of British civilization. Moreover, the assertion that the Irish model was uniquely British enabled its advocates to ignore, conveniently, its similarities with the Gendarmerie model that had been developed for rural France and which had spread across Europe in the wake of the armies of Napoleon Bonaparte.[20]

Beyond Britain and her empire there were many who bought into the distinctiveness of London's Metropolitan Police. Gendarmeries might be useful for showing the flag and pacifying peasants. But European liberals also aspired to seeing their streets patrolled by a largely unarmed, civilian police responsive to the needs of respectable society. The London model acquired an additional aura of success from Britain's avoidance of revolution in the early nineteenth century and the good behaviour of the massive crowds at the Great Exhibition. Napoleon III, somewhat surprisingly, claimed to be a liberal. While in political exile in London he was sworn in as a special constable during the Chartist disorder of 1848. When he reformed the police of Paris in the 1850s he incorporated elements of the London model. The parliament of united Italy were struck by the virtues of *il Bobby inglese*, but regretfully concluded that their fellow citizens were not yet ready for such a police. German liberals also looked to London, and so too did civic reformers in the United States. But in the United States there were also old English practices where men like Thomas Hunt Dann, the constable of Wimbledon, and George Bakewell, who believed that as a new policeman he should have the spirit and independence of a traditional constable, would have found themselves at home.

The constable system crossed the Atlantic and was deployed and developed in the thirteen American colonies both before their war of independence and afterwards. Alongside it went the Freeborn Englishman's suspicion of a standing army and of spies and informers. Cities in the United States began to expand under similar pressures to those in Europe in the early nineteenth century and American civic reformers, like many European liberals, looked to London's Metropolitan Police and its idea of prevention as the model for solving their own problems of crime and disorder. But a different political and social context meant that American variants of the new police evolved in different ways from those in Britain. For many years, for example, there was a reluctance to put American police officers in uniform; uniforms smacked of the hierarchical structures and the master-and-servant relationships of the old world. Though he came from the same root, the American cop possessed a personal authority and discretion that was in some ways closer to that of the old constable. George Bakewell would have approved of much of this, and perhaps too of the egalitarian democracy that meant that the job of police chief – just like that of other civic officers – was often filled through election. The whole policing structure remained (and remains) fragmented, with thousands of tiny police forces staffed by men who patrolled their beats, but often just as they wished. 'He wears a uniform, to be sure,' explained the *New York Times* at the end of 1857,

but he disdains to button it in a military fashion, and exposes his snowy linen and its California diamond with as much ostentation as a railroad conductor. To put one's hands in one's pockets while on duty is a grave military offence. Your New York policeman hardly ever puts them anywhere else. He smokes vigorously. If he meets a friend, he takes a drink with him in a good-natured way, just as any other citizen might. He gossips pleasantly at the corners of streets, and in doorways, and 'loafs' with all the nonchalance of a man who knows the rights secured to him by the Constitution, and means to exercise them . . . He is not the servant of the State, and would feel insulted if you called him so.[21]

All of which was very different from the discipline and the work regime imposed on the Bobby who was often spoken of by British advocates of the new police system as the visual manifestation of the law, an institution rather than a man.

— CHAPTER 5 —

'An Institution Rather than a Man': The Victorian Police Officer, 1860–1880

AS MUCH AS any Victorian factory worker the Victorian police officer had his time at work strictly regulated. In a city or town he clocked in for a parade before going on duty. He began his beat at a set hour and paced it like clockwork, always with the chance of a check by his superiors. Unlike the factory worker, he was required to keep a careful record of what he had done. Each man had his personal notebook. The police stations had occurrence books, charge books, refused charge books (books that contain details of alleged offences, but which for a variety of reasons were never proceeded with), discipline books.

On his beat the individual officer had discretion about how he perceived an incident and how he chose to proceed with it. Yet this was not how his superiors and the most fervent advocates of – apologists for – the new police liked to portray his role. The author of a mid-century article in the *Quarterly Review* captured the essence of the official portrayal with a description of a London Bobby on the beat.

> Amid the bustle of Piccadilly or the roar of Oxford Street, PC X58 stalks along, an institution rather than a man. We seem to have no more hold on his personality than we could possibly get hold of his coat buttoned up to the throttling point . . .[1]

If Bobbies were an institution they were also men, and men with different origins and aspirations, whose careers and family lives followed different and very personal trajectories.

A London Bobby: Alexander Hennessy

In June 1867 Queen Victoria had been on the throne for exactly thirty years. She was also five-and-a-half years into her long widowhood and her eldest son, Edward, Prince of Wales, was taking her place at many public engagements. On two days in the first week of that June the prince visited the race meeting at Ascot. He did not attend on Friday 8 June to watch the six scheduled races, but John Cooper of Leicester Street, Birmingham did. Cooper attempted to get into the Grand Stand without paying the 10 shillings entrance fee. He was apprehended by Alexander Hennessy, one of the Metropolitan Police constables sent to Ascot to help police the meeting. Cooper was remanded on bail to appear at Bow Street Magistrates' Court on 1 July. Neither Cooper nor his surety appeared; nevertheless, the stipendiary magistrate still discharged him. The trustees at Ascot did not wish to prosecute. Cooper's was, after all, a very petty offence. It was probably not even registered among the crime statistics for the year. The story survives because it is entered on the first page of the pocket book kept spasmodically by Alexander Hennessy during his twenty-five years' service in the police.[2]

A day or two policing the races at Ascot was probably the nearest thing to a holiday that PC Hennessy knew in his years as a policeman. Ascot during a race meeting was busy, but it was nothing compared to the bustle of central London. The metropolis had grown enormously since the beginning of the century. The population had increased from one million to more than two-and-a-half million. The distinct entities of the City of London, the City of Westminster, the Port of London and the East End were sprawling into each other. Farmland, heath and common had been built upon as, first, ribbon development had spread along the roads running into the centre and then as builders began to fill in the spaces between. In the centre new roads were cut, slicing a route through some of the worst rookeries; most notable in this respect was New Oxford Street which cut through St Giles, heralding the complete destruction of the old slum area where Dickens had ventured with Inspector Field. Traffic was still largely horse-drawn but, as well as the long-distance trains steaming to the hub of London from the four corners of the country, there were also the beginnings of a few commuter lines, and the first underground stations had opened in 1863.

This changing metropolis was the birthplace of just under a third of the constables that worked alongside Alexander Hennessy; nearly another third came from counties bordering the metropolis. Many joined the police initially, it seems, to tide themselves over a period of unemployment and also, perhaps, just to see what the job was like. Hennessy himself was born in 1834 in Stratford, a fast-growing ward of the parish of West Ham. The parish was situated in the county of Essex though, from the beginning, it had been included within the jurisdiction of the Metropolitan Police. By 1851 the young Hennessy had moved into the City proper and was working as a servant and errand boy in Cheapside, the great thoroughfare that linked St Paul's Cathedral with the Bank of England. Five years later, stating his trade as a calico printer, he joined the police and was posted to 'E' Division, the Holborn Division of the Metropolitan Police. 'E' Division was one of the smaller police divisions in central London: it covered an oblong running about one-and-a-half miles east–west from Gray's Inn Road to Portland Place and Regent Street, and about one mile south– north from a line running between Covent Garden, Soho and Oxford Circus to the Euston Road. When Hennessy joined, the south central area of the division contained both Bow Street and the squalid, stinking, teeming courts and tenements of the remnants of the St Giles rookery. But the period of his service saw major changes; in particular the Artisans Dwelling Act of 1875, which enabled local authorities to make compulsory purchases of land for slum clearance, and the construction of strictly regulated moral dwellings for the poor by organizations like the Peabody Trust, were thought generally to have improved the darkest quarters of the district.

The personnel of 'E' Division occupied five clusters of buildings in the district when Hennessy joined, but only gradually were the police acquiring purpose-built stations and residences. A group of old houses had been rented in Bow Street since 1831; here there was accommodation for three unmarried sergeants and sixty-six unmarried constables. These old houses also contained seventeen rooms designated as cells It was only in Christmas 1880 that the police took up the lease of a purpose-built police station in Bow Street with room for one hundred unmarried men. A married inspector, four single sergeants and sixty-six single constables occupied 36 and 37 Whetstone Park, described by a Home Office committee in 1881 as 'two miserable tenements, dark and unhealthy'. Clarke's Buildings had been leased in 1843 and housed a married inspector, a married sergeant and forty-two single constables. The single men were moved from here into Bow Street when it became available, and Clarke's Buildings became married quarters. Other houses were rented for the police stations in Brunswick Square and Tottenham Court Road; and these also had accommodation for unmarried police officers and cells for offenders.[3] Hennessy began his service sharing with other young constables in Clarke's Buildings.

In a jointly authored late-Victorian survey of the police, Charles Tempest Clarkson, a former policeman with thirty-three years' service, and J. Hall Richardson, a London journalist, gave a glowing account of places like Clarke's Buildings – places that were often referred to as police barracks. Frequently these 'barracks' were run by a married sergeant or inspector, together with his wife, and the men who lived in them had a small sum deducted from their weekly wage for rent. 'The influences of residence in barracks are good', declared Clarkson and Richardson.

[T]he men have the advantage of home association with each other, comfortable, separate beds, clean and well-warmed apartments, and properly cooked food. They have reading, smoking, and recreation rooms, and a good dining-room; and can, at their pleasure, retire from or seek the society of their companions – in short, enjoy all the privileges of a well-respected private home.[4]

What Clarkson and Richardson did not mention was the squalor and appalling sanitation of much of this accommodation. Admittedly these were problems across Victorian London, but the *Report on the Condition of the Metropolitan Police Stations* published less than a decade before Clarkson and Richardson's book was occasioned by an outbreak of typhus in one police station. The report found sanitation to be generally poor and the investigators were so concerned at Wandsworth that they immediately cut off the water supply.

Equally Clarkson and Richardson avoided mention of the horseplay and the inconvenience of living in a police station. But we can look to other sources for such insights, such as the reminiscences of Timothy Cavanagh, a contemporary of Hennessy's. He was the son of an Irish cordwainer and was born in London about 1827. In March 1855 he left his job as a warehouse clerk and joined the Metropolitan Police. His first posting was to Stone's End Police Station in 'M' Division on the south bank of the Thames. The station was under the walls of the Queen's Bench Prison and the dormitory for the young constables was directly over the station's cells so that, when prisoners were brought in and out, and especially when men came back off their beats in the morning, there was a considerable din. Perhaps more annoying, no matter how long a man had worked at night, or had spent taking prisoners to court the following morning, he was not allowed to be in bed after 1.00 p.m. But many of these Bobbies were young men, full of energy and testosterone and, when off duty, they were likely to be rough and rowdy. In his memoirs Cavanagh described the constables throwing eggs at each other and making so much noise larking around in the station kitchen that magistrates in the neighbouring police court several times ordered them to be quiet as they could not hear the proceedings. Cavanagh and his mates also conspired to strap an unpopular colleague to a bench and hold him under the station pump, while an Irish constable, who fancied his luck with the ladies, was drenched with a bucket of whitewash. But the rough and tumble of the barracks could also involve self-regulation. Tom Divall, who joined the Metropolitan Police as Cavanagh and Hennessy retired, recalled that if a dispute could not be settled amicably then the tables of the mess would be pushed back, seconds would be appointed, and the issue was settled in a formal fight. And rather than reporting any constable to a senior officer for breaking the rules of the barracks – not putting things away, for example, or not hanging clothes properly – an unofficial court of the man's peers would be convened. If he was found guilty, the man was fined, and no one ever refused to pay the fine.[5]

By the late 1860s Hennessy had married and moved out of the barracks at Clarke's Buildings. The 1871 census identifies him as living at 19 Burton Street, St Pancras at the northern end of 'E' Division. The street ran parallel to the wealthy Tavistock Street but was also close to some rough areas. At the turn of the century, when the philanthropist and social investigator Charles Booth launched his massive inquiry into London and its population, Burton Street was noted as abutting Brantome Place. Brantome Place was poor and grim; it had a common lodging house for 'women of a disorderly character' and overcrowded buildings with 'patched and dirty' windows where there was much drunkenness, where women sat on the doorsteps suckling babies and where the children were pale and dirty. Hennessy's Burton Street, however, was described as having a mixed population with some comfortable and some poor working-class families.[6] He lived here in 1871 with his wife Sophia, a native of Gloucestershire, and two children: Alexander aged two years and Emma aged two months. Ten years later they had moved along the street to number 7, and the family had grown with the addition of another three children: Alice aged seven, Louise aged five and Alfred aged four. On 30 March 1881, still resident in Burton Street, Hennessy resigned from the police after more than twenty-four years' service. He was suffering from bad varicose veins, a complaint brought on by years of pounding the beat and, while it was not the main cause for men being invalided out of the force – rheumatism, bronchitis and tuberculosis were greater – it was one that was common among policemen. His conduct was noted as good and he was given a pension of £52 a year. He and Sophia stayed in Burton Street, at least until the turn of the century.

When Hennessy joined the Metropolitan Police in 1856 the force was just over twenty-five years old. The men still wore a uniform much like that of the constables who first trod the beat in 1829; it was almost another decade before a tunic replaced the swallow-tail coat and a helmet replaced the top hat. The men still carried a rattle to spring when they needed assistance; the first experiments with whistles to replace the rattle did not begin until 1883, two years after Hennessy's retirement. They were still advised that their principal objective was the prevention of crime, and their modus operandi remained the beat patrol at a steady pace of two-and-a-half miles an hour. The men worked in shifts, with approximately two-thirds of the beat patrols taking place at night. Night-time beats were generally shorter than those of day-time and consequently more men were required to be deployed. At night-time the constable was expected to check doors and windows, waking up householders and the proprietors of shops to secure any property that was open, unlocked or appeared otherwise unsafe. In his annual report for 1875 Superintendent James J. Thompson, the commander of Hennessy's division, recorded: '1683 doors and windows found open during the night and secured by inhabitants on request of the police, frequently after a minute search of premises or buildings.'[7] Unofficially a constable could also make a few extra pence a week by giving men an early-morning call by knocking on their windows to ensure that they got to work on time. Timothy Cavanagh was lucky enough to land one of the best beats in his division for this when he began his service.

There was a good deal of money to be made on this ground – as many as forty calls belonging to the happy possessor of the beat. A 'call' meant that a man (and here they mostly belonged to the Borough Market) wanted calling at four or five, or even earlier, in the morning, for which service he paid on Saturday night with great regularity the sum of sixpence. Should he, however, fail to pay up, matters were soon put right by failing to call him on Monday morning, when, in consequence of losing half a day's work, he was certain to be in the way with the stipulated 'tanner' the next night.[8]

Sergeants followed the men round on their beats to ensure that they were doing their duty, not sleeping in doorways or idly chatting to each other or to anyone they met. Stopping, questioning and searching people out after dark, however, especially if they were carrying bundles or moving property in a wagon, remained important to the policeman's task. The moonlight-flit, with the furniture from rented accommodation, continued to be a problem. Absence from a beat, or missing a crime committed on a beat was serious and, if there was no valid excuse, was liable to heavy punishment – a fine, demotion or even dismissal.

The work was often boring; on the extended rural beats especially it could be extremely lonely. 'No-one, not having gone through the ordeal', Cavanagh wrote of his patrols in the Borough, 'can possibly imagine the dreary work it is tramping about for eight hours in such a filthy neighbourhood.'[9] It was also sometimes dangerous and, with the strict discipline, it was not to every recruit's taste. The turnover in men continued to be considerable. One commentator estimated that between 1856 and 1867 the force of around 6,800 had an average annual turnover of 1,069 men.[10]

While the prevention of crime continued to be the principal object of the police, the men were also expected to enforce new levels of public decorum on the streets. This was unpopular in many working-class districts where the street was a major arena of commercial activity and of leisure. The middle-class Victorian might have considered an Englishman's home as his castle, but the picture looked very different to those in the poor working class still crammed into dingy courts and tenements where everyone could not help but know everyone else's business. There were some areas where the police did not go, except in pairs. Cavanagh recalled being advised by an old Irishman to keep out of the slum and cul-de-sac of Ewer Street; if there was a fight, it was politic to let them get on with it.[11]

Around such areas, and elsewhere, the number of assaults on the police was high and such assaults did not decline in the same proportion as other criminal assaults recorded in the annual criminal statistics during the second half of the century. On 16 February 1868 Hennessy was assaulted by Eugene Stack in Fitzroy Market. Only twenty years old, Stack already had two convictions for assaulting policemen. He was sentenced to fourteen days' hard labour without the alternative of a fine. The last entry in Hennessy's notebook also concerns an assault on a policeman; this was in August 1880 when he went to the assistance of a colleague who had sought to arrest a drunken sailor and had been hit for his pains. The seaman's solicitor requested a fine, but the magistrate would have none of it and passed a sentence of two months' hard labour.

The early years of Hennessy's police career coincided with the great panics about garrotters – the name used in the press to describe street robbers in Victorian London. The robbers themselves, according to PC William Good, who gave evidence in a major trial of street robbers at the Old Bailey in November 1862, preferred the term 'mug' to 'garrotte'.[12] During these panics many respectable gentlemen went out after dark carrying coshes, euphemistically labelled 'life preservers'. Hennessy did not record ever coming into contact with a street robber; not surprisingly, perhaps, given that, whatever the panic engendered by the press, such robbers were few in number. Nor did he record meeting any gentleman armed with a life preserver. In this respect he was much more fortunate than PC Matthew Maddock who, one night at the beginning of 1866, while patrolling in plain clothes, had approached a gentleman in Sydenham. The gentleman promptly drew his life preserver with which he knocked down and injured the unfortunate Maddock.[13] The press largely lost interest in garrotting from the mid-1860s; however, in 1879 Superintendent Thomson reported that for a short period 'E' Division experienced

> an epidemic of the crime known as 'snatching' . . . where persons while passing through the streets . . . were suddenly confronted by one or more men, generally lads, snatching whatever valuables [were] visible, and instantly vanishing, the time and the place being, of course, calculated, and the very audacity of the crime so astounding the victims, that identification was rare, the whole resulting in the perpetration of very serious crime almost with impunity. A concentration of Police, uniform and detective, in the localities followed, and it died out.[14]

Hennessy was almost certainly involved in this 'concentration', but few of the offenders with whom he came into contact were people that fit the popular perception of professional criminals. Some were repeat offenders, but these were rarely violent or dangerous. Samuel Baldwin was one such. Eight years after Baldwin's conviction for theft of a leg of mutton, Hennessy appeared in court to testify to that conviction when Baldwin was found guilty of stealing money from his master. In December 1876 Hennessy was involved in the arrest and prosecution of fifteen-year-old John Tierney, who had taken four shillings' worth of copper coin from a shop till. Tierney was sentenced to ten days' imprisonment to be followed by four years in a reformatory. Eighteen months later, after Tierney had absconded, Hennessy travelled fifty miles north of London to Bedford to confirm Tierney's identity and former conviction when the youth – now using an alias – was prosecuted at the borough sessions for picking a lady's pocket. This may have been the furthest that Hennessy ever travelled from the immediate vicinity of London.

The most serious thief that Hennessy ever encountered – serious to the extent that his actions brought him before a judge at the Old Bailey – was one Robert William Shepherd. Shepherd, also known as Shepherd Hoppey because of a lame right foot, appeared at the Old Bailey charged under the names of William Thompson, in August 1861, and Henry Smith, in October 1865.[15] On the first occasion Shepherd, then aged twenty-three, was accused with John Thompson, aged seventeen, of breaking into the house of the brothers George and Myrthyl Brunswick, who ran a cabinet-making business in Newman Street just off Oxford Street. John Thompson had been employed by the brothers and it seems that he and Shepherd planned to take money that was sometimes left in the house on Friday night to pay the workforce on Saturday. They found no money but made off with a watch valued at £10, two coats valued at £3, a one-shilling comb and a few miscellaneous pieces of property. The haul was dispersed around different local pawn shops. On his beat Hennessy came across Shepherd keeping watch during the robbery. His testimony at the Old Bailey is illustrative of the way that the police sought to move on suspicious loiterers; it also suggests that Shepherd was already a marked man. 'I know the [Brunswick brothers'] house,' Hennessy explained to the court.

On the evening of 5th July, I first saw William Thompson about ten minutes past 10 o'clock – I did not speak to him then – I saw him near a passage that runs from Newman-street to Upper Rathbone-place – I afterwards saw him in Newman-street at the other end of the passage, about twenty minutes past 10 – I stood and looked at him for a second, and said, 'You have a waiting job to night' – he said, 'I don't know what you mean, I don't understand you' – I said, 'I spoke plain enough for you to under-stand, you have a waiting job on to night' – he said, 'Oh! it is not a late hour' – I said, 'Whether it is a late hour or not I shall not have you about here, I shall see you away' – I followed him through two or three streets – he had been pointed out to me before . . .

PC Joseph Lambert, also of 'E' Division, testified that Thompson's real name was Shepherd, and added that he had known him and his mother for years. A third constable, William Hepher, gave details of Shepherd's previous conviction at the Middlesex quarter sessions in December 1856 for the theft of 448 pounds of lead from a building, an offence that had earned him four years' penal servitude. Shepherd got six years for the theft at the Brunswicks' house.

In October 1866 it fell to Hennessy to testify to the 1861 conviction when Shepherd, now going under the name of Henry Smith and the trade of a shoemaker, confessed to a burglary at the house of a tallow chandler in Charlotte Street. Before reliable record keeping and the ability to use fingerprints, such 'proving' of previous convictions by police officers in the courts was a commonplace. In 1866, as in 1861, Shepherd's haul had been meagre: two coats and a few other articles. This time he was sentenced to seven years' penal servitude. At the foot of the page on which he reported this case, Hennessy made a personal note that suggests how he and his mates saw Shepherd, and how they expected to have to watch out for him on his release: '66/ 67/ 68/ 69/ 70/ 71/ 72/ 73/ time will expire.' There was a vicious circle here. The police were expected to make lists of habitual criminals in their districts, though the term 'habitual criminal' was never precisely defined. They were expected to keep an eye on men released early from prison on a 'ticket-of-leave'. Many men released from prison protested that the system led to police harassment and that, under such circumstances, it became extremely difficult to go 'straight' and to find any steady employment. Charles Hunter, for example, who had served a sentence of transportation and who appeared at the Old Bailey in November 1856 on a charge of robbery, protested to the court that a particular Police Sergeant had harassed him from one job to another.

> When I came home from transportation, I obtained a situation at a beer house in the Waterloo-road, where I was getting a comfortable living, and supporting my wife and aged mother, I had been there a few weeks when sergeant Broad came and told the landlord I was a ticket-of-leave man, and if he allowed such characters in his house he should indict it; he told me to go, after that I drove a costermonger barrow, and he followed me about the streets, telling my customers to see that their change was good, for I was a ticket-of-leave man; I was compelled to give that up; I went to live with my parents, and worked at tailoring, and every time I came in or out of the court where I lived, he would stop and search me, if any of the neighbours or their children were about; so that at last I could get nobody to trust me with anything; what had I to do? I would work if they would let me, but they will not.

Similar complaints were made directly to Lord Carnarvon, a leading figure in Victorian penal policy, when his lordship brought a group of ticket-of-leave men together early in 1857 to recount their problems. As one put it: 'If a mat was stolen from the next door to his, ten to one but that the police would be down upon him for it.'[16]

Most of the offences that Hennessy recorded were minor: the occasional beggar, drunks, petty theft, prostitutes and the violation of street regulations. (See Table 1, p. 132.) It is unclear what prompted him to make an entry in his notebook; the recorded average of six offences a year must reflect only a fraction of the total that he dealt with during his service. He appears to have been particularly assiduous in 1873 when he recorded forty-seven separate offences, rather more than a third of the total in the book. The regulatory offences with which he dealt generally involved members of the crew of an omnibus or a cab driver. As London expanded during the nineteenth century, so the demand for transport to bring commuters in to the centre also expanded. There were a few short stage coaches running in and out of the centre at the beginning of the century but George Shillibeer's regular omnibus from Paddington to Bank, via the Angel, which began two months before the first Metropolitan Police constables took to the streets, is commonly credited with being the first full regular service. By the mid-1850s around 200,000 people still walked to work in London each day; some 6,000 may have been using the new railways, and 15,000 travelled along the Thames by steamboat. The omnibuses could carry well over 25,000. The buses, the hackney cabs and various commercial wagons jostled for road space, and while there had been some road-widening schemes there were still nasty bottlenecks, particularly leading into the City proper. In 1868 one commentator noted the 'disproportionately large number [of police] in the main thoroughfares' because of traffic problems, '[a] circumstance which must tend to withdraw the Police from those retired courts and bye-streets where people stand most in need of protection against such crimes as garrotting and robbery with violence'.[17] And Hennessy's 'E' Division had particular problems with its bustling theatre traffic in the evenings and the early morning activity round the great fruit and vegetable market of Covent Garden.

Hennessy summonsed bus conductors for not having the appropriate licence, for delaying so as to pick up additional passengers and for carrying more than their specified quota of passengers. Such offences, when unobserved by a police officer, were generally to the omnibus crews' advantage since they were well known to pocket a percentage of the fares. Hennessy summonsed cab drivers for loitering and also for driving their carriages while drunk. In September 1863 he issued a summons for yet another kind of regulatory offence. E.W. Simmons, a shopkeeper in Tottenham Court Road, had created an obstruction to the footpath by putting furniture for sale in front of his shop.

Table 1: Offences recorded by PC Alexander Hennessy 1857–80

Offence	Male	Female
Burglary	3	–
Petty Larceny (including pickpocketing)	24	3
Assault	12 (5 also involved drunkenness)	–
Begging	2	1
Drunk and Disorderly/Incapable	15	17
Drunk in charge of a vehicle	28	–
Omnibus/Cab Offence	26	–
Other	7	1
Total	117	22

(*Source:* MPHC, Notebook of PC Hennessy)

Most of the offenders with whom Hennessy dealt were ordinary people rather than individuals who were regularly in conflict with the law; their offences commonly involved doing silly things to the disadvantage or the annoyance of others. The fourteen-year-old boy arrested for letting off fireworks in the street on the eve of Guy Fawkes's day 1874 is, perhaps, the most extreme illustration. From the addresses that he wrote alongside each offender it appears also that Hennessy was commonly dealing with neighbours. These were people who lived in or very close to 'E' Division's patch. Even Shepherd Hoppey was a local; indeed, the only times that he appears not to have been resident in the division was when he was in prison.

Criminal statistics and court records all point to young men as the principal offenders in any period. It is not surprising, therefore, to find that most of the offenders noted by Hennessy were male. It is initially surprising, however, that the number of women apprehended for being drunk and disorderly or drunk and incapable was greater than the number of men. The key element here is prostitution and, perhaps also, the perception of prostitution among the police. Some of the teeming streets in and around 'E' Division were noted for vice. In the later 1860s and early 1870s Superintendent Thomson expressed concern about the lewd literature and prints that were trafficked in Holywell and Wych Streets. But 'the sorrow and shame of prostitution' that 'afflicted' his division was his main concern when it came to vice. Of the sixteen women that Hennessy arrested for drunken behaviour – he arrested Charlotte Wood twice, once in February and once in March 1874 – he labelled nine as prostitutes. In some instances he described their offences as being aggravated by the propositioning of male pedestrians. Thirty-two-year-old Elizabeth Loudon, alias Jackson, arrested in the busy thoroughfare of Tottenham Court Road, was also accused of using obscene language and exposing herself; she was given the particularly harsh sentence of a month's hard labour. Elizabeth Philips, aged twenty-four, worsened her offence by being seen soliciting, by uttering obscenities and by spitting in Hennessy's face; she was given the choice of a 20-shilling fine or two weeks in prison. Loudon and Philips appear almost deliberately to have been playing the role of the incorrigible 'fallen woman' that Victorian society had cast for them. But the question has to be whether all of these arrests were of 'prostitutes', or whether Hennessy, like others, made the assumption that a woman who had been drinking and who was out alone after dark was bound to be a prostitute. Respectable women, it was assumed, did not behave in such a way. Indeed, evidence from later in the century suggests that there were police constables who commonly assumed that any young woman out alone after dark, whether he could smell drink on her breath or not, was a prostitute. Julia Bevan, a thirty-year-old needlewoman arrested by Hennessy for being drunk and incapable in September 1874, adopted the role of the inconsolable penitent; she attempted suicide while in the police cells.

Hennessy's biography, such as it can be constructed, is not startling. His conduct may have been good but, as a police constable, he did nothing out of the ordinary. He provides a contrast with – perhaps a useful antidote to – most of those policemen who wrote autobiographies during the late nineteenth and early twentieth centuries. Typical of such biographies were those of detectives like Andrew Lansdowne, Benjamin Leeson and John Littlechild. They were commonly written to a formula, celebrating careers which took a man from lowly origins to senior rank, and almost always by way of a string of notable arrests and court cases. Indeed, they often wrote of avoiding the mundane and deliberately selecting stories that would excite and engross the reader.[18] Hennessy's working life as a policeman in Victorian London was more typical of the majority of such lives. His home life and his working life were confined to a relatively small area of the metropolis, and his horizons may never have stretched much beyond that area. He seems to have shared the prejudices of his trade with regard to recidivists like Shepherd Hoppey. He seems also to have adopted the assumptions of the respectable classes in his attitude to women, and especially towards 'prostitutes'.

Hennessy's pocket book was not an official record, but we can draw a final, significant point from it: how he referred to people. There was not much description of the petty criminal offenders that he arrested, but he usually gave their name, age, trade, if they had one, and address. Bus drivers and conductors, in contrast, were referred to only by the number of their badge. Admittedly, unlike the petty offenders, it was the badge number that was crucial in the summons. But bus drivers and cabbies were not necessarily locals whose actions were affecting their neighbours; they were functionaries whose offences were often victimless breaches of the rules. Policemen were also functionaries and in his book, Hennessy also referred to them by their divisional numbers, occasionally noting their name afterwards. In reporting the second offence of Samuel Baldwin, Hennessy wrote: 'PC 84 E proved a former conviction.' In this case PC 84E was Hennessy himself, and in referring to himself and his comrades by number rather than by name it would seem that, to some extent at least, Hennessy was acknowledging the official image of himself while at work. Once on his beat he ceased to be Alexander Hennessy and became a human cipher representing the law.

A Country Bobby: James Jackson

In spite of the bustle and clamour, it was probably far easier to play the role of a straight-backed personification of the law striding along the London streets than trudging the lanes and fields of the countryside. The fields and villages of the Victorian countryside were a different world from the smoggy, traffic-congested metropolis and the industrial towns, but the rural policeman's life had a similar rhythm. As PC Hennessy pounded his beat in Holborn, so James Jackson patrolled an isolated beat in his native Hertfordshire.

James Jackson was born in Standon, Hertfordshire, in 1844, the son of a carman. In November 1865, after a period as a labourer on the railways and during which time he still lived in Standon, he joined the Hertfordshire Police. Hertfordshire was a relatively small, predominantly agricultural county. Its two main towns, St Albans and Hertford, had their own separate police forces of seven and six men respectively. The county police, in keeping with the county itself, was one of England's smaller forces. There was an overall increase of twenty men in the year that Jackson joined, which brought the complement up to 112 men, roughly one police constable for every 1,400 persons in the county. In his annual inspection for 1865–6, Her Majesty's Inspector of Constabulary for the region declared the force to be efficient and therefore eligible for the Treasury grant of one quarter of the costs of clothing and pay.[19]

For eight of his eleven years' service in the force, Jackson and his wife lived in the village of Great Hadham less than ten miles from his birthplace. Their two daughters were born in the police house there. During the nineteenth century the way of life in the two villages of Great and Little Hadham changed little; around

2,000 people lived here, largely working the land. The villages straddled the River Ash; the roads were little more than pressed earth and patrolling often meant struggling for miles along muddy paths by night to reach a 'conference point' with one of the constables on a neighbouring beat.

Jackson's surviving journals are much fuller than Hennessy's notebook, but then these books were the official record of his duty that his superiors inspected at regular intervals.[20] Entries were required to be made daily. They ran across two pages of the book. The left-hand page contained the date, the number of patrols made during the day, the number of fellow constables with whom he conferred, and at which conference points. The right-hand page contained 'Remarks', which included any arrests, court attendances or attendances at events such as fairs or fires or meetings with his superintendent. Jackson wrote in an elegant copperplate, which outshone his occasional, idiosyncratic but phonetic spelling as with, for example, an entry for 19 June 1870: 'Apprehended William Eureah Barns on suspetion of beean disarter & took him to [Bishop's] Stortford.'

Serious crime was a rare occurrence for Alexander Hennessy and, as might be expected given his posting, it was similarly rare for James Jackson. It was exceptional for there to be as many as 200 indictable crimes reported annually in Hertfordshire during the 1860s and 1870s. Jackson had to make inquiries about burglaries in March 1869, April 1872 and April 1873; there was also a robbery at a farm in February 1872, an attempted highway robbery and forced entry into a cottage with the theft of £72 in 1874. There were a few other thefts, but these were mostly petty, involving growing crops, animals or items of clothing. In May 1868, for example, he arrested Elizabeth Chipperfield for stealing a dress worth 12 shillings and 6 pence. A few years later he helped in the arrest of three men who had stolen a sheep; this was regarded as a serious offence and the men received, respectively, five years' penal servitude, eighteen months and twelve months. The prevention of theft was seen as a significant part of the rural officer's role and Jackson records several stake-outs, often with a fellow constable, observing walnuts or fields of potatoes or turnips. The eleven years covered by the diaries record Jackson's involvement in twenty-six arrests and the delivery of fifteen summonses for theft, the apprehension of four poachers, and the serving of two summonses on Samuel Warner, an agricultural labourer and army pensioner, for poaching.

Acts or threats of violence were not a great problem in the Hadhams, and very few made their way into Jackson's diaries. The most serious incident was in August 1868 when sixteen-year-old Aron Warner stabbed Robert Renols (the spelling is Jackson's). Young Warner took up two more days of Jackson's time two years later when he was killed in a railway accident. The recurrence of certain names in the diaries makes an important point. The Hadhams were a small place where all of the inhabitants probably knew each other at least by sight, and some of these individuals, often whole families, occupied a disproportionate amount of Jackson's time. The Thakes offer one example. William Thake was arrested with George Anson for the theft of thirty trusses of straw in May 1869; Jackson had given evidence against Anson for being drunk and disorderly six months earlier. Frederick Thake was arrested on suspicion of stealing a fowl in April 1870, and for being drunk and disorderly the following September. In December 1871 Jackson had to serve a summons on Frederick's wife Mary. But the most troublesome family for Jackson were the Warwicks ('Warricks' in Jackson's spelling). William Warwick was charged with assault on 6 June 1870; less than three weeks later Frederick Warwick was arrested for a similar offence compounded by an assault on Jackson. In November of that year eleven-year-old Henry Warwick was arrested for stealing carrots. Charles Warwick was arrested in February 1872 for threatening a widow. Richard Warwick, however, was the real pest. He was an agricultural labourer, born in Great Hadham about 1839. Jackson had to deal with him for being drunk and disorderly in 1870, for deserting his wife, for poaching and for threatening his wife in 1872, and for threatening her again in 1873.

The Hertfordshire police checked the weights and measures used in local shops and markets; the constables acted as assistant relieving officers for vagrants. Jackson recorded moving on gypsies and, on one occasion, impounding their horses. He spent more time serving summonses than arresting offenders. In addition to those noted above for theft and poaching, he served summonses for drunkenness; there were over 700 pubs in the county and over 600 beer houses and between 300 and 400 people were taken before the magistrates every year for being drunk and disorderly. He served summonses for failure to pay the poor rates, failure to support a family, for riding without reins, cruelty to a horse, breaking a work contract. Two men were summonsed for making a fire on the highway on 5 November, and Jackson also gave evidence against a woman for selling fireworks to under-age boys. Few of these offences would be perceived as crimes, but resolving them added to the general maintenance of what was considered orderliness and the proper regulation of society. In struggling over tracks and fields Jackson and his fellows may not have shown the steady pace and swagger of PC X53 in Piccadilly, but they were fulfilling a similar role; they were the regulatory institution in human form.

Jackson's career looked promising. He was promoted to second-class constable in August 1868 with the corresponding pay rise from 17 shillings and 6 pence a week to 19 shillings. He was promoted to the first class four years later when the whole force was given a pay rise apparently because of vacancies and difficulties in attracting recruits.[21] Jackson was now earning 23 shillings a week. In March 1876 he moved to a new posting in the village of Letty Green some ten miles west of the Hadhams and close to the county town of Hertford. Here Jackson appears to have committed a serious disciplinary offence; family tradition had it that he failed to doff his hat to the squire's daughter. He was dismissed on 7 March 1877, at about the time that his wife gave birth to their son. The Jacksons moved to the small market town of Ware and in 1881 he was described in the census as a

General Servant and Domestic; ten years later he was a foreman agricultural labourer living in Tottenham on the outskirts of the metropolis.

A Detective: Jerome Caminada

Police officers like Hennessy and Jackson had their uniforms 'buttoned up to throttling point' to contribute to their image of 'an institution rather than a man'. But not every police officer wore a uniform. Jerome Caminada was the son of Irish-Italian parents and was born in Manchester in 1844. He spent five years in the Royal Lancashire Militia and a short period in a Salford ironworks before joining the Manchester City Police in 1868. Like Hennessy and Jackson, and thousands of others, he started his police career on uniformed patrol experiencing the usual tedium and occasional danger. Caminada recalled being assaulted on his beat by a man who punched him in the face protesting that he had 'to pay rates and taxes to keep such lazy fellows . . . walking about the streets'. He pursued his assailant into a beer house, up a flight of stairs and, in the ensuing scuffle, 'he managed to get my hand in his mouth, and began to bite away in right good fashion. Fortunately, he had no teeth, but he worked away so vigorously with his gums that I could feel the pain for weeks after.'[22]

But early on in his police career Caminada handed in his uniform and joined the police detectives. It was while still serving as Chief Detective Inspector of the Manchester Police in 1895 that he published his memoirs, *Twenty-Five Years of Detective Life*.

Caminada's memoirs were among the first written by a British police officer, but they read much like those that were to follow. As with Thomas Woollaston's memoir published ten years before, there was no chronological narrative but rather a series of chapters each recounting a case or series of cases involving types of offenders or particular offenders. Caminada described pursuing various kinds of swindler, fraudster and the various quacks who were always ready to sell cures for a host of different ailments.

Sometimes arrests were violent. Sometimes he disguised himself and paid street lads to get information. But he also knew the local pawnbrokers and, above all, he gave the impression that he knew his quarry. In the same way that Hennessy and his comrades knew their local offenders and ticked off the months or years till their release and the likelihood of arresting them again, so Caminada, rather more elegantly and for the vicarious delight and satisfaction of his readers, described his knowledge of known criminals. No doubt his respectable readers slept more soundly having read a long chapter in which he described breaking up a group of thieves that he met in his first year as a police officer. Some of the group, however, had criminal careers that stretched the length of his police career. Among the most significant of them was Tommy Lewis and an individual with several aliases but who Caminada refers to principally as 'Little Alf'. In the early 1870s Caminada was instrumental in sending the group to prison for some twenty-eight house-breaking and burglary offences.

> As time went on, my colleagues often said to me, 'How would you like another Little Alf and Tommy case?' To which inquiry I invariably replied, 'They will probably turn up again, and give us a startler one of these days.'

Little Alf turned up again in the following decade and, even though he 'had sworn he would never again be taken alive', Caminada recounted with pride that he took him. Little Alf was released in the early 1890s and several offences immediately smacked to Caminada of his handiwork. When they met in the street Caminada recalled urging Alf to go straight and giving him half a crown.[23] For all that he portrayed offenders like Little Alf as incorrigible, Caminada was also aware of the problem of stigmatization and the difficulties that faced people when they were released from prison. At the outset of his book he explained:

As long as our system of punishment for the repression of crime is accompanied by degradation, it will tend more to foster criminal propensities than to remove them. Degradation strengthens evil propensities, prevents repentance, and renders reform impossible. You have wandered from the right path. You wish to retrace your steps, and in all sincerity and earnestness to lead a new life. Your desires are in vain. Society has excommunicated you. You are an outcast. You have no hope. You have undergone the sentence of the law, and public opinion carries on the punishment and you are worse off than ever . . . The freed prisoner is a pestiferous thing which society detests and abhors.[24]

Well before his memoirs were published, avid readers of the police court reports in the Manchester press would have known of 'Detective Caminada'. He appeared regularly, often after having arrested small-time, but persistent thieves and pickpockets who he had observed in action or subsequently identified.[25] Occasionally there were more sensational stories, such as the case picked up by *Reynolds's Newspaper* in December 1875 that vicariously appealed to the class prejudice of this popular newspaper's readers and their fear and dislike of paedophiles. A Cheshire magistrate and captain of the local volunteers had propositioned a boy and urged him to bring a friend with him to a meeting place. The boy informed Caminada and the detective followed him to the rendezvous, where he arrested the gentleman at the moment he opened his trousers and exposed himself. The gentleman offered a bribe of first one and then two guineas, but when Caminada refused the gentleman set about him with his heavy walking stick. A violent struggle followed during which Caminada's baton was broken; only with the arrival of two other gentlemen and two police officers was the offender overpowered and handcuffed. *Reynolds's Newspaper* considered that the fine of £20 for assaulting Caminada, £5 for assaulting a witness, together with £2 and costs for exposing himself was insufficient for such 'disgusting bestiality'. 'The fellow should have been sent to prison.' It trusted that he would be banned from the bench of magistrates.[26]

By the 1890s Caminada was a celebrity in Manchester and respected, it seems, even among those on the wrong side of the law. In 1892, after William Willan, a sixteen-year-old cooper, had been sentenced to death for the murder of Peter Kennedy in a fight between two of Manchester's 'scuttling' gangs, Caminada was called to the condemned cell and was begged to initiate a campaign for a reprieve. And this was in spite of the fact that he had had no previous involvement with the case. Four years later when he led a raid on a notorious pub to prevent an illegal prize fight, the publican protested to the local magistrates that most of the crowd had turned up because of Caminada: 'It went round the neighbourhood that the wonderful Caminada had come. People who had never been in the house before came in when they heard that Caminada was there.'[27]

In addition to the seedy back streets of Manchester, Caminada's career took him to various parts of England in pursuit of suspects or to keep an eye out for old offenders that he knew at events such as, for example, the Grand National at Aintree and races at Goodwood. He served for just over thirty years, retiring in 1899 as a superintendent. He remained living in central Manchester with his wife Amelia, who was twelve years his junior, his young daughter Mary and a maidservant. But he did not opt for a quiet life. In 1907 he was elected as an Independent for Openshaw on the Manchester City Council. He died a few months before the outbreak of the First World War.

The police careers of Caminada, Hennessy and Jackson had different outcomes, yet in many ways they were all exemplars of the Victorian police officer. They were working-class men charged with the supervision and surveillance of other working-class people. They were not exceptional in their origins. From time to time there was an interest in attracting rural labourers as recruits to the urban forces; agricultural labourers were thought to be fitter and healthier than the urban working class and more willing to take orders and to fit in with the hierarchical structure of the police. But a high proportion of recruits were always drawn from the unskilled and semi-skilled working class and, like Caminada, Hennessy and Jackson, served in the town or county where they were born.[28] Jackson was unlucky to have lost his post, possibly through failing to observe the strict class divisions of the period.

These men joined an institution; on the streets of towns or in the countryside they represented the police institution and, in the eyes of their supporters and spokesmen, ultimately they represented the law. The old parish constables had also represented the law, but they were individuals; at the end of their period of service they were replaced by another local individual. The policeman was different in that the force of the bureaucratic police institution was behind him. The institution's paperwork provided a memory of districts, individuals and offences which could be passed on and which could facilitate forward thinking. But this did not mean that, during the nineteenth century, a police officer's personal authority no longer counted. Victorian policemen dealt with tough men, and sometimes tough women. Many working-class jobs during the nineteenth century continued to depend on physical strength and fostered the cult of the hard man. Policemen patrolling in the areas populated by working-class hard men, as has been implicit in the stories of Caminada, Hennessy and Jackson, needed to possess, or else cultivate rapidly, a similar physicality and toughness.

— CHAPTER 6 —

Hard Men and Harder Coppers: Bobby on the Front Line, 1860–1914

THE SECOND HALF of Victoria's reign did not witness the scale of hardship and the massive political agitation of the 1830s and 1840s, but police officers still had grim slums to patrol, the Queen's peace to maintain and various forms of political activity to watch and suppress. The statistics suggest that crime began to level out from the 1850s and that some offences even declined. But there were occasional crimes that electrified the public, most notably the cluster of savage killings in one of East London's poorest districts in the autumn of 1888 – the killings that contemporaries attributed to Jack the Ripper. The police's failure to catch the Ripper brought considerable adverse comment.

Periodic criticism in the media was counter-balanced by periodic praise of and pride in 'the best police in the world'. The jibes about Dogberry-like stupidity also continued, which rankled with officers who were increasingly developing a professional consciousness. But while words and songs could not injure physically, there were still plenty of sticks, stones, fists and boots directed at men on some beats. In 1875 the Chief Constable of Staffordshire, a former army officer, told a select committee of the House of Commons that the assaults committed on his men made their lives more dangerous than those of soldiers.

The other day in Birmingham we had a man killed; not a week passes in the Black Country but what a man is almost killed; a soldier may be in the army for 20 years and never be hurt, but the policemen in the Black Country are liable to be hurt every day; certainly they would not go five years without being hurt.[1]

While the figures for assault were among the criminal statistics that declined in the second half of the century, those in the special category of assaults on police officers declined at a lesser rate. A policeman's beat could still be a dangerous place and it needed a tough man to walk it.

Policing the Working Class

Nineteenth-century Manchester appeared to many contemporaries as the archetypal industrial city, and the image has persisted in the popular mind to the present. During the 1830s and 1840s as more and more factory chimneys added to the sooty clouds over the city and as more and more men, women and children poured into the fetid, humid, ear shattering maws of the factories of cottonopolis, the whole was regarded with a mixture of admiration and horror. Karl Marx's friend and collaborator Frederick Engels, himself involved in cotton manufacture in Manchester, wrote of 'the filth, ruin, and uninhabitableness, the defiance of all considerations of cleanliness, ventilation, and health which characterise . . . the heart of the second city of England, the first manufacturing city of the world.' The Frenchman Alexis de Tocqueville occupied a very different point on the political spectrum, but he had a similar impression. Manchester was 'a foul drain' and 'a filthy sewer', though from it flowed 'pure gold'. 'Here civilization works its miracles, and civilized man is turned back almost into a savage.'[2] Jerome Caminada began his memoir with a description of the poorer districts of central Manchester in his youth. It is a description that resembles, and might well have drawn upon, Dickens's grim picture of St Giles.

Manchester had been the site of the Peterloo Massacre and the growth of the factory system accentuated the division of social classes, fostering fear among the Manchester elite and among other social commentators that the new industrial proletariat had the potential for violence, pillage and revolution. From the middle of the century considerable improvements were made in the city and in the surrounding industrial areas. Even so, to quote Caminada, 'with all its great moral, religious and political associations, its commercial enterprise recognised in every part of the world, and its corresponding wealth, [Manchester still had] its dark spots.'[8] And while a significant part of the Mancunian working-class leadership adopted a conciliatory tone, there were still enough meetings of socialists and trades unions to feed the concerns of wealthy property owners and their families. There were also violent youth gangs, the Scuttlers, infesting the poorest districts. In the last three decades of the century vicious Scuttler gangs defended their shabby squalid territories and invaded those of their neighbours swinging their brass-buckled belts as weapons, lashing out with their pointed clogs as well as wielding all manner of knives, cudgels, pokers and iron bars.[4]

At the beginning of the twentieth century, possibly taking their cue from Caminada, two police officers who had spent their working lives in the Lancashire Police wrote and published their memoirs. James Bent and Richard Jervis enjoyed similar careers in the industrial districts around Manchester as the shock city of the first half of the century sought to transform itself into a beacon of Victorian civic pride. They were both tough customers, and proud of it.[5] James Bent was the elder of the pair. He was born in Eccles in 1828. His first job, at the age of seven, was in a silk mill. When he was nine his family moved to Manchester where his father joined the local watch. In 1848 James signed up with the Lancashire Constabulary. He served for forty-two years, rising to command the Manchester Division. Richard Jervis was born in Ightfield, Shropshire in 1832. His father joined the Lancashire force when it was established, was quickly promoted and, by the early 1840s, he was an inspector based in Southport. Jervis claimed to have joined the force in 1850 aged eighteen, but the census for 1851 lists him as still in Shropshire, in Donnington, a servant boy in the house of the Revd John Meredith, vicar of Uppington. Whatever the truth, Jervis was in the police by the mid-1850s.

Both Bent and Jervis enjoyed rapid promotion. Bent was made a sergeant in 1857, an inspector five years later, and he became superintendent of the Lancashire force's Manchester division in 1868. Jervis's rise was faster. In 1857 he replaced his father as inspector in Southport; he became superintendent of the Bacup and Rossendale Division in 1864 and moved from there to Ormskirk in 1877, where he saw out his career, retiring thirty years later in 1907. Jervis boasted that he had been the youngest member of the Lancashire force when he had joined and that he was the oldest serving police officer in England when he retired.

The two men married and raised families in police accommodation. Within a year of his appointment Bent had married Martha, a widow slightly older than himself. Martha had two young sons from her first marriage. She had two daughters with Bent. At least one of the stepsons followed Bent's career and, by 1891, was an inspector in one of the police forces employed by the railway companies. Jervis delayed marriage. Frances, his wife, was ten years younger than him. The eldest of their children was encouraged to climb the social scale and in 1881 Alfred E. Jervis was listed on the census as a medical student. For some reason things did not work out as planned and a decade later Alfred was an ironmonger in Widnes with a wife and young family. As superintendents both Bent and Jervis lived in police houses and were sufficiently comfortable to employ a domestic servant. In each instance their houses were part of a cluster of police buildings. In 1871, for example, Bent lived at 7 Union Street, Stretford; PC Chappell and his wife Anna lived at number 4, with four constables as boarders; PC Alston, his wife and baby daughter were at number 5; Police Sergeant Keighley and his wife lived in number 6. In 1881 Jervis

was at 7 Derby Street, Ormskirk, which was next to a police
station that housed two married and two single constables.

The memoirs of both men, like most memoirs, need to be treated
with care. Nevertheless, they provide a vivid and believable picture
of police service. They both commented on how tough the life
was for a recruit, particularly in the early months. Bent recalled
that, 'having been previously accustomed to go to bed at a regular
hour, I found it hard at first to keep awake in the night-time.' He
also confessed to being frightened of ghosts and hobgoblins on
his night-time patrols, something that he put down to his reading
of 'cheap trashy literature'. But he soon learned to cope; and he
soon learned the dodges, such as disappearing for a night's sleep
in a dyeworks when it was especially cold.

Jervis seems to have been rather officious and a stickler for
enforcing the law. He described instances in which he appears to
have pressed his authority to the limit – one reason, perhaps,
why he stood out to his superiors and was promoted so rapidly.
He boasted of making 'almost a special feature of stopping and
searching tramps and suspicious-looking characters on the road,
and the results justified the means – a great many did I pick up
with stolen property in their possession'. He claimed also to
have clamped down on a popular pastime of bowling stones down
the highway. 'Many a contest took place for wagers,' he explained,
'and as in the excitement of the game little heed was taken of the
traffic, pedestrians as well as horses were frequently injured –
several seriously.' Jervis's actions against the stone bowlers made
him enemies and some of the young men that he had taken before
the magistrates planned to get him. Warned of the conspiracy
Jervis surprised his ambushers from behind and set about them
with his 'logwood', as he called his truncheon. One would-be
assailant suffered a broken arm and promised a civil action in the
county court but, in the event, nothing came of the threat. Bent
did not admit to any similar incident of getting his retaliation in
first, but he was quite open about the rough way in which he
handled some prisoners. He wrote unashamedly of pulling one

man downstairs by the foot, and then dragging him similarly along the road.

It was not only in the industrial conurbation around Manchester that tough policemen clashed with local hard men. While the typical English gentleman was supposed to abhor violence, never to strike the first blow, fight fairly and, generally, only in defence of women, children and other supposed 'weaker vessels', in many working-class districts of Victorian and Edwardian Britain men continued to gain and maintain a reputation by physical strength and aggression. If police officers were to survive in these areas, to apprehend the drunk and disorderly, and to pursue and arrest criminal offenders, then they had to be as hard as the local hard men.[6]

Middlesbrough had a very different economy to Manchester and its environs. Its rapid expansion from a settlement of four houses and twenty-five people in 1801, to over 5,000 inhabitants in 1841 and nearly 40,000 thirty years later, was based on its position as a railway hub and port and a booming iron industry. Gladstone called it the 'infant Hercules' in 1862, and doubtless some of the young men who poured into the booming town saw themselves as cast in Hercules's mould. The town suffered all the problems of a fast-expanding centre packed with young male workers and seamen. Policemen who tried to arrest drunks were often assaulted. The usual weapons were fists, feet and teeth, but sometimes clubs, hammers, knives and pokers were used; dogs also were set upon the police. The statistics suggest that, during the 1860s, a Middlesbrough policeman might expect an assault twice a year, and, of course, these statistics reflect only those cases where the officer involved decided to make an arrest or a report. In an organization where a man's toughness and physicality won respect among his mates as well as from his opponents, some assaults, especially those in which a man had been bested, might never have been reported for fear of implying weakness. Middlesbrough policemen had to be tough and to show themselves as tough. Indeed, some of the more respectable locals were concerned about police brutality and about police officers participating in fights with rather more enthusiasm than ought to be expected from guardians of the law. But others, who made no critical comment in the local press, were probably content to give the police a free hand in chastising drunks and roughs.[7]

It was the same situation beyond the booming centres of new industry. Birmingham was industrial, but not a centre of either textile factories or massive iron works. Here, too, in the poorer working-class districts there were stories of ferocious violence against the police and of police brutality. In May 1867 the *Birmingham Daily Gazette* protested about 'the terrible and cruel punishment inflicted upon lads by irate and passionate policemen'.[8] Eight years later came the most notorious anti-police incident in the city. Navigation Street was a poor area, stigmatized by the press and respectable inhabitants as the dwelling place of 'roughs'. One Sunday evening in March 1875 two police detectives visited the home of a suspected burglar and arrested him. The moment that they left the house with their quarry and began walking along Navigation Street, they were surrounded by crowds of angry locals intent on rescuing the suspect. Hearing the commotion, uniformed officers in the vicinity hurried to the scene. A ferocious fight ensued during which a police sergeant and a constable were stabbed. Thirty-year-old PC William Lines, married with a young daughter, had been in the Birmingham City Police for eleven years and on three occasions, when making arrests, he had suffered serious injury. Following the Navigation Street riot he clung to life for two weeks, giving a statement about the fight from his hospital bed, before dying of his wounds.[9]

The poorer areas of London, as might be expected, were no different. The occasional violence faced by Alexander Hennessy and the advice to Timothy Cavanagh to steer clear of an Irish slum were described earlier. In 1897 one of Charles Booth's investigators made abbreviated notes of the comments of Inspector Carter as he showed the investigator around his East End 'manor'.

The Block of streets between Gale Street and Furze Street are the worst in the District, worst than almost any district in London. Three policemen wounded there last week. This block sends more police to hospital than any other in London. 'Men are not human'[,] they are wild beasts. [If you] take a man or a woman, a rescue is always organised. They fling brickbats, iron, anything they can lay their hands on. All are Irish cockneys. Not an Englishman or a Scotchman wd. live among them.[10]

Some hard men within the Metropolitan Police, like Tom Divall and John 'Tin Ribs' Monk, seem positively to have relished opportunities to demonstrate their toughness and their fighting prowess. Divall remembered the first question asked of him by his inspector when he was posted south of the Thames to the dockers' district of Deptford: 'Can you fight?' Some nights, he went on, 'our charge room at the station [was] more like a slaughterhouse than a place for human beings'. 'We made no attempt to arrest anybody,' Monk recalled of one confrontation that began in a pub in central London. 'We knew the kind of treatment that that sort of rough understood.'[11] Given this pattern of violence it is small wonder that several liberal commentators described the policemen that patrolled the poorer districts of the East End as resembling an army of occupation and as believing that any courtesy and kindness would be taken for weakness.[12]

There was more friction between the police and the working class during industrial disorders. The police were required to enforce the complex and frequently revised law on picketing – a law which rarely worked in favour of strikers. Bobbies were called upon to protect the blackleg labour imported to break a strike and to protect bailiffs employed both to evict strikers and their families from company housing and to seize property from a worker's home in payment of a debt or fine. In August 1862, for example, a Salford court directed bailiffs to seize the furniture of a man named Fitzpatrick who worked at the Norton Steel Works in Newton Heath. Fitzpatrick was out when the bailiff called but one of his fellow workers, Patrick Whelan, came to the assistance of Fitzpatrick's wife and beat up the bailiff. The following day the bailiff returned with five colleagues and two police officers from the Lancashire Constabulary. They had begun to load the Fitzpatricks' furniture on to a cart when a score or so steelworkers attacked them. Bruised on his head, arms and body, PC Shaw ran to his superiors for assistance. Inspector Richmond and James Bent, then a sergeant, courageously strode with Shaw into the steelworks to apprehend the assailants. Bent approached one worker, who dropped his hammer, appeared prepared to leave quietly with the police, but then gave what seems to have been a pre-arranged call for help. The three police officers suddenly found themselves confronted by a number of men armed with red-hot iron bars and abusing the police with language that the Victorian press could only report with evocative blanks. Richmond and Shaw were knocked to the ground, but the angry steelworkers appear to have focused their attention particularly on Bent. He was jabbed with the red-hot bars and thrown on a coke pile. He fought his way to his feet and was thrown on a wheelbarrow and struck across the head with one of the hot bars. 'Ram it down the —'s throat!' cried one of the attackers, and as Bent fought off the renewed attack he was burned on his mouth and hand. Eventually Richmond and Shaw, still groggy from their beatings, dragged him away. Bent was confined to his bed for several days nursing his injuries. But Bent was a hard man; he survived the beating and the burning, saw Whelan and another of his assailants, Denis Brady, sentenced to twenty years' penal servitude at the Lancashire Assizes, and proudly recorded the event in his memoirs.[13]

The steelworkers' attack on Bent was particularly violent, but it was not unique and it underlines just how rough Victorian and Edwardian Britain's industrial relations could be. Following a strike on the London Docks in the summer of 1912 Chester Jones, one of the London stipendiary magistrates, was directed to make an inquiry into a disorder in Rotherhithe. Jones found that, even though the crowd was 'large and dangerous', some people 'undoubtedly [had] a right to complain of the treatment they received' from the police. Bottles and glasses had been thrown; but some of the police had swung their heavy rolled capes in preference to truncheons and women and children had been. hit. The Transport Workers resolved to organize their own police from former soldiers and sailors so that, as their instructor put it, 'his men would be ready to charge the police if the police charged them'.[14]

Violence between the police and local hard men was not confined to Saturday-night brawls and industrial disputes. Some of the poachers on the young Constable Bent's rural beat were organized gangs that operated from the industrial towns and cities. Some men poached on a grand scale for a large commercial market that asked no questions. The poaching gangs declined in the second half of the century and gamekeepers were their real enemy, but interfering policemen might also be attacked with murderous ferocity. In January 1878, for example, a gang of six poachers severely beat Constable John Hughes of the Merioneth Constabulary, leading local magistrates to offer a significant reward for information and a local paper to query whether the assailants were native Welshmen or English. During the next seven years two constables in the neighbouring forces of Caernarfonshire and Flintshire were shot and wounded by poachers.[15]

The Bobby in Words and Music

The newspapers revelled in tales of 'orrible murder and, as Bent's career drew to its close, the press seized the opportunity of Jack the Ripper's killings to push back the limits of what could be reported in terms of the female body and to lambast the police. In 1888, during the autumn of the Ripper murders, the press was especially critical of the CID, as it had been in the past when detectives had failed to catch killers. The satirical malapropism 'the defective police' had been first used by *Punch* when it appeared that

Inspector Whicher's inquiries into the Road Hill House murder were going nowhere. Now it was trundled out once again with the Ripper killings.[16] Yet, at other times, the Bobby was also a hero.

When PC Lines was killed the *Birmingham Daily Post* made a eulogistic comparison with the military.

> Soldiers have by no means a monopoly of fighting, nor are battle-fields the only places in which personal valour is called for. Many a desperate hand-to-hand encounter that takes place between the police and armed burglars or murderous highwaymen by night, and cruel savage mobs by day, is [as] worthy of the poet's homage as the most brilliant exploits recorded in naval and military annals; and if courage and fortitude, without reference to the wearer's coat, conferred a claim to the decoration, we know of no man who could advance a better right to the Victoria Cross than the deceased policeman Lines.[17]

A decade later the *Police Guardian*, a journal primarily written for the police, quoted with satisfaction the similar comments of another daily newspaper:

> In the rough localities . . . police officers are often seriously knocked about, and do daring deeds, which if performed by a soldier would receive distinct marks of approbation. The police officer, however, labours under the disadvantage of being considered as a humorous person, derided by the clown in the pantomime, and suspected of yearnings for cold mutton. But all who have seen him really at work will recognise his genuine pluck and power of quelling the 'rough' when he happens to come his way.[18]

In the crowded music halls, most of which retained boisterous, non-deferential, plebeian pub traditions until the end of the century, policemen were mocked and branded as brutes and tricksters. C.P. Cove's song and patter 'The Model Peeler' was a particularly sharp example.

Oh, I'm the chap to make a hit,
   No matter where I goes it.
I'm quite a credit to the force,
   And jolly well they knows it.
I take folks up, knock others down,
   None do the thing genteeler,
I'm number 14, double X,
   And called the Model Peeler.

The patter continued explaining how he took bribes and lied in court. And of course, he also dallied with cooks and maids: 'Yes, all the little cook maids have a welcome for me, and no wonder for . . . I always do my duty, and by the help of my trusty staff, I do it like a man.'[19]

The celebrated music hall song 'Ask a P'liceman' first appeared in print and performance in the autumn of the Ripper murders. For the next thirty years it was the centrepiece of the entertainer James Fawn's act. The initial chorus, and best remembered part of the song, ran:

If you want to know the time,
Ask a P'liceman!
The proper Greenwich time,
Ask a P'liceman!
Ev'ry member of the Force
Has a watch and chain of course.
If you want to know the time,
Ask a P'liceman!

The implicit joke for the knowing working-class audience, was that the 'p'liceman' would have acquired his watch and chain from the drunk that he had rolled out of the road. The jokes in the other verses and following choruses were more explicit, and more traditional, picking up on the 'p'liceman's' ability to know where to get

a drink when the pubs were shut, to know the whereabouts of
maidservants, and

> Watch a Bobby in a fight,
> In a tick he's out of sight;
> For advice on rapid flight,
> Ask a P'licemen![20]

The newspaper press and the humorous weeklies continued to joke
about the policeman's interest in cooks and servant girls, but they
also commented on Bobby's courage and the danger of his job.
In August 1866, for example, *Punch* carried a drawing of a dazed
constable, blood streaming from a head wound as he faced a crowd
waving sticks and throwing bricks; the unsubtle caption read:
'Ruffianly policeman about to perpetrate a brutal and dastardly
assault on the people.' Ten years later, *Fun*, a similar weekly but
generally far more critical of the police than *Punch*, showed a young
constable stepping between a battered wife, a 'wife kicker' and an
'amiable person'.

AMIABLE PERSON *(to wife kicker)*: 'Wot a lark! 'ere's the pleeceman
   a comin', Bill!'
WIFE KICKER: 'Is he? Then blowed if he don't get one too!'
AMIABLE PERSON: 'Well, after you knock 'im on the 'ed into the
   gutter, Bill, let 'im come to a bit 'afore you begins to kick 'im,
   or he won't know what you're a doin', and he'll lose half the
   fun!'

The media and many social and political commentators appeared
to have little difficulty in criticizing and admiring the Bobby in
alternate breaths. But it was a celebratory discourse that began to
dominate among the respectable classes towards the end of the
century as English/British policemen began to be spoken of increasingly as 'the best in the world'. In 1879 came what was to become
one of the clearest manifestations of the English middle class's

satisfaction with its police – the policemen's chorus in *The Pirates of Penzance*.

When a felon's not engaged in his employment,
Or maturing his felonious little plans,
His capacity for innocent enjoyment,
Is just as great as any honest man's.

Our feelings we with difficulty smother,
When constabulary duty's to be done.
Ah, taking one consideration with another,
A policeman's lot is not a happy one.

Gilbert and Sullivan's Savoy Operas were pitched between the burlesque of the low-life music hall and pantomime and the sophisticated concert hall. They drew on both as they presented to their non-intellectual, moral, middle-class audience a gently comic celebration of Englishness and the social order. Gilbert and Sullivan's policemen were natural successors to Shakespeare's Dogberry and Verges and natural ancestors to the avuncular Dixon of Dock Green. The Savoy Opera patrons could sleep safely in their beds, fully aware that, while a policeman's lot was not a happy one, he was uniquely English, therefore honest and upright, and earnestly devoted to his duty.

Arming the Constable

The respectable classes' ability to sleep safely in their beds while policemen faced dangers on the streets was highlighted in the mid-1880s by a scare about armed burglars. Many sections of the press drew attention to the fact that the Bobbies who pursued and occasionally confronted them were unarmed. 'It is not only foolish but absolutely cruel,' declared the *Evening Standard* following two incidents in the summer of 1883, 'to send policemen out to combat men possessed with revolvers, without any other arm than a short club.' The number of incidents recorded in the Metropolitan Police District and passed on to the Home Office was small (see Table 2) but the repercussions were significant.

Table 2: Incidence of burglars using weapons in the Metropolitan Police District, January 1878 to December 1886

	Firearms	Other weapons
Number of police killed or fatally wounded	2	–
Number of police wounded	13	11
Number of private persons killed or wounded	5	9
Number of burglars escaping arrest by using weapons	18	21
Number of burglars on whom such weapons were found when arrested	14	21
Total	52	62

(*Source:* Home Office file in The National Archives: H.O. 45.9605.A1842B)

In September 1883 an official questionnaire on arming was sent to sergeants and constables in the outer divisions of London, where beats were longer and more isolated. Scotland Yard and the Home Office were surprised, and perhaps a little shocked, when the results revealed that more than two-thirds of the men (4,430 out of 6,325) were keen to carry guns. Accepting the verdict of the questionnaire would have meant overthrowing the unique, unarmed nature of Bobby. This had been a key element in his creation and, a generation earlier, it had led the Home Office to stand firm against the requests of chief constables that their men should be trained and equipped for potential military deployment in case of invasion. In response to the questionnaire the Home Office and the Commissioner decided that there could be a limited issue of revolvers. The issue was to be confined to men patrolling beats known to be dangerous and where assistance could not easily be summoned by the constable's rattle or by the new whistle that was replacing it. Some senior officers clearly put pressure on the men not to carry guns, and used the requirement that men issued with firearms had to be absolutely dependable to refuse the issue to many others. Even so, the policy of arming a few men was adopted also by some of the provincial forces.[21]

The revolvers were very rarely used. Training and practice was limited to each man who was permitted to carry a gun being allowed to fire six shots a year at a target. A confrontation between armed burglars and armed police outside Hatfield House, the country home of the Prime Minister Lord Salisbury, during which twenty-one shots were fired and no one was hit, prompted one official in the Home Office to query whether '6 practice shots [were] enough'. And even when the use of a revolver appears to have been a sensible last resort, there were senior officers who took exception. PC Henry Owen, for example, had a remote beat in 'P' Division on the edge of the Metropolitan Police District where it abutted the county of Kent. In the early hours of a February morning in 1887, as he plodded through the village of Keston, he saw that the general store was on fire. He knew that the family slept above the shop and when all other efforts to waken them had failed, he drew his revolver and fired six shots into the air. His inspector added to Owen's report: 'I think the PC acted wisely in using his revolver under the circumstances.' But the divisional superintendent differed, and he had the last word: 'PC Owen is not a stalwart man, and I do not think the firing of the revolver is justified.'[22]

Policing Politics

The respectable classes of Victorian and Edwardian Britain prided themselves on a constitutional structure that had avoided the political revolutions of Continental Europe. Nevertheless, politics, like industrial disputes, could get fractious and occasionally violent. In the second half of the nineteenth century elections could lead to fights: parliamentary candidates, or their agents, still occasionally recruited toughs to bolster their chances at the polls – especially before legislation of 1872 introduced the secret ballot and before limits were put on the 'treating' of voters. Voting sometimes continued for several days, which extended the opportunities for trouble at the polls. The General Election of 1868 was especially turbulent, with violent incidents in over a quarter of the contested constituencies.[23] Thomas Woollaston's police career was discussed earlier; during the 1868 election he was divisional superintendent at West Bromwich in industrial South Staffs, which was among the most disturbed areas. When the poll opened at Wednesbury Woollaston had to rescue two men from a crowd, and was struck on the head with a stone for his pains. A few days later, with about forty-five policemen under his command, he faced a bigger, more violent confrontation at Oldbury. A crowd attacked the Conservative committee rooms in a local hotel. The Riot Act was read but, rather than dispersing, the crowds switched their attention from the Conservatives to the police and began to hurl stones at them.

Sections of the men were now detached; these pursued the offenders, often running them down, and when caught, chastising them. This continued for several hours. I myself was engaged in many chases, and was positively tired by thrashing those attempting to injure us.

After Oldbury the election continued in Rowley Regis and Old Hill and again Woollaston and his division were called out. On this occasion the crowd was armed with a 'nasty sort of missile called "Rowley Rag," which having serrated edges, inflict[ed] very awkward wounds'. Woollaston and his men were armed with cutlasses. Rowley Rags were thrown, and cutlasses were drawn to drive off the crowds.

I believe many received some severe blows. These being given with the backs or flat side of the cutlass, no serious wounds were inflicted, at least that were known. The hilts of the weapons were also effectively used . . . These, when skilfully wielded, give severe punishment. I may mention that my own weapon was so used, and the blade of it so bent, that it could not without difficulty be placed in its sheath.[24]

It might be a matter of opinion whether the 'chastisement' administered by the police resulted in 'no serious wounds'. 'Chastisement' with a police baton may have been bad enough; Richard Jervis, after all, broke a man's arm with his truncheon and, clearing a crowd at the Malton Steeplechase in 1870, PC John Norman killed Alfred Bowes Barugh, with a baton-blow to the head.[25] But the cutlass was an edged weapon. Always using the flat of the blade, when a cutlass grip was designed to ensure that the edge was used, and using it in such a way in the middle of a fight, seems fanciful. Similarly a punch in the face with the knuckle guard of a cutlass could give a significant injury to a cheek or jaw bone and, in the midst of a mêlée, the face would have been the most obvious target for such a blow. No wonder then that, during such instances, there were commonly complaints of unnecessary violence by the police.

There was disorder in various parts of the country again during the General Election held in November 1885 and serious complaints were levelled against the police in Nottingham. It was alleged that the local police, assisted by men from other forces, notably Birmingham and Derbyshire, set about crowds with their truncheons before any serious disorder had occurred. In response to the allegations the local watch committee set up an inquiry chaired by the Recorder of Lincoln. The inquiry heard conflicting evidence. The police defence was that they had been stoned by a crowd for a considerable time before being given the order to clear the streets. Nevertheless, the inquiry found that the police disobeyed instructions as to the use of truncheons and behaved intemperately, and that the second detachment of reserve police, consisting mainly of Derbyshire and Birmingham officers, together with a few Nottingham men, drew their staves and used them most improperly.

Not surprisingly, perhaps, none of the offending officers could be identified.[26]

Although they had to deal with election disorders, the police were not required to supervise the hustings or other political meetings. These were regarded as private affairs at which, when confronted by toughs hired by their opponents, candidates were expected to show their pluck. The police did their best to keep out of such confrontations. In 1909 the Head Constable of Liverpool explained candidly and, perhaps rather surprisingly, to a departmental committee at the Home Office: 'If you consider that your meeting is going to be disturbed by fifty roughs you must have seventy-five roughs who can throw them out.'[27]

Militant Women

For all that the respectable British gentleman might have regarded his political system, like his police, as the best in the world, at the turn of the century there were increasing numbers of women who objected to the concept of separate spheres that restricted their participation in public life and denied them the vote. In the mid-nineteenth century many Chartists had acknowledged the woman's right to vote and there were women involved with the movement. The suffragettes' campaigns were a logical extension of earlier demands for an extension of the franchise, but they put the Bobby in a new situation for which he was ill-prepared. Police officers were used to confronting working-class males. These were the people that usually had to be moved on for gathering on street corners and for selling goods illicitly in the streets; and young adult men were the social group most commonly associated with criminal

offending. The only women that police officers had regular dealings with were those – again members of the working class – that
they identified, rightly or sometimes wrongly, as prostitutes. During
the steadily escalating campaign of militant suffragette violence in
the five years or so before the outbreak of the First World War,
however, the police officer found himself having to confront and
even arrest not simply members of a superior social class to himself,
but female members of that class – and these women invariably
refused to go quietly. No doubt many of the police involved as
detectives in watching these militants and opening their letters, or
as uniformed officers arresting them for creating disturbances,
breaking windows and committing arson, considered these women
as, at best, odd. Many of the police's social superiors, male and
female, were appalled and shocked by the way in which the militants broke taboos of class and sex. But every rough act by an infuriated policeman dealing with a struggling, shouting suffragette
was a recruiting sergeant for the militants.

'I was baking cakes at the time,' recalled Grace Alderman, a
suffragist in Preston, 'and Mother came into the kitchen with the
paper – it was when the Press first began taking photographs –
"just look at this!" she said . . . Until then I'd thought England
stood for fair play.'[28]

Suffragette militants were fully aware of this. As a result of a
childhood illness May Billinghurst could not walk without crutches
and she attended political meeting in her wheelchair. In confrontations she propelled the chair at the charge into police lines; but
when it came to public accounts, she described how police officers tipped her out of the machine, pinioned her arms behind her,
or moved her into a 'hooligan crowd' and disabled the wheels.[29]

Terrorists and Anarchists

Occasionally in the second half of the nineteenth century and in
the decade before the First World War, a few individuals injected
a lethal element into politics and on to the streets. First there

was the problem with Fenian terror and then with foreign anarchists. The Fenians, who sought to establish a republic in Ireland,
launched their first campaign in England in 1867. An aborted
attack on Chester Castle was followed by the attempted rescue
of two men from a prison van in Manchester during which a
police sergeant was shot dead. The attempted rescue of four
Fenians from Clerkenwell Prison in London involved exploding
a bomb against the prison wall, which left twelve people dead
and over a hundred injured. Irish police officers, drafted in to
assist, expressed amazement at what they considered to be the
incompetence of their English counterparts. In the early 1880s
there was a second wave of bombing by Irish republicans, which
included an attempt on Scotland Yard. Out of the groups organized to combat the terrorist threat emerged the Metropolitan
Police Special Branch; initially, because of its focus, it was known
as the Special Irish Branch. By the end of the century it was
investigating a variety of political offenders as well as people that
appeared to threaten what was understood as the unique qualities of British life because of their advocacy of, or interest in, for
example, erotic literature and free love.[30]

A generation after the Fenian terror the country was shocked
by the violent crime of anarchists from Eastern Europe. In January
1909 the Tottenham Outrage saw two Latvian anarchists rob a
wages clerk and then seek to escape by hijacking a tram. The
ensuing gun-battle left a police officer and a schoolboy dead; the
two anarchists used their last bullets on themselves. Nearly two
years later three more police officers were shot dead, and another
two wounded, during the robbery of a jeweller's shop in
Houndsditch. Once again, foreign anarchists were the culprits and
this incident led, ultimately, to the celebrated siege of Sidney Street
in January 1911 when police and guardsmen trapped two men in
a terraced house in Stepney.

Sir Robert Peel (1788–1850) who, as Chief Secretary for Ireland (1812–18), created the precursor of the Royal Irish Constabulary and, as Home Secretary in 1829, steered the legislation that created the Metropolitan Police. The nicknames 'Bobby' and 'Peeler' come from Peel's name.

The front page of the short-lived *Policeman* newspaper, 21 September 1833. The image shows two constables of the new Metropolitan Police taking a tray of sweets from a young street-seller and ignoring youths throwing stones just around the corner. The constables also seem oblivious to the various missiles, including a cat, being thrown at them.

PC James Jackson, Hertfordshire Police 1865–77 (see pp. 135–9).

THE "NAB" LIGHT.

Respectfully dedicated to the Patrons of the Metropolitan Police.

A cartoon from *Judy* in 1868 which portrays the police as their superiors wished them to be seen – catching burglars in the act.

The idea that Victorian Bobbies spent their evenings wooing house-maids and cooks was popular with satirists. This cartoon is one of the earliest and comes from the anti-police paper *Policeman*. Similar illustrations can be found in *Punch*. A second constable can just be seen enjoying a meal in the room below stairs.

A cartoon from *Fun*, September 1883, commenting on the decision to allow police officers on remote beats to carry guns because of the threat from armed burglars. Generally speaking the press was in favour of the move.

One of the last watchmen (note the 'VR' for Victoria Regina on his truncheon). These men were denigrated by police reformers and, subsequently, by many police historians. Evidence shows, however, that many of them were as courageous and competent as the best of the new police.

The scene of the last act of the Tottenham Outrage, 23 January 1909 (see p. 164). Jacob Lepidus, the surviving gunman, ran into this cottage occupied by a mother with two young children. He locked himself in the upstairs bedroom pursued by armed police. He shot himself as the police fired through the bedroom door.

The funeral of PC William Tyler, 29 January 1909. Tyler, who had joined the Metropolitan Police in 1903 after ten years' service in the Royal Artillery, was shot and killed as he attempted to arrest Paul Hefeld during the Tottenham Outrage. Hefeld shot himself a few minutes later.

News article showing police and Scots Guards at the Siege of Sidney Street, January 1911 (see p. 164). The gentleman wearing the top hat in the picture top right is the then Home Secretary, Winston Churchill. Note the police officer armed with a shot-gun, bottom right.

Epsom Police Station shortly after the attack by Canadian soldiers in June 1919 during which Police Sergeant Thomas Green was killed (see p. 191).

Cable Street, 4 October 1936. Crowds withdraw from a barricade built by locals to prevent a march through the district by the British Union of Fascists (see pp. 219–20).

A group of Metropolitan Police officers from 'P' (Catford) Division, 1941. Most of the men in flat caps are war reserve or special constables. The constable seated on the extreme right in the front row is Ernie Emsley, the author's father.

Above: Two WPCs patrolling outside Bow Street Police Station in the interwar period.

Left: Metropolitan Police constable at an early stage of the Second World War. He carries a gas mask in the pack across his chest. The blue and white striped armlet on his left cuff was worn to indicate that he was on duty. It was first issued in 1830 and discontinued in 1968.

PC Arthur 'Old Pick' Pickering is in discussion with a Bedfordshire farmer c.1950. Note the bike on the left of the picture. Pickering said that no rural Bobby ever went out without a bag on his handlebars to pick up food from local farmers (see p. 228).

Brixton, April 1981. Police crouched behind long shields come under attack from missile-throwing rioters.

PC Norwell Roberts. This *Sun* newspaper story from 1972 shows the way in which he was used by the Metropolitan Police publicity machine at precisely the time that he was abused and ill-used by many of his colleagues (see pp. 263–4).

Metropolitan Police officers of the late twentieth century doing their bit for community relations.

Detective Policing

The public was appalled to see Bobbies and others gunned down in the streets, but sections of that same public were also suspicious about the political undercover work that countering these threats entailed, and suspicious too of undercover work that implied entrapment. One case that prompted considerable outrage in this respect involved a young chemist, Thomas Titley, prosecuted at the Old Bailey at the end of 1880 for 'selling a noxious drug for an unlawful purpose' – specifically an abortifacient. The Titley affair showed Metropolitan Police detectives going to considerable lengths to make a case against a suspect individual. Martha Diffey, the wife of a policeman who also worked as a 'searcher' of arrested females, went into Titley's shop posing as the mother of a pregnant woman who wanted an abortion. When Titley showed himself reluctant to help, Inspector John O'Callaghan wrote a letter claiming to be the young woman's seducer and offering 'to pay any sum which was reasonable for the service rendered'. Howard Vincent, who had recently reorganized the metropolitan detective department, had provided O'Callaghan with £25 with which to tempt Titley. The chemist, however, remained suspicious and it was only when Mrs Diffey returned to his shop accompanied by Sergeant William Stroud, who became the physical presence of the imagined daughter's seducer, that Titley agreed to sell two bottles of drugs, and these for a mere 4 shillings. In court, Titley was found guilty as charged and sentenced to eighteen months' hard labour. But the case caused considerable disquiet. Titley may have been a suspect person when the police began their moves against him, but *Reynolds's Newspaper* was not alone in condemning the 'myrmidons' – a popular word with the press in this instance – of the new CID who had shown themselves 'thorough adepts at lying and every other means of deception'. Nearly 300 miles away from the scene of the affair the *Newcastle Courant*, amidst references to the Bible and Shakespeare, could not resist reviving the sinister bugbear of half-a-century earlier – the French police.[31]

The fear of French-style police – that is, both a military body designed for overt oppression and a detective body designed for spying on ordinary members of the public – had faded in English eyes by the last quarter of the nineteenth century. Concerns continued to be expressed occasionally that the Bobby was becoming militarized, particularly during General Sir Charles Warren's tenure as Commissioner of the Metropolitan Police (1886–8). Fortunately, perhaps, few outside of the Home Office and the senior officers of the Metropolitan Police appear to have been aware that Howard Vincent had spent time in Paris studying the police there and that he had drawn on the Parisian model for his reorganization of the detective department in London. Vincent, who had already enjoyed a varied career as a soldier, war correspondent and barrister, was only twenty-nine at the time of his appointment and had no police experience. No doubt some of the hoary heads among the detectives ruminated on the triumph of social status over experience when he assumed command, but some of their previous superiors had provided the opportunity for his appointment. Vincent took over the department in the aftermath of the Turf Fraud Scandal of 1877 and a Departmental Commission established by the Home Secretary. The Turf Fraud Scandal, or Madame de Goncourt case, had seen four leading London detectives tried at the Old Bailey for involvement in a scam based on fraudulent racing tips. One of the four, Inspector John Meiklejohn, was revealed to have been taking payments from bookmakers and swindlers for several years.[32] Vincent's reforms, however, were largely organizational. They had no impact on how detectives did their jobs and could not prevent them from occasionally falling prey to temptation.

In the same way that there was no great change in the way that uniformed men had plodded their beats from the days of increasingly competent eighteenth-century parish watchmen, so there had been no great developments in detection since the days of the Principal Officers of Bow Street. Photographs had been available since the mid-nineteenth century; a system for cataloguing fingerprints was introduced in the 1890s and a Fingerprint Bureau was established at Scotland Yard in 1901. But both photographs and fingerprints required sophisticated cataloguing systems that enabled them to be easily and rapidly searched; these were not things that could be established overnight. Moreover, it is clear that, well into the twentieth century, the daily *Police Gazette* that included photographs and descriptions of suspects and recidivists often remained unopened when it arrived at a provincial (and perhaps also at a metropolitan) police station.[33]

As Caminada's memoirs suggest, the detective's job involved knowing where to look, who to question, who was likely to reoffend. There was also an element of dogged determination, persistence and a common-sense ability to put two and two together to make four. The unfortunate Jack Whicher possessed such attributes and so too did some of the young men that he mentored, such as Richard Tanner. Born in Egham, Surrey, in 1831, Tanner left his job as a clerk and joined the Metropolitan Police in 1853. He was rapidly recruited for the detective department of 'A' Division and achieved significant fame in 1864 when he arrested a young German tailor, Franz Müller, for the robbery and murder of Thomas Briggs. This was the first murder committed on an English railway train, but what also captured the public imagination was the fact that Tanner had to pursue the suspect by steamship to New York before he could make his arrest.[34] While a romantic aura continued, on and off, to surround the detective, the dogged and successful pursuit of an offender, even overseas, did not require a policeman to have the title 'detective'.

William Ashe joined the police in Middlesbrough in 1866. He was twenty-one years old and had already served for a few months in the Leeds Police. There did not appear to be anything particularly exceptional about him. Like his mates in Middlesbrough he was assaulted on several occasions and, like many of these mates, he was reprimanded for being drunk and unfit for duty. But in Ashe's case, the offence was not repeated. In 1870 he was promoted to sergeant and, although there were detectives in the

Middlesbrough force, six years later it was he who was given the task of pursuing Thomas Cameron Close, the Borough Accountant who had embezzled some £2,500 from the Town Council. Ashe pursued his quarry, quite literally, to the far side of the world, delayed only by an outbreak of cholera in Ceylon. He caught up with Close on Sandridge Pier in Melbourne, Victoria; and then brought him home again. In the style of the ideal, unassuming English 'gentleman' Ashe eschewed publicity. He brought Close quietly to Middlesbrough in a cab sent by the chief constable to Darlington Railway Station, and then promptly reported for duty at the Police Station. He was promoted to inspector and, seven years later in 1883, he became the town's chief constable, a post that he held until 1901.[35]

The tenacity of men like Ashe and the sacrifice of men like Sergeants Robert Bentley and Charles Tucker and Constable Walter Choate, shot dead in the Houndsditch affair, played well with people of property and respectability. By the third quarter of the nineteenth century, as the statistics of criminal offences levelled out, police reformers like Edwin Chadwick were looking forward to the time when the prevention of crime had prevailed and the police could emphasize its 'moral usefulness' by cultivating its 'beneficent services and provide for its occupation on occasions of accident or calamity'.[36] The police had been involved in welfare tasks since the beginning. The roles of Poor Law Relieving Officer and Inspector of Lodging Houses could, in part, be seen as central to the police role of supervising that social group suspected as being the principal perpetrators of crime. The role of police officers in running boys' clubs might be seen in the same way. Yet it is too cynical to dismiss a policeman's earnest commitment to what he saw as a good cause as ultimately motivated by the desire to establish a restrictive social control. Moreover, there were other aspects of the police welfare role. In some urban forces the police also provided the local fire brigade. Constables were given first aid training that was available in an emergency whatever an injured person's social class. In the bitterly cold winter of 1878 Superintendent Bent organized a soup kitchen for poor children in Old Trafford out of his own pocket. The Chief Constable subsequently reimbursed him for his losses and the soup kitchen was continued until the First World War. The Lancashire force also organized an annual picnic for poor children and supplied the poorest with clogs and clothing, and if some wore the clothes with reluctance because they were stamped with 'POLICE', the value of the clothing could not be ignored. Jervis explained that the various kinds of welfare work that he and his men undertook were looked upon 'as a mere matter of duty which we regarded as something more than the prevention and the repression of crime'.[37]

The Growth of Professional Consciousness

But if the God-fearing Victorian and Edwardian policeman believed that he had a duty to help others, he also recognized the need to help himself, his mates and his family. It was understandable that a spirit of camaraderie and mutual support would grow up in the section houses and police stations. This was sometimes translated into backing up mates when engaged in street fights, or when in trouble with members of the public, with superior officers, or with the courts. When John Monk was the only constable among twenty to support the complaint of a fellow officer against the loutish behaviour of another, all of the others refused to speak to him for several weeks. Monk also recorded an incident when an individual well-known to the police had been struck, deliberately, by a detective sergeant in a charge room in the presence of an inspector and five other constables. The inspector decided to overlook the incident, but the 'bad character' was granted a summons for assault. At the subsequent trial

The Judge expressed the hope that the Inspector and his five men, together with the accused [detective sergeant], had not conspired to commit perjury, but he did characterise their evidence as 'a tissue of inconsistencies'. The jury, however, returned a verdict of 'Not Guilty'.

In the early summer of 1868 PC John Hamblin brought a charge of assault against John Hollanby; he was backed up by another constable from the Whitechapel district. There was, however, evidence that the initial assault had been made by Hamblin when Hollanby threatened to report him for misconduct with a woman. During the inquiry into the trouble at Rotherhithe in 1912 Chester Jones heard several witnesses testify that a coal porter was struck round the face with a Police Sergeant's cape when all he was doing was saying 'Goodnight' to four friends. Several police witnesses insisted that nothing of the sort had occurred. Jones concluded, however, 'that some such incident must have taken place; it is impossible to believe that all these persons can have conspired together to fabricate a false charge of this description'.[38]

Police support for workmates was varied in its nature and did not necessarily involve glossing events when in the witness box or before tribunals. In 1887 in the aftermath of the failed prosecution of a seamstress, Elizabeth Cass, for soliciting, PC Bowen Endacott was charged with perjury. Members of the Metropolitan Police petitioned the Home Secretary for permission to start a subscription to pay for his defence. The Home Secretary, and the Commissioner, agreed; the case against Endacott failed. But ten years later, when there was an attempt to raise a subscription for Police Sergeant Robert Birnie on his retirement, the Commissioner refused to allow it. While he was no radical trouble-maker and was opposed to the idea of the police taking strike action, Birnie had been a key figure in organizing the rank and file to petition for improvements to their superannuation scheme. Following the Commissioner's refusal a subscription was, nevertheless, organized by the journal *Police Review*, allegedly collecting money only from men in the forces outside London.[39] The action of the *Police Review* in this instance is illustrative of the growth of craft consciousness within the police and the way that this was fostered by what might be termed the police trade press.

Few, if any, jobs are perfect and from the beginning there were complaints about pay and conditions among members of the new police forces. In many instances, as the high turnover of manpower testifies, men simply voted with their feet and quit the job. But many others embarked on different forms of labour protest. In November 1848 eleven Metropolitan Police constables signed a petition:

> Men joining the Police service as 3rd Class Constables and having a wife and three children to support on joining, are not able properly to do so on the pay of 16/8d a week.
>
> Most of the married men on joining are somewhat in debt, and are unable to extricate themselves on account of rent to pay and articles to buy which are necessary for support of wife and children.
>
> We beg leave to state that a married man having a wife and 2 children to support on joining, that it is as much as he can do upon 16/8d per week, and having to remain upon that for the first 12 or 18 months,

There were strikes in Hull and Manchester in the 1850s and among the Metropolitan Police in 1872, 1889 and 1890. In the latter instance, much to the concern of the authorities, the police delegates held meetings in working-men's clubs and even on the premises of the Social Democratic Federation, Britain's first Marxist political party.[40]

From the 1860s newspapers began to appear aimed directly at a police audience. This press helped to develop ideas of a brotherhood of policing that stretched beyond the shores of Britain. The *Police Service Advertiser*, which began publication on 1 February 1866, called itself a 'Journal for the Police and Constabulary Forces of Great Britain and the Colonies'. It went through two name changes; in 1873 it became the *Police Guardian* and then in 1888, until its closure in 1934, it was the *Police Chronicle*. But the most significant and long-lasting of these journals was the weekly *Police Review and Parade Gossip*, the first edition of which was published on 2 January 1893. These journals aimed to give the policeman a sense of his worth and to challenge the continuing portrayal of him as a bumbling Dogberry. 'Probably no public servant is so ill-used by his employer as the policeman,' declared the *Advertiser* in 1867. 'Placed by the public to protect the peace, the first thing the public does is to bring its officers into ridicule, and the next to ill-treat them.' In its first issue the *Police Review* lamented similarly:

> [T]here is a tendency, all too prevalent, as evidenced on the stage and in the comic Press, as well as on the public foot path, to treat a policeman with less regard for his own self respect than should prevail amongst men towards their fellow-men in all ranks of life. One aim of the REVIEW will be to change this state of things, and, by cultivating the self-respect of the Constabulary of this country, to raise them in the esteem and regard of all their fellow citizens.[41]

Serving officers, writing in the correspondence columns, took a similar line on jokes about the police. John B. Nobbs, a PC in Liverpool, seems to have known his Kipling and, in an early edition of *Police Review*, he sought to pen the police equivalent to Kipling's 'Tommy Atkins'.

> Who is that one, at whom you sneer,
> And oftentimes will cheek and jeer,
> What do you call him far and near?
> Why, 'Bobby'.
>
> Yet, when there comes a vicious fight,
> Or when mad dogs begin to bite,
> Whose coming hail you with delight?
> Why, 'Bobby'.[42]

Journals like these became the mouthpiece for men to express pride in their job, as well as resentment about the way that they were mocked and, more importantly, the way that they were sometimes treated by their superiors and their employers.

One of the perks of the job of policeman was the promise of a pension when a man retired. Unfortunately the initial system of superannuation was poorly structured and uncertain. In the 1860s men complained that, unlike soldiers, they were required to contribute to their pensions; moreover, the award of the pension was dependent on the discretion of a borough watch committee or a county chief constable. When PC James Baverstock retired from the Worcestershire force in 1866 after fourteen years' service he received only a gratuity of £14. In the following year PC Clare left the Bedford Borough force aged sixty-seven and after thirty-six years' service; he was promised a pension of 12 shillings a week, but was also warned that, should he enter an almshouse, his pension would be withdrawn.[43] A parliamentary select committee was established in 1875 to investigate and recommend a solution to the problem of police superannuation, but the bill based on its recommendations that appeared before Parliament in 1882 was rejected. It was only in 1890 that a Police Act required a full pension for any man retiring after twenty-five years and for any man retiring on medical grounds after fifteen years. But even after this, parsimonious local authorities quibbled. In 1894 the *Police Review* took up the case, and paid the legal fees, of PC William Wood Cant in his dispute with the Lancashire Police Authority. Cant had retired after twenty-six years of police service, but Lancashire claimed that it did not owe him a pension as the first eight years of his career had been with the Roxburghshire Police.[44]

The police newspapers enjoyed celebrating the careers of men like Cant who had served loyally, and especially those who, from humble beginnings, had risen to significant rank. They printed letters, often anonymous, and used leaders to voice complaints about favouritism and secretive methods of promotion. One major area of criticism in this respect, and one that linked relatively modern ideas of fairness and transparency with the older hostility to a military presence in policing, was the opposition to the appointment of army officers to the post of chief constable. In the spring of 1867 the *Police Service Advertiser* expressed concern, picked up by some of its correspondents, when the Glamorgan magistrates failed to shortlist Superintendent Wrenn of Merthyr Tydfil for the post of chief constable. Wrenn was a career policeman, and the shortlist consisted of five colonels, two army captains and a commander from the Royal Navy.[45] Nearly forty years later the *Police Review* noted with distaste that of the forty-four county chief constables in England, thirty-three were former army officers, three were naval officers and only another three had risen through the ranks of the police. The situation in Wales was marginally better: here, only six of the twelve chief constables were former army officers and two men had risen through the police.[46]

For some at the close of the nineteenth and beginning of the twentieth centuries, the only way to ensure that the police officer's rights could be established and maintained was through the formation of a trade union. The letter columns of the *Police Review* fairly buzzed with arguments generally for, but occasionally against, such a union. The application of heavy-handed, ill-conceived disciplinary measures towards a rigidly principled but blinkered and increasingly paranoid Metropolitan Police inspector on the eve of the First World War hastened the creation of such a union.

John Syme was born in Ayrshire in 1872. He began his working life as a solicitor's clerk before moving to London and joining the Metropolitan Police in 1894. Syme was an able man and his promotion was rapid; in 1899 he became a sergeant; in 1908 he was made an inspector. In the early hours of 18 August 1909 two drunks were brought into Gerald Road Police Station, roughly midway between the railway terminus at Victoria and Sloane Square, where Syme was the inspector on duty. The drunks had been creating a noisy disturbance at the door of a house in Warwick Street. What the two arresting constables had not realized was that one of the drunks, Costa by name, was clumsily and very noisily, trying to get into his own home. Mrs Costa identified her husband; but neither she, nor any of the neighbours that had been disturbed, wished to make a complaint. Syme decided not to press charges and entered the details into the Refused Charge Book. Unfortunately, Syme's superiors decided to take the matter further by reprimanding and disciplining the two arresting constables. Syme objected strongly to this and, when he persisted, he was transferred to another station and labelled as both unreasonable and too familiar with his subordinates. This only served to stoke the fires of Syme's unyielding Presbyterian self-righteousness. He protested to the Commissioner, which led to him being suspended while his complaints were investigated. He protested to the Home Secretary. A disciplinary board recommended his reduction to the rank of station sergeant. He announced that he would take up the matter with his MP. He was dismissed.[47]

John Kempster, the editor of the *Police Review*, took up Syme's case. In his eyes this was another example of unreasonable behaviour by the senior ranks of the police. By the middle of 1911, however, as the affair drew on and on, Syme's behaviour became more and more extreme. Threats to the Home Secretary and to a former superior led to his prosecution and to six months' imprisonment. On his release in 1912, Syme cashed in on continuing public sympathy by forming the John Syme League and, in the following year, the League announced in the *Police Review* the formation of the Metropolitan Police Union. Kempster grew concerned. Whereas he had always supported police officers in trouble with their superiors, urged self-improvement upon them and had campaigned for improvements in their conditions and pay, he was wary of any police union claiming the right to strike. Kempster urged his readers to consider a Police Federation that would defend its members' interests but never take strike action. It is symptomatic of the frustration with their situation that when he circulated 21,000 forms inviting rank and file officers to join his Federation, only 100 were returned.

When the Metropolitan Police Union met in December 1913

Syme claimed, probably with as much wishful thinking as accuracy, that there were nearly 5,000 members. In the following year the organization spread beyond the capital and became the National Union of Police and Prison Officers. But also in 1914 the catastrophe of the First World War engulfed Britain and the rest of Europe and while this was to have a profound effect on policing and the embryonic police union, initially the conflict pushed all such activity into the shadows.

— CHAPTER 7 —

War, Women and Wages: Policing the Home Front, 1914–1918

THERE IS AN image of the summer of 1914, perpetuated in many history books, as bright, sunny and idyllic. In the words of *Punch* reflecting on the conflict: 'We were thinking of holidays, of cricket and golf and bathing, and then were suddenly plunged in the deep waters of the greatest of all Wars.' The juxtaposition of a beautiful summer shattered by the horrors of trench warfare in the Flanders mud makes the war that much more terrible. In fact much of the summer of 1914 was overcast. *The Times* described the weather during the last week of July as 'dull' and concluded that 'the wandering thunderstorms that have been a characteristic, . . . as they were of . . . June and May, explain the variableness of the harvesting experiences.'[1]

The assumption that accompanies the image of the idyllic summer is that the populations of the combatant countries assumed that the war would be over by Christmas. Quite how many of those involved in government believed this remains an open question. Yet whatever members of the British government, their civil servants and their General Staff had thought about the potential duration of the war, they had not planned for the unprecedented demands for men, money and materiel. Initially the British fought the war with professional soldiers and sailors; reservists were recalled to the colours and volunteers came forward. Only in 1916 was conscription established.

There were many reservists scattered through the different police forces, and there were many fit young constables who volunteered in the early months of the war. Police ranks were consequently depleted, but the demands of the unprecedented war meant that, as their numbers thinned, so their tasks increased. Women filled the gaps created by men leaving for the front in many professions, services and trades. Women came forward to serve as police during the war, but their responsibilities were limited largely to matters involving women and children. In addition, very few of them were formally sworn in as constables and hence had no powers of arrest. For the male officers that remained the increased wartime duties became more irksome as wartime inflation eroded their pay. Long hours and financial difficulties were persuasive recruiting sergeants for industrial militancy.

Women Policing Women in Wartime

Women police officers were a creation of the First World War. It had long been recognized that there could be problems when women were arrested and supervised in custody by male officers only. The affair of Inspector Wovenden in 1834, described in Chapter 2, had indicated what might arise when women were held in police cells overnight with only male officers present. An ad hoc system of police matrons recruited to search and to keep watch on female suspects brought to police stations, was seen as one way of reducing the opportunity for such charges. The matrons were usually the wives of station sergeants, already present in the stations since they lived there with their husbands and took charge of the domestic needs of the young constables also quartered there or in a neighbouring barrack. Martha Diffey, who had assisted in the arrest and prosecution of the chemist Thomas Titley in 1880, was one such matron. While no one appears to have taken it up at the time, she also showed the potential value of having women available for undercover work.

During the 1880s the system of police matrons became more

formal. In 1883 a woman was employed to visit women convicts released on licence; a second woman visitor was employed three years later. In 1889 fourteen women were recruited formally as police matrons to search and supervise women that had been arrested, but proposals that women police officers should be appointed for the care and supervision of women offenders were peremptorily rejected. In 1907 Sir Edward Henry, then Commissioner of the Metropolitan Police, employed a woman to look after and to take the statements of girls and children involved in sexual assaults; payment was organized through the Police Fund and various charities. Outside London the use of women by the police was ad hoc. In the smaller, often one man country police stations, it was the police officer's wife who was expected to undertake such tasks; and while there might be some remuneration in the big urban forces, in the countryside such tasks were simply expected of the wife and went without pay.

The outbreak of war raised fears for the morals of young women. First there was the problem of the numbers of young women and girls that were loitering in the vicinity of large army camps. In addition there were concerns for those women that volunteered to work for the war effort, most notably in munitions factories. They were seen as vulnerable, exposed to new and dangerous temptations, especially because their patriotic commitment took them away from the normal protection of family and friends. The moves for women police were thus less concerned with filling gaps left by men going to the front and more inspired by the notions of separate spheres. The leaders of the push for women police built on the traditions of middle-class voluntarism as well as feminism, but they also included militant suffragettes and feminists who pressed for the recognition that the men who frequented prostitutes were as 'guilty' of sexual offending as the prostitutes themselves.

But for all their feminist and suffragette credentials, these women also had close links and friendships with men in influential positions. Margaret Damer Dawson, a wealthy gentlewoman who, before the war, had been deeply involved in philanthropic causes and constitutional feminism, established the Women Police Volunteers with the like-minded journalist and novelist Nina Boyle. Unashamedly Dawson used her friendship with Sir Edward Henry in setting up the force. At roughly the same time a somewhat less militant grouping dedicated to social work, the National Union of Women Workers, established the Voluntary Women's Patrols (VWP). The organizer of this body was Louise Creighton, the widow of the Bishop of London and an anti-suffragist.[2]

Dawson and Boyle's group was the more professional of the two organizations. Its desire to establish a new career for women became more apparent when Boyle was ousted from the leadership early in 1915. Dawson became the Commandant of what was now termed the Women's Police Service (WPS). The sub-Commandant was Mary S. ('Robert') Allen, a former militant suffragette and one of the first to use the hunger-strike weapon in gaol. The WPS's aim was to get women engaged in regular police duties on an equal footing with men. Between 1914 and 1920 it trained 1,080 women and the first attested woman police officer in the United Kingdom, Edith Smith, was one of them. Smith was posted to Grantham in the spring of 1915; she replaced two other women who had been given no formal status but who had been rushed to the area towards the end of the previous year because of concerns over prostitution in the vicinity of Belton Camp, the base of the 11th Infantry Division. But while Smith, and a few other members of the WPS, began by working around army camps with the blessing, often hesitant and reluctant, of local chief constables, the institution got itself on a firmer financial footing in January 1917 when it signed a formal contract with the Ministry of Munitions to supervise women in the munitions factories. Nine out of ten of the women in the WPS were deployed on these duties, among them the young daughter of a clergyman, Gabrielle West.[3]

Gabrielle West had spent her early years in Eastbourne, where her father, the Revd George H. West, ran a preparatory school for some fifty boys. When she was about ten years old her father accepted a living and the family – mother, father, three sons and two daughters – moved to a parish in rural Gloucestershire. Gabrielle finished her schooling about the age of eighteen, a few years before the outbreak of war. She began to play the role of the clergyman's dutiful daughter – visiting the sick and teaching Sunday School. When the war broke out, like several of their neighbours, the Wests accepted a Belgian refugee family into their home for a few weeks. In the spring of 1915 Gabrielle had her first opportunity to do her bit when Lord Sherborne handed over his country house to be converted into a military hospital; Gabrielle worked in the kitchen. In the summer she moved to a bigger hospital, converted from a school in Cheltenham. Her work was voluntary and unpaid and, before long, she felt that she simply could not afford to continue. In January 1916 she accepted an offer from Lady Lawrence's Canteen Committee to run a canteen for women working in the Royal Aircraft Factory at Farnborough; the pay was £60 a year and two meals a day. Over the next eleven months she managed, or acted as assistant manager for a series of factory canteens moving ever closer to London. At Woolwich she crossed a police officer who objected to her taking her small terrier, Rip, with her into the arsenal. Gabrielle was small, but she had a steely resolve and was not prepared to kow-tow to pettifogging regulations that she considered irrelevant. Her response to the policeman was to pull strings and arrange for Rip to have his own pass to assist in the preparation of food – a pass that she kept to her dying day and which is now deposited with her journals in the Imperial War Museum. But Gabrielle and her close friend 'Buckie' Buckpitt were not inclined to settle down as canteen managers for the duration of the war. They considered becoming, respectively, cook and housemaid to a lady. And then they heard about the Women's Police Service and decided to apply.

On 4 December 1916 Gabrielle and Buckie began their two weeks' training. 'There are about 20 other recruits', Gabrielle noted in her journal. 'Most are ladies or middle class women, all are a better class than the average policeman.' They had been told at their interview that members of the WPS aimed to be the same as male police officers, though with an emphasis, perhaps, on matters concerning women and children. They were also aware that they were likely to be sent to police the women working in munitions factories, but none of the training addressed this probability. They had lectures with 'a certain amount of talk about sex troubles and so on'. They visited courts and, in the evenings, they went on patrol with police women in some 'lively neighbourhoods'. At the end of two weeks Gabrielle and Buckie found themselves posted to a munitions factory in Chester. They were both able and efficient, but their experience of working in factory canteens had ill-prepared them for what they were to experience especially when, after less than a month, Buckie was promoted to sub-inspector, Gabrielle was made a sergeant, and they were both sent to Pembrey in South Wales.

Pembrey, in Gabrielle's estimation, was 'the back of beyond, a little coal mining village with a minute harbour and the remains of a large silver works'. The munitions factory was built on sand hills, 'the most desolate spot in the world'. It was below sea level, which created sanitary problems, and to make matters worse, when Buckie and Gabrielle arrived, there were no lights in the toilets, which were dirty and infested with rats. Persuading the factory manager to get lights was not part of their job as police, but this, together with other reforms for which they pressed, won them some popularity, or at least a greater degree of toleration with the women workers. This, in turn, was something that helped in a difficult job. The task of making munitions was unpleasant and dangerous, not simply from the risk of explosion but also because of the chemicals used in manufacture. When Buckie and Gabrielle moved to a munitions factory in Hereford in the summer of 1917, Buckie believed that the prussic acid used there was making her ill and causing her gastric upsets. The workers suffered headaches, sometimes collapsed or had fits because of the chemicals, and it was the duty of the WPS officers to carry them from the shop floor to the recovery rooms for medical assistance. The danger of explosion was aggravated by the determination of some women to take cigarettes and matches into the workplace. The women police had to search women workers for such items on the way into the factories, as well as for any metal buttons, buckles or other items that could cause a spark. They also searched workers leaving the premises; the brass and other metals used for shells had a high value on the black market and some women sought to smuggle such materials out under their clothes. Such searches caused annoyance even among those who were not trying to bring in potential fire hazards or to take things out for their own profit. The women police were also resident enforcers of factory discipline and regulations and, even though they did not meet the kind of ferocious violence that was meted out to James Bent half a century earlier as described in Chapter 6, they could still find themselves involved in scuffles and having to break up fights.

Buckie's predecessor as sub-inspector at Pembrey had been threatened with a ducking by a group of workers. Shortly after their arrival Buckie, Gabrielle and three constables were faced with a protest in the canteen when the women workers refused to leave and go back to work. The reason for the protest is unclear, but the five police were hooted and booed and the women said that 'they would down the first policewoman that came near them'. Buckie and Gabrielle courageously strode into the middle of the the protesters and ordered them back to their tasks. 'By and bye one or two cried out to the booers to "shut up" as we'd got a bit of pluck any how.' But it took ninety minutes to get all the women back to work.

In the Hereford factory they had to deal with trouble between English women and a group that had come over from Ireland. The Easter Rising had occurred the year before and the British army's clumsy and ruthless response had given Pádraic Pearse and his comrades the martyrdom that he, particularly, had sought. The Irish women workers sang 'Sinn Fein songs and made offensive remarks about the "Tommies"'. One evening in August 1917 the trouble spread outside the factory and resulted in a fight on the

platforms of Hereford railway station. Gabrielle and some constables became involved and, when the situation had calmed, they
were required to escort the Irish women through the town back
to the factory. A crowd gathered and began to hoot and pelt the
women with mud.

> One girl fell and was kicked by a young man in the crowd. I and
> another W.P. grabbed him and called to a policeman who had seen
> it done, but instead of taking him the p.man [*sic*] slunk off, so
> we had to let the man go.

The problem here was that, like most of the early women police,
Gabrielle was not formally sworn in as a constable and, as a consequence, she needed a male officer to make an arrest.

In the late summer of 1917 Gabrielle and Buckie were feeling
frustrated with their situation in Hereford. Buckie was keen to
leave because of the periodic sickness brought on by the prussic
acid. 'Also', Gabrielle confided to her journal,

> it is rather disheartening to work under a manager who is constantly
> inventing new rules for us to enforce, but does not back us up
> by punishing those who disobey them.
>
> But the real reason is that B. has been fighting to get us sworn
> in. In a factory like this where we have a good deal of genuine
> police work to do (i.e. prosecuting for bringing in matches, for
> theft, blackmail, etc. and our work during strikes and riots) it is
> really important that we should have the power to take out and
> serve a summons, and carry through a case without being obliged
> to pass everything over to the men police. B. was promised that
> we should be sworn in, but some hitch has occurred, so she has
> now said that if we are not sworn in she will resign. We have not
> been and so she has resigned, and has been appointed by
> Headquarters sub Insp. of Waltham Abbey Royal Gunpowder and
> Royal Small Arms Factories.
>
> As an instance of the importance of being sworn in. During

the strike the girls attacked a policeman, and knocked off his helmet, and also knocked down a police woman. For assaulting the police [*sic*] they were liable to 6 months hard labour. Assaulting the p. woman counted only as a common assault; as we, not being sworn in, count only as private individuals; and the maximum penalty is 1 month.

Alongside the practical difficulties that were created by not being sworn in and attested as a full constable, the women also had to face patronizing attitudes from some of the men with whom they worked. Gabrielle was incensed by the Superintendent of the Special Constables at Hereford who insisted on calling her 'my dear lassie'. On one occasion, in spite of her diminutive form, she barged him out of her office and when she reported her actions to the more sympathetic military officers in charge of the factory, she noted how they were stifling giggles. Sometimes, though Gabrielle does not appear to have experienced it, male attitudes were aggressive and insulting. In Weybridge patrols by women police volunteers of the National Union of Women Workers were disparaged as 'the DIPs' – damned impertinent patrols. One patrol member recalled being stopped by an angry Canadian soldier who 'proceeded to give me a piece of his mind . . . and advised me to stay at home and bring up my family instead of walking the streets in a way no decent woman should'. Such male aggression, however, did not often extend to violence against the women police. Indeed, Sergeant Gladys King who, as a member of the WPS, policed the Beaver Hut hostel established for Canadian troops in the Strand in London, remembered being summoned on several occasions to pacify violent, drunken soldiers at the request of their comrades or male police officers.[4]

In addition to the insults, the patronizing attitudes of some men, and the sexual harassment by others, it appears also that the women's police may have attracted some aggressive lesbians looking for partners. At Pembrey Gabrielle met Sergeant Guthrie who, 'like a man', had close-cropped hair, a thickset figure, big feet and a tenor voice. The factory women refused to be searched by her believing her to be a male detective. Among the police women she caused alarm by stroking their hands, kissing them and calling them 'darling'.

Overall the WPS might have been rather more professional in the way that it approached policing than the volunteer patrols, but it smacked too much of militant feminism and the suffragette campaign to be welcomed by the Home Office and by senior police officers once the wartime emergency had ceased. Not that every member of the force shared the aspirations of Margaret Damer Dawson and Mary Allen. Gabrielle West, for example, appears to have accepted that her policing career would end once peace came. She returned to Gloucestershire and opened a tea room. The Voluntary Women's Patrols had a less overtly feminist agenda than the WPS. Their membership was also largely middle-class and their wartime role was couched much more in terms of welfare, and particularly overseeing the morals of young working-class women in the towns. But their duties and their presence annoyed some police officers, who considered the women as interlopers in a man's job. Others, like the elderly London magistrate Frederick Mead, were appalled by the necessity of their involvement in 'filthy and disgusting cases'. Indeed, some of the women police were also shocked by these duties. One recruit to the WPS, for example, who appears to have been much more sensitive than Gabrielle West and Buckie Buckpitt, resigned after her training and sent a letter to the *Weekly Dispatch* explaining that:

> The shock of hearing and seeing the things I did in my three weeks' training altered my whole outlook on life. We spent the mornings at the police courts hearing unspeakable things and the nights in patrolling Leicester-square, etc., seeing unspeakable things, the intervals being filled up with lectures on subjects mostly, to my mind, quite indecent . . .[5]

But most of the women, both in the WPS and the VWP, took such things in their stride and by 1918 both the Home Office and the Commissioner of the Metropolitan Police were keen to experiment with a body of 100 women to be attached to the Commissioner's force.

Not surprisingly, given the aspirations and the radical pedigree of the WPS leadership, the Home Office and the Commissioner turned to the leader of the Voluntary Women's Patrols in London. Thus Sophia Stanley, the wife of a member of the Indian Civil Service, was invited to organize the new women's department of the Metropolitan Police. Margaret Damer Dawson protested to the Home Office that her force had established excellent and indispensable training facilities and instructors. The Home Office's response was to issue a circular to chief constables advising them of the value of police women but, by emphasizing that such women should be considered as part of the local force, it obviated any need for a national training centre such as that created by the WPS. In the event, only a few chief constables acknowledged that women had any value in the police. One such was Captain J.S. Henderson of the Reading Borough force. He had been impressed by the performance of two women officers that served in his force during the war. At the end of 1919, however, both of these women chose to leave. Henderson promptly appointed Gladys King and her friend and fellow WPS veteran from the Beaver Hut, Lena Campbell. Gladys served until 1940, when she resigned but continued full-time probation work for another nine years. Lena resigned through ill-health in 1941.

The WPS itself battled on after the war as an independent body with an increasingly explicit feminist agenda. It continued to offer training for women officers and it sent its own members to some difficult trouble spots. A few travelled to Ireland to assist in the policing of women suspects as Britain extricated itself from what was to become the Irish Free State. Others went to Germany, to help enforce the curfew on 'undesirable women' in the region controlled by the British Army of Occupation.

The young women recruited into the Metropolitan Police in the immediate aftermath of the war were never intended to take over men's responsibilities. They were to be confined to the female sphere of supervising other women, children and families. 'We had not been given power of arrest,' recalled Lilian Wyles, daughter of a well-to-do brewer, a veteran of the wartime patrols and one of the first women police sergeants,

> the reason being that as we were to be an experiment it might be dangerous to give us too much authority. I have a shrewd idea, however, that the real reason we had not been given the full powers of a constable was that the authorities feared what might happen if they were to let loose on London streets one hundred women, completely armed with authority that would enable them to arrest all and sundry according to their whims and fancies. Why a young man of nineteen or twenty, who had most likely come from a remote Cornish hamlet or from the bogs of Ireland, should have been considered as more suitable to hold the power of arrest than women who for the most part were London bred and who had considerable knowledge of the seamy side of life in the Metropolis, I could never understand. There it was! 'Women', quoth the wiseacres of Whitehall, 'are so unpredictable, so impulsive.'⁶

The Specials and Policing Disorder on the Home Front

The impact of the war on the police might have been predicted had the matter been given much thought before 1914, but it was not. For male officers the war years created new burdens. Their ranks were depleted by the call-up of reservists. There were more than 1,000 reservists in the Metropolitan Police, about 5 per cent of the force. These men disappeared virtually overnight. And there was no impediment to prevent patriotic young officers from volunteering. Police numbers were only maintained by keeping men on after retirement age and by using special constables.

Special constables had been enrolled throughout the nineteenth century, generally when there was the threat of disorder. Alongside the legislation for the development of more regular police institutions during the 1830s, Parliament had also allowed for the recruitment of Specials. It became possible to nominate them when magistrates received reliable advanced warning of disorder, to pay them for their time and trouble, to permit men to volunteer for the position rather than wait to be nominated and to allow them to be used outside their immediate locality. Their performance had been patchy during the Chartist period; they were at their best when deployed in support of regular, full-time police and there were concerns that middle-class special constables being used against working-class demonstrators would inject an additional level of class confrontation into disorder. But the recruitment of Specials, specifically when public order was perceived to be under threat, continued throughout the Victorian and Edwardian periods. In the immediate aftermath of the industrial disorders of 1911, when large numbers of Specials had been sworn in, a Home Office circular advised local authorities to compile lists of reliable men that might be called upon in the future. Few appear to have bothered but within a month of the declaration of war in 1914 thousands of special constables had been sworn in up and down the country, and their tasks over the next four years were to be much more extensive than those of earlier Specials. In some instances they took over beat patrols; they also guarded potential targets for enemy attack such as power stations, reservoirs, roads and railways. As respectable middle-class, often middle-aged men who had volunteered out of patriotic duty, some of them resented being ordered about like the regular police. They also resented the initial lack of uniform, believing that a badge, armband and baton were insufficient marks of authority; and when the provision for uniforms was made early in 1915, many resented the fact that they were given flat caps rather than the distinctive police helmet. Nor was the resentment all one way. Some of the regular police believed that the Specials received more favourable treatment and a better rate of pay.[7]

While the Specials took over some of the duties of the regular police who were not recalled to the colours as reservists and who, for a variety of reasons, did not volunteer for the military, the tasks of those police officers who stayed on the home front did not diminish. Far from it; from the moment that war broke out the regular police acquired a cluster of war-specific tasks. These included the billeting of troops, the apprehension of deserters and absconders, and sometimes the supervision of prisoner-of-war camps. Probably the most distasteful duty was checking the conduct of those in receipt of the pension granted to war widows and of the separation allowance granted to the wives and dependents of soldiers and sailors. If the women were found to be cohabiting with new men, then their money was withdrawn. There was also the more obvious wartime need to protect against sabotage, spies and subversion. Spies and saboteurs were rare, but this did not lessen the concerns about them, or the directions to the police to keep tabs on aliens, to be watchful and to investigate people sketching or painting or taking photographs near the coast or other sensitive places. The Russian Revolution intensified the fear of subversion and ensured that it continued beyond the armistice.

Food shortages created long queues and short tempers that could lead to disorder, and the potential for such trouble was not entirely settled by the issue of ration books in February 1918. The reduction of beer in quantity as well as in strength and flavour also provided opportunities for trouble, especially after the armistice; soldiers who could not buy a drink could be as difficult and dangerous as those who had drunk too much.

Before the war soldiers had often proved a problem for police by getting drunk and fighting among themselves. The situation was aggravated by the enormous increase in service personnel during wartime, and particularly the arrival of large numbers of men from Australia, Canada, New Zealand and South Africa. The arrest of a soldier by the police could provoke a violent rescue attempt by other soldiers. The worst of these incidents occurred at the end of the war and involved Canadians keen to get home.

In June 1919, after two Canadian soldiers were arrested and locked in the cells of Epsom Police Station, about 400 of their comrades besieged the station demanding their release. Throwing discretion and arguably common sense to the winds, Inspector Pawley attempted to disperse the angry Canadians by ordering the fifteen policemen present in the station to make a baton charge. Among Pawley's forlorn hope was 51-year-old Station Sergeant Thomas Green. Green had served in the Royal Horse Artillery before joining the Metropolitan Police twenty-four years earlier. Married, with two teenage daughters, he had spent the last eight years at Epsom. In the fracas that ensued from Pawley's order, Green was struck a severe blow on the head; the following day he died from his injury.[8]

Violent wartime disorder was not only caused by drunken soldiers and by angry people in food queues. Weary policemen, supported by Specials and sometimes by soldiers, had to suppress anti-German riots in the early months of the war. A few months later, following the sinking of the *Lusitania* in May 1915, a new and particularly serious wave of disorder enveloped the whole country as furious crowds attacked shops, restaurants and individuals with German-sounding names. Two years later it was Jews who were the target. Relatively recent young male immigrants from Russia, who had settled in London and Leeds particularly, were suspected of avoiding conscription; and the old anti-Semitic standby of the profiteering Jewish businessman was invoked to increase still further the temperature of the crowds' passions.

Part of the Union: Bobbies on Strike

Wartime inflation and the additional burdens created by the wartime emergency were powerful recruiters for the National Union of Police and Prison Officers (NUPPO). The union was at its strongest in London where it had been founded by John Syme on the eve of the war. During the war Syme's obsessive behaviour, which included accusing the police of perjury to secure a murder conviction, led to his being voted off the executive committee. The union had to develop underground; the police authorities were aware of its existence and tried to stop its activities and discipline its leadership. In February 1917, for example, Military Police were sent to break up a meeting in London. As the MPs sought to push their way into the meeting, single men held the door to enable their married comrades with family responsibilities to escape. Fourteen police constables were dismissed. But such solidarity was not universal. PC Tommy Thiel, a former drill sergeant of the Guards and a veteran of the Boer War, was the provincial organizer for NUPPO. Thiel, based in Hammersmith, had been in contact with a fellow constable in Manchester but, on promotion to sergeant, the Manchester PC decided to hand over all of his union correspondence to his Chief Constable. It was this action that led, ultimately, to the police strike of August 1918. In the new sergeant's favour it might be noted that the Chief Constable in Manchester, Robert Peacock, was sympathetic to his men's situation and that, less than a week before the London officers took action, Peacock persuaded the local watch committee to pay an increased war bonus and to reinstate the weekly rest day. But that was of little interest to the men in London when the police authorities there, armed with evidence from Manchester, set out to punish Tommy Thiel for his union activities.

Chief Constable Peacock had sent Thiel's correspondence to London and, towards the end of August 1918, Thiel was summoned before a disciplinary board and dismissed. The union leadership promptly wrote to both the Prime Minister and the Home Secretary demanding his reinstatement together with an immediate pay rise and recognition of the union. The letters, sent on Tuesday 27 August, warned that if the government had not complied by midnight on 28 August, then the leadership would bring the Metropolitan Police out on strike. It is unclear whether those ministers and civil servants left in London during the summer holidays failed to recognize the seriousness of the situation, or simply sought to call the union's bluff. By noon on 30 August 6,000 policemen, about a third of the force, were on strike and soon only a few, mainly in the outer divisions, were reporting for duty. When the authorities sought to bypass and ignore the union, it responded with a successful call to the City of London Police to join the strike.

The rank and file seem to have had little hesitation in taking strike action. 'We want more pay, Sir,' PC Gates protested to his superintendent at Notting Hill. 'I don't get sufficient money to keep my children in boots. My second son has just been called up by the Army and I have to go care-taking to keep out of debt.' Such complaints were not exceptional. But a police strike in the capital, just as the troops on the Western Front were recovering from the spring offensive of Ludendorff's storm troops and beginning to turn the tide, looked suspicious to some. Sections of the press noted the German-sounding names of Tommy Thiel and Jack Zollner, another former Guardsman, a veteran of the retreat from Mons and now a serving City of London policeman and union activist. But the Prime Minister, Lloyd George, did not believe that there was time to quibble and debate. The Home Secretary and the Commissioner were ordered back to London from their summer breaks and together with the Prime Minister they met union leaders in Downing Street on the morning of 31 August. An immediate pay rise was promised, Thiel was reinstated and there was a strong implication that a representative body for the rank and file would be recognized at the end of the war. The strike was called off; the men went back to their beats; the union leadership was elated; and the government prepared its next moves.[9]

On 1 March 1919 the government appointed a committee, under the chairmanship of William Henry Grenfell, Baron Desborough, to look into the recruiting, the conditions of service, the rates of pay, allowances and pensions of the police in England, Wales and Scotland. In the six months between the end of the strike and the appointment of the committee the war had ended, the membership of NUPPO had become open, had expanded and was seen to extend well beyond the metropolis. The police in Scotland had established their own union, but while equally incensed by the deteriorating situation of police officers, the Scottish union had agreed not to use the strike weapon.

Desborough's committee was urged to report quickly and, by the middle of May, the Home Secretary was aware that its broad recommendations would involve much higher pay rates and a standardization of pay and conditions across the 200 and more police forces in Britain. In reaching its conclusions the committee heard evidence from a range of police officers – from Sir Edward Henry, Commissioner of the Metropolitan Police at the time of the strike, and his replacement, General Sir Nevil Macready, to representatives of the rank and file. Constables, sergeants and inspectors from across England, Wales and Scotland, gave powerful testimony about the stresses and strains of the job. They complained about unjust treatment and favouritism in the way that promotions were made and men were disciplined. They drew attention to the problem of maintaining the level of respectability expected from an officer and his family on the rates of pay provided. In the opinion of Inspector Thomas Griffiths and PC C.A. Joslin of the Southend-on-Sea Borough Police:

> The restrictions under which the policeman works bear no comparison in other walks of life. Generally speaking, he has to reside where required; he has to live in a highly respectable neighbourhood; clothe himself and his family decently (his boots and underclothing have to be the best procurable) . . .
>
> A constable is expected to keep up a better appearance than a skilled artisan, yet his pay at present is not equal to that of the unskilled labourer. When the industrial worker leaves the workshop he knows that he has finished for the day, but the constable must study at home to keep up to the ever-changing laws.

Other officers made similar points. Sergeant George Blackburn and PC Zollner from the City of London, for example, began their testimony with an eloquent plea for improved status and also sought to situate the police officer within the broader perspective of a working class demanding social improvement:

> We wish to say that hitherto a constable has been paid a wage that has kept him very low down the social scale. He has always had to exercise the greatest possible economy in order to eke out the slender income at his disposal. He has had to seek the cheapest accommodation and to put up with its attendant evils. His wage has never exceeded the bare subsistence level. In recent years, however, the constable, in common with others of the class of the community to which he belongs, has become dissatisfied with this condition of affairs.

Blackburn and Zollner spoke of men applying to serve on permanent night duty because of inadequate accommodation, and getting into bed in the morning a few moments after their wife and daughters had left it. They stressed the man's need for a good diet to enable him to perform his tasks, and for good boots; even though there might be a boot allowance, they noted how the cost of good boot leather had increased enormously as a result of the war.[10]

The impact of wartime inflation on police pay was something to which witness after witness referred. The men had picked up on the Board of Trade's assessment of inflation over the period of the war as about 130 per cent, and most appeared to consider that, even with various war-time bonuses and subsequent pay awards, their wage had fallen in real terms by 60 to 70 per cent from what they were earning in 1914. When a member of the committee suggested to men from Newcastle upon Tyne that they had a good pension to look forward to, the response was that most men would prefer the money put aside for the pension to be put in their weekly pay packets. Inspector Thomas Dale from Newcastle warned further that the policeman 'was subject to temptations that the ordinary man in the street cannot know of'. His comrade, Sergeant Robert McBirney, added: 'You can have no conception. It is hard to be honest when your pocket is empty.'[11]

Among the witnesses that appeared before the Desborough Committee was Metropolitan Police Sergeant John ('Jack') Henry Hayes. Jack Hayes was born in 1887, the son of a Wolverhampton police inspector. His brother had become a policeman and, in 1909, Jack himself joined the Metropolitan Police. His abilities were quickly recognized. After a year on the beat he was transferred to the divisional office and, three years later, promoted to sergeant. After only a short period as Commissioner, Macready had him marked out for further promotion and for a career in the senior ranks. But Hayes was a Labour Party man through and through, and he was committed to his mates at the sharp end of policing. He had not been a significant figure in NUPPO during the war and the strike but, in the tense period following August 1918, he resigned from the police to take up the full-time, salaried post of the union's general secretary.

Whatever was or was not said about recognizing a police union at the meeting that had ended the first strike, neither the government nor Macready was prepared to countenance such an organization. On 1 July 1919 the Desborough Committee published its first report which suggested, among other things, the creation of a body that provided police officers below the rank of superintendent with the right to confer over pay and conditions. Exactly a week later a Police Bill was introduced into the House of Commons that provided for what was to become known as the Police Federation. The new organization was not to be a trade union or affiliated to the Trades Union Congress; it was not to involve itself in individual cases of discipline or promotion; and it was not to be permitted to initiate any industrial action. These clauses were a direct challenge to NUPPO and the union executive recognized it. Jack Hayes advised against calling another strike urging that, as government agreement to a substantial pay claim was in the offing, the membership would be reluctant to take strike action again. He was outvoted. On 31 July the union leaders called a new strike, and they rapidly discovered that Hayes had been right.

Just over 1,000 men in the Metropolitan Police responded to the second strike call with around another sixty from the City of London. Men in the counties and most of the boroughs simply carried on working. In Manchester a union meeting voted against action; the men appreciated some of the recommendations of the Desborough Committee, the promised pay increase and the moves already made by Chief Constable Peacock and the city's watch committee. They did, however, request that the Federation be permitted to address individual matters of promotion and discipline. In Birmingham the call from NUPPO received support largely because of the local situation. Charles H. Rafter, the former RIC man, was still Chief Constable; he showed overt hostility to his men having any right to confer and the watch committee was notorious for its lack of sympathy with their constables' problems. In Liverpool tension between the rank and file, the Chief Constable and the watch committee was even more pronounced. The principal grievances here focused primarily on the conviction that there was manifest favouritism in promotions and unfair treatment in disciplinary matters. It is unclear how many men struck work in Birmingham as some, quickly recognizing that the strike was a failure, hurried back to work without really being missed and others, with good records and long service, were not reported as striking by their senior officers. Nevertheless, 119 out of 1,340 men were recorded as striking and were summarily dismissed. In Liverpool the situation rapidly got out of hand. At least 1,000 of the 2,200 men in the force took action. Men who reported for work were abused and intimidated. At the same time looters took to the streets. Warships sailed in to protect the docks. Troops clashed violently with rioters and looters, and one man died from a bayonet thrust.

The men who were identified as participating in the strike were summarily dismissed. This included men with fine records who had served twenty years and more and who were approaching retirement, as well as men passed retirement age but who had been kept on because of the manpower shortage created by the war. Most of these men appear, eventually, to have got their pensions. One or two younger men seem to have succeeded in joining other forces and Macready, together with some other officers and members of watch committees, helped some of the dismissed men to find other jobs.[12] But for many others there were no such opportunities. Calls for reinstatement and for the restoration of the benefits to which the men had contributed were made by local Labour politicians and activists from other trade unions, but when Labour formed its first government in 1924, and again in 1929, Labour ministers' ears remained deaf. Hayes was devastated and insisted that his pay as general secretary of NUPPO be significantly reduced. He campaigned ceaselessly for those members that he considered to have been 'locked out' and he kept their case prominent in a journal, *The Bull's Eye*, which began publication in August 1920.

The Bull's Eye, which took its name from the lamp carried by constables on night duty, focused, naturally enough, on issues regarding police and policing. It adopted a typical, radical Labour stance and returned regularly to the old concern of a militarized police. Hayes had expressed his concerns about militarization before the Desborough Committee and, when the police broke up a meeting of the National Federation of Discharged Soldiers and Sailors in May 1919, he had issued a press statement on behalf of NUPPO apologizing for the violence, which he put down to militarization, and calling for better links between the police and organized labour. A particular target of *The Bull's Eye* was Lieutenant Colonel John Hall-Dalwood, the Chief Constable of Sheffield, who couched many of his instructions in military terms. In December 1920, with apologies to Rudyard Kipling, the journal published a poem, the 'Military Police-to-be', that envisaged what ordinary policing would be like in five years' time:

> I wish me mother could see me now
> A-goose-stepping down the Strand,
> With a rifle on me shoulder
> And a Mills' grenade in me hand.
>> We used to be in the police force once;

What a sweet little, dear little police force once;
What a true little, blue little police force once;
But now – We're 'M.P.'

The Emergency Powers Bill of 1920, labelled by the journal as 'Prussian Politics', was seen as a further manifestation of militarization. So too were the grim events in Ireland that saw the violent birth of the Irish Free State and its truncated neighbour, the still British province of Northern Ireland, together with the end of the Royal Irish Constabulary.[13]

The Bloody End of the Royal Irish Constabulary

If the outlook was bleak for those English policemen identified as striking in 1919, for many of their Irish equivalents the eventful period following the Great War was far more traumatic, and sometimes fatal. The Easter Rising of 1916 began a new process of isolation for the Irish police that reached a climax with the outbreak of the Anglo-Irish War at the beginning of 1919 and saw the police reaching, once again, for their guns rather than their batons. The RIC, which was a little under 16,000 men at its peak in 1921, bore the brunt of the fighting between 1919 and 1922; an authoritative estimate has concluded that 588 men died violently during the period with nearly another 700 wounded.[14]

Ireland was a heavily policed country and different English people had different opinions about the Irish police. Jack Hayes told the Desborough Committee that he disliked its national structure and feared that it was a militarized body. But others saw it as a part of the broad family of British policing and different only in as far as the national characteristics of the Irish required something a little different from the English – the late nineteenth and early twentieth centuries were, after all, the heyday of the notion of the significance of inbred national characteristics. In reality the RIC and the Dublin Metropolitan Police had increasingly come to resemble the English forces following the Land War of 1879–82;

and over the next thirty years they had lost much of their military edge, were concerned more and more with ordinary patrolling, and with batons rather then firearms.

Patrick Shea was the second son of an RIC constable. He was born in 1908 shortly before his father's posting to Athlone in County Westmeath. His recollection of his early childhood was coloured by what came after, but there seems little reason to doubt his happy memories of growing up in the constabulary barracks. As he readied himself for school in the morning, he watched the constables parade before going on patrol, almost always it would seem without their guns. He recalled games between the men from his father's barracks and constables and soldiers from elsewhere. His bedroom was over the cells and he heard and saw petty thieves and boisterous drunks brought in and locked up. Patrick's father and mother were nationalists and supported Irish Home Rule, but this did not protect him and his brother in the aftermath of Easter 1916. The boys were abused and beaten on their way to school and things were to get worse. The police at Athlone Barracks, and the families that lived with them, were shocked and shaken by the news that reached them at the end of January 1919.[15] Constable James McDonnell, a widower in his fifties with a young family and just a few months away from retirement, and Constable Patrick O'Connell, a man in his early thirties, were protecting a cart of gelignite destined for a stone quarry near Limerick. The cart was ambushed by eight Irish Volunteers at Soloheadbeg, and both constables were shot dead. The shooting is generally regarded as marking the start of the Anglo-Irish War and set the standard for the cold-blooded viciousness of much of the fighting.

The next three years witnessed ambushes and murders committed by both sides. More RIC men were ambushed and killed. RIC men, and the auxiliary force recruited to assist them, the Black and Tans, were implicated in killings and atrocities, notably the shooting of Tomás Mac Curtain, mayor of Cork and commander of the mid Cork brigade of the IRA. In April 1919 the new Dublin parliament, the Dáil Éireann, agreed to a boycott or 'social ostracism' of members of the RIC, and even after the truce of July 1921 between the British government and the leadership of what was to become the Irish Free State, attacks on policemen continued. It rapidly became apparent that there would be no room for the RIC in the Free State and the force was disbanded in the early summer of 1922.

The brothers Con and Michael Sullivan had joined the RIC in the less combustible days before the Easter Rising. They were born into a large farming family in County Cork. Con enlisted in March 1911 and served in the south-east of the country for eight years before transferring to a clerical job in Dublin Castle. Michael enlisted in September 1914 and served in Limerick, rising to the rank of sergeant. Their parents were proud of them. They returned home for annual holidays when they helped out on the farms of their parents and their parents' neighbours, and joined in any local festivities. But once the fighting started in 1919, while their parents were happy to see them, they always made their twice-yearly visits together, never attended mass, dances or parties, and while one slept, the other sat watching the door with two loaded revolvers. By 1921 even these visits were considered to be too dangerous. While Con drove his desk in Dublin Castle, Michael was involved in some of the heaviest fighting in Limerick and Tipperary, and was told that he was marked for death by the IRA. When the RIC was disbanded the brothers left for England. Some of their comrades transferred into other imperial forces; a few were welcomed into the new Royal Ulster Constabulary that was set up in the British province of Northern Ireland. Con settled in Leicester, and did not visit Ireland again until 1960. Michael followed the route taken by many RIC men of earlier generations; he moved to Australia, and never returned.[16]

— CHAPTER 8 —

Good Cop, Bad Cop: Bobby
Between the Wars, 1919–1939

THE FIRST WORLD War was seen as 'the war to end all wars'. Probably a majority of the men that returned from the battlefronts, and of the families to which they returned, expected to be able to pick up life from where it had been interrupted in the summer of 1914. Prussian militarism had been defeated and in the popular mind this looked like a triumph for Britain's values and virtues. In the immediate aftermath of the war all adult males were finally granted the vote, together with all women aged over thirty years. There were some anxieties. There were concerns about the behaviour of men brutalized by the war; and while the outcome of the Russian Revolution was still in the balance in 1919 and 1920, the overthrow of the Tsar and the triumph of Bolshevism aggravated fears about working-class unrest. In the euphoria of military victory few among the general population were aware of the economic cost of the war, but there were those who recognized that, potentially, this was much more destabilizing than the human cost.

Most seasoned police officers, whether they had gone to the battle fronts or remained at home, expected to be able to carry on as they had before the war. Thanks to Desborough, however, they now enjoyed improved pay and conditions. In a few instances, some men had the continuing novelty of women colleagues. There were a few other novelties that began to try the police, such as the spread of motor traffic and the expansion of suburbs. Yet, in the space between the two world wars, much policing did return, more or less, to Victorian and Edwardian practices – both good and bad.

A Tale of Two Sergeants

Among the men who had policed the home front during the war were two Metropolitan Police sergeants, Bob Josling and George Goddard. On the surface they would have appeared similar; in reality they were chalk and cheese. Born in 1889, Horace Robert (Bob) Josling was the son of an engine driver. He attended Brentwood Grammar School and began his adult life working as an untrained schoolteacher. In July 1912, hoping to better himself, he joined the Metropolitan Police. Josling's abilities were quickly recognized. He was promoted to sergeant and, at the end of the war, was appointed as an instructor in the Police Training School at Peel House. Almost immediately, however, financial cuts forced a reduction in the school staff and Josling rapidly found himself transferred to Great Marlborough Street Police Station, one of three stations in the centre of the metropolis supervised by 'C' Division.

At the heart of 'C' Division's relatively small manor lay Soho, a cosmopolitan district developing a notoriety as a centre for leisure and, above all, for vice. The officer responsible for supervising the night-clubs and 'disorderly houses' in the division was Sergeant George Goddard. Born in Guildford, Surrey, in 1879, Goddard had begun his working life as a bricklayer. He had joined the police in 1900 and had served across the range of metropolitan districts from busy Marylebone, to the mixed suburbs of Wandsworth and Hampstead. Goddard had a drink problem early in his career and in 1910 he was severely reprimanded, fined and cautioned. Shortly before the outbreak of the First World War, however, he was regarded as 'practically a total abstainer', and it was then that he had been posted to 'C' Division. Josling and Goddard were two of some sixty sergeants in the division; but while Josling was virtuous to a fault, Goddard luxuriated at the centre of a web of corruption.

The Street Betting Act of 1906, designed to limit working-class gambling, had prohibited the taking of bets in the street. Senior police officers had feared that the legislation would be unenforceable, and so it proved. More seriously it led to some bookmakers making 'arrangements' with some police to turn a blind eye to the runners who took bets. The police also tipped off bookies when arrests were to be made, while paid stooges were hired to stand in for, and be arrested in place of, the runners. Goddard was a key figure in the weekly distribution of bookies' bribes in Great Marlborough Street Police Station. Even after he had refused to participate, Josling claimed that he found envelopes filled with money pushed into his locker. Concerned that they had the same superior officers within the station, Josling reported the matter directly to the Commissioner, Brigadier General Sir William Horwood, who had taken over in the late spring of 1920 when Macready was sent to take command of the British military forces engaged in the Anglo-Irish War.

Josling faced Goddard at a Disciplinary Board which met at Scotland Yard in July 1922. But, as Josling later explained, he felt that he was the one on trial. Goddard was permitted two witnesses, but Josling was not permitted to question them. No bookmakers were asked to give evidence. 'I was cross-examined for two days to the point of almost physical and mental exhaustion,' Josling recalled.

> On the first day I was examined for eight hours with a break for luncheon. On the second day I was kept before the Board from 1 o'clock until 20 minutes to 8 at night. The members of the Board had tea, but I was not offered any.

In an echo of the case of 'Juicy Lips' Jeapes in the middle of the previous century and described in Chapter 2, the accusing sergeant was condemned and Goddard was exonerated. Josling was found guilty of making false allegations against a fellow officer, and was called upon to resign. He lost his pension rights and went back to teaching, though for two years his wife became the breadwinner while he undertook a course of formal training at Goldsmiths College in London. Goddard returned to Great Marlborough Street, and continued to profit from a variety of scams that involved not only bookies, but also restaurateurs and night-club owners.

During 1927 Superintendent Charles Morton, the commander of 'C' Division, received anonymous letters alleging that certain restaurants and hotels in the district were linked with prostitution and that night-clubs were selling drinks after hours and had become centres for trafficking in cocaine. He passed the letters on to Goddard for investigation even though Goddard himself was accused in some letters of both enjoying free meals, courtesy of the restaurateurs, and tipping off night-club proprietors about police raids. In March the following year, possibly as a result of information sent to the Commissioner from the Home Office, Morton organized an early-morning raid on Kate Meyrick's '43 Club' without informing Goddard. The raid was a complete success; between 250 and 300 people were found to be in the club consuming alcoholic drinks at 1.30 a.m. But no questions were asked of Goddard or of those working with and under him.

Six months later the Commissioner received an anonymous letter accusing Goddard of taking bribes from night-clubs and of having a personal financial interest in them. It also drew attention to his expensive house and car, and reported that he had established his brother-in-law in a pawnbroker's business. Inquiries were begun without Goddard's knowledge, though a phone call from the firm from which he had purchased his car, asking if the details might be passed to the police, inadvertently warned him and he tried to conceal some of his assets. The investigations revealed that Goddard, whose weekly wage was £6.15s., had assets amounting to nearly £18,000. At a disciplinary board convened at Scotland Yard on 29 October 1928 he admitted guilt in two of the accusations levelled against him: neglect of duty, in that he had failed to give a satisfactory account of large sums of money that he had received; and discreditable conduct, in betting and associating with bookmakers and undesirable characters. He was dismissed from the force. He was then arrested and charged with corruptly receiving and obtaining money from Kate Meyrick and Luigi Ribuffini, a restaurateur and night-club proprietor. Meyrick and Ribuffini were charged with paying him money; and all three were charged with conspiracy to pervert the course of justice.[1]

The trial of Goddard, Meyrick and Ribuffini was sensational. They were all found guilty. Goddard was sentenced to eighteen months' hard labour, fined £2,000 and ordered to pay the costs of the prosecution. But amid the evidence of Superintendent Morton's myopia, and of the way in which Goddard was able to draw over £100 a month in Treasury bills to finance young constables investigating night-clubs, there was no mention of weekly share-outs from bookmakers and no serious suggestion that any other officers were significantly involved. This has been the subsequent line taken in police histories; Goddard was simply a rotten apple. What has been glossed over in these histories is the aftermath in 'C' Division. At the beginning of November the Commissioner informed the Home Secretary that he wanted answers from the division about why senior officers had failed to detect what Goddard was doing. Within a week of this letter Brigadier General Horwood was replaced as Commissioner by Lord Byng of Vimy. Whether the inquiry was progressed is unclear but in the summer of 1929 two sergeants and two constables from Great Marlborough Street Police Station were dismissed for accepting free meals in restaurants and associating with brothel keepers. Two years later an inspector and twenty-six constables were dismissed from the same station for accepting money from bookmakers and other tradesmen; and at least one other inspector and twenty-three men were separated and moved to other divisions. The press picked up on this activity and raged about the police failure to make any official statement. In the Metropolitan

Police itself the rumour spread that 'something like 200 men of all ranks' had been dismissed.[2]

One name conspicuous by its absence during Goddard's trial was that of Bob Josling. At the time of Goddard's conviction he was the headmaster of a small village school in Shropshire. Having read of the trial, and prompted by Jack Hayes, who was now the Labour MP for Edge Hill on the fringe of Liverpool and an unofficial spokesman for the police in Parliament, Josling decided to submit a claim for compensation. The Home Office eventually agreed to amend his resignation to 'voluntary' and awarded him £1,500 from the Metropolitan Police Fund. Josling remained with his school in Shropshire and died at the beginning of 1941 aged only fifty-one.

Tangentially it is interesting to note that, two years after settling with Josling, the Metropolitan Police also settled with the sad and now slightly deranged John Syme. In 1924, while ignoring all requests to reinstate the strikers of 1919 or to grant the pensions to those still denied them, the first, short-lived Labour Government had appointed a Lord Chancellor's Committee to inquire into the Syme affair. The committee concluded that, while Syme's dismissal had been justified, his initial behaviour had been perfectly correct and that the disciplinary action had been heavy-handed. Seven years later a new Labour Government acknowledged Syme's integrity stated that he had been wrongly transferred and agreed to pay his pension back-dated to 1909 – a sum amounting to over £1,200.[3] The claims of the dismissed strikers were still ignored, but it was as if the authorities were seeking to draw a line under previous, high-profile problems within the service and to restore faith in what many still liked to boast of as 'the best police in the world' in spite of a recent succession of blemishes on that image.

Problems of Class and Gender

Goddard's arrest and prosecution were reported in the press alongside accounts of the deliberations of the Royal Commission on

Police Powers and Procedure, an investigation launched as a response to several complaints about high-handed police behaviour in the decade following the First World War. The press, and others, talked in sensational terms about 'the third degree', a method of interrogation supposedly popular with police in the United States. According to *The People*, this was a 'merciless, ceaseless, nerve-shattering bombardment of questions and accusations' that left the suspect prepared 'to say anything which will end his intolerable mental anguish'.[4] In addition to concerns about the 'third degree', some of the complaints about police behaviour almost certainly became public because of the social class of the complainant. The voice and person of a gentleman carried far more weight with authority than did that of a member of the poor working class. Thus, when the clerk to the Privy Council was arrested for annoying women in Hyde Park in 1922, proceedings were dropped entirely because of his social standing and regardless of the fact that he had been arrested for a similar offence five years earlier.[5]

Two rather different cases, in which the police appear to have been at fault, involved army officers and hence men of a social class which could raise a voice that attracted some attention. In June 1925 Major R.O. Sheppard DSO was mistakenly identified by a woman as the soldier who had taken property from her rooms. The major accompanied his accuser to Vine Street Police Station where, according to a tribunal of inquiry, a succession of police officers of different ranks, either deliberately or through ignorance, denied him a whole series of his legal rights. Two years later the Home Secretary appointed another committee which concluded that Major Graham Bell Murray of the Indian Army had been similarly poorly treated following a charge of drunkenness. The committee's report was not published, but the major was offered £500 from the Metropolitan Police Fund. Hard on the heels of the Major Murray affair came the case of Helene Adele, charged with insulting words and behaviour. Miss Adele had an arrangement with a man who washed taxicabs that she might sleep overnight in an empty cab. Two policemen on patrol, who came across Miss Adele alone in the cab, appear to have considered that she should share her favours with at least one of them. Her vociferous resistance resulted in the charge, and while she did not have either the class or the authority of an army officer, she was able to draw upon her youth – she was only twenty-one – and her attractiveness to win media and hence popular support. The case against her was dismissed and the shoddy police evidence resulted in the two constables being tried and found guilty of perjury and attempting to pervert the course of justice. They were each sentenced to eighteen months' hard labour and both they, and their sergeant, were dismissed from the force.[6] But the best known of the incidents of high-handed police behaviour, and the one that ultimately prompted the Royal Commission, was that surrounding Sir Leo Chiozza Money and Irene Savidge. In this instance it was class snobbery that initially got the police into trouble, but it was their subsequent behaviour that cast an unfavourable shadow over their interrogation practices and their behaviour towards women.

Sir Leo Chiozza Money was a noted financial expert, a friend of Lloyd George and a former Liberal MP. Irene Savidge was a factory girl. One evening in April 1928 they were discovered by two plain-clothes constables committing, in the contemporary parlance, 'an indecent act' in Hyde Park. When apprehended Sir Leo insisted that he should be allowed to go as he was not 'the usual riff raff'. The magistrates at the Great Marlborough Street Police Court appeared to agree; they dismissed the case and awarded costs against the police. Sir Leo, however, was not prepared to let matters lie and he urged his friends in Parliament to raise the matter. He wanted the arresting officers charged with perjury; the Home Secretary ordered the police to conduct an internal inquiry. Chief Inspector Alfred Collins and Detective Sergeant Clarke were directed to interview Miss Savidge; they were also directed to take Inspector Lilian Wyles with them when they drove to fetch the young woman from her place of work. According to Wyles, Collins seemed to resent having to take her along and, when Miss Savidge was settled in an interview room at Scotland Yard, he told Wyles that she could leave. The story rapidly spread that Collins had treated Savidge with a mixture of avuncular familiarity and hectoring, but Wyles doubted that Collins had shouted at Savidge as the walls of the rooms were very thin and loud bullying would have been heard. The story was aggravated by Savidge having to share a teaspoon with the officers when cups of tea were provided. Detective Sergeant Clarke, possibly with innuendo and certainly with a paternalistic foolishness, asked her: 'Will you spoon with me?' More questions were asked in Parliament, but this time about the treatment of Miss Savidge. Wyles was brought to Parliament for questioning. She confessed to feeling tempted, 'after years of insults, slights, [and] frozen faces', to tell her interrogators how police officers had treated her; but she recorded that she was 'ashamed of her unworthy thoughts' and consequently answered the questions simply and to the point. She was infuriated when Inspector Collins announced that he would dictate the statement that she was to sign for the formal inquiry that was to be held and she insisted on writing her own statement. The three members of the inquiry were split two to one in support of the police, but all three were unanimous in recommending that henceforth, whenever a male officer questioned a woman over 'intimate' matters, a policewoman or police matron should be present. On 1 August 1928 a Metropolitan Police Order was issued to this effect. Wyles used this as the opportunity for extending the role of her own women detective officers. Trained by Wyles herself, women in the Metropolitan Police increasingly took responsibility for taking the statements of women and children involved in cases of sexual assault.[7]

Ten years after the Metropolitan Police Order, when the women who worked in provincial forces met at their second annual conference, it was recorded that, where women officers existed, they were taking statements 'in the majority of cases' where women were the victims of indecency. Indeed, the Birmingham City Police had introduced such a practice before the London order. But, on the eve of the Second World War, women officers were still only to be found in 45 out of the 183 forces in England and Wales and a sixth of these women were not attested as constables. Most forces continued to employ police matrons for searching and supervising women. The matrons also sat in on interviews to ensure that no accusations could be levelled against male officers.[8]

The Royal Commission that followed the Savidge affair, and that ran concurrently with Goddard's trial, gave the police a clean bill of health and 'formed a very favourable opinion of the conduct, tone and efficiency' of the service. It found little support for the allegations that the police were 'generally more arbitrary and oppressive in their attitude towards the public' than they had been before the Great War. It recognized that, in an organization with 52,000 men across England and Wales, there was bound to be the occasional 'black sheep'. It was also impressed with the role undertaken by the 150 women serving in the police and considered that 'the time is ripe for a substantial increase in their numbers'. But the implementation of this recommendation was to be left to local discretion.[9] Given the tight restrictions on budgets and the continuing hostility of many chief constables, this meant that nothing happened. And it was not only chief constables that disliked the presence of women in the police.

Most men serving in the police regarded their women colleagues as inferior, even though a large number of women police were drawn from a higher social class than the average Bobby. Worse still, there were assumptions that women officers were denying their femininity by taking on the job. The first woman officer's uniform did not help matters; the wide-brimmed helmet, the tunic and the wide skirt were considered 'mannish'. Some women police were assumed to be lesbians, and Mary Allen, who continued to direct the Women's Auxiliary Service, as the rump of the WPS had become, fuelled such assumptions with her cropped hair, monocle, and personalized military-style uniform and riding boots. The gradual feminization of the uniform in the

1930s and 1940s helped to remove some of this prejudice, but by no means all of it.[10]

Police culture was vigorously heterosexual. Bobbies might snigger and joke about their 'mannish' female colleagues; they also had the power to arrest any men that they caught engaging in homosexual practices. It was not until the Sexual Offences Act of 1967 that homosexual acts among consenting adults were decriminalized. There were probably few homosexual officers among police men, but such as there were appear generally to have kept their preference a secret. Silence was the best way to avoid becoming the butt of jokes and, perhaps, worse. Harry Daley, the son of a Lowestoft trawlerman who had been lost at sea in the September Gale of 1911, had joined the Metropolitan Police in 1925. Daley was incautious about his sexuality, and while he managed to avoid arrest and dismissal, he was subjected to spiteful bullying by some of his workmates. 'Their malicious remarks,' he remembered, 'disguised as jokes, continued almost non-stop in my presence and presumably in my absence. A hole in the office wall was altered with pencil to represent an arsehole, and "love from 308", which was my number, was written underneath.'[11]

Hard Men and Crooked Men

Coming to terms with women officers was a novel matter for the Bobby, but many of the problems that he faced at the sharp end of policing in the inter-war period would have been recognizable to his predecessors. There were still working-class districts where the police were regarded at best with suspicion and where a weak or nervous constable was seen as fair game. In the summer of 1927, for example, a magistrate in London's East End condemned the practice of 'police baiting' that seemed to him to be 'a form of big game hunting. I hold no brief for the police,' he went on, 'but it is dirty and cowardly for a gang to set upon one or two men . . . The people of this district must be taught to find some amusement other than knocking the police about.'[12]

Such districts still possessed hard men who proudly established and maintained reputations based on their strength and ability to fight; and there were still tough Bobbies who were prepared to take them on and who were posted to beats where they might do so.

Marwood George Mullins was born in Bromley, Kent, in 1898. He gave up his trade as a carpenter and joiner in April 1920 and joined the Metropolitan Police. 'Ginger' Mullins, as he was known to his mates, served as a constable for twenty-six years in 'Y' Division and he acquired a formidable reputation in the rougher parts of Highbury and Islington. He broke up fights in the street, always placing his neatly folded tunic on the kerb with his helmet on top, while he did so; and no one dared to touch 'Mister Mullins's' uniform as it rested there.[13] Ted Lyscom, a young constable from the East Riding recently appointed to Highbury, was seconded to a beat in Holloway that was, fortunately, close by that of the legendary 'Ginger'. As one of his first evening patrols was drawing to a close, young Lyscom was asked by a publican to eject three troublesome drunks from his premises. 'I entered the pub with an air of authority,' Lyscom recalled.

I saw that the floor was littered with broken glass. They had delib erately broken three pint glasses when the licensee refused to serve any more liquor.

They were drunk and did not seem too afraid of my uniform. I asked them quietly to leave the pub and I was told to go and get stuffed. The three men advanced towards me and one had an empty bottle in his hand. I backed into the corner with my back to the wall and got a little scared. Never draw your truncheon except as a last resort[,] I was taught at Peel House. I was sure this was the correct time and I pulled out 'Charley Wood' from my truncheon pocket.

I felt a lot braver with it in my hand and waited for the next move. The three men stopped, they had not expected this, and the other occupants of the bar stood watching and did nothing. I wondered whose side they would be on when the fight started, but it never did start.

The bar door swung suddenly open and in the doorway was the tall and burly figure of PC 'Ginger' Mullins . . . He had been told by a passer-by that a PC had just gone into the pub to square up to some trouble.

My feeling of relief was enormous . . .

Mullins strolled over to me, told me to put my truncheon away, turned to the three men and said simply 'Out'. Two of them sidled towards the door and crept out quietly, but the third one, still brandishing his beer bottle was undecided. He seemed to have gained more courage from his beer than his two comrades. Ginger moved towards him, took the bottle firmly from his hand and again repeated 'Out'. The man slowly and obviously undecided backed away towards the door and eventually into the street. There was no sign of his two pals . . .

Ginger said to the man . . . 'Go home and don't come back here tonight'. The man replied with a torrent of abuse and bad language and made it clear that once we had gone, he would return to the pub. Ginger did not waste any more time. 'Drunk and Disorderly, you're nicked', he said and we propelled the man up Seven Sisters Road towards Holloway police station.[14]

In some instances it may have been simply because an officer was known that trouble was averted. Newly promoted to sergeant and posted to Notting Dale Police Station, West London, in the mid-1930s, another Yorkshireman, H.B. Green, prepared to break up a scuffle outside a notorious pub on a Saturday night.

A PC strolled up and said 'Leave it to me Sergeant.' The PC walked into the crowd, which soon started to drift away. The PC came back. 'I know them', he said. 'I know their names. You might have been in trouble being new round here.'[15]

Some of these tough policemen were probably far rougher than was necessary. PC Birtles, a fisherman from Grimsby who served in the Liverpool City Police between the wars, was remembered by former comrades as a terror to the local 'Bucks' and rather too enthusiastic in a fight. 'Birtles gets there before me and it was like a hurricane sweeping through. "Thwack, bash!" They're lying on the floor and there's blood everywhere, broken glass. He dropped a fellow at the bat of an eyelid.'[16] And it was not just in the capital and the big industrial cities and towns that policemen were tough. Arthur Pickering, who joined the Bedfordshire Police in 1932 after service in the Royal Artillery, prided himself on being 'rough and ready'. His sergeant in Dunstable chose him to deal with 'Shiner', a road builder working on the construction of the A5 trunk road who was notorious for getting into Saturday-night brawls. And in the villages where he subsequently served, 'Old Pick' generally preferred to deal with problems himself, using 'a wet cape, a sting inside the ear-hole', rather than taking people to court.[17]

One or two of the working-class hard men in the cities found employment as strong-arm men in bookmakers' gangs. The violence between such groups, immortalized in Graham Greene's *Brighton Rock*, sometimes spilled over into pubs, clubs and streets with the use of brass knuckles, razors, knives and guns. On 2 June 1921 Police Sergeant Joseph Dawson achieved national fame for arresting twenty-seven of these gangsters in a pub on Kingston Hill. Sergeant Dawson was one of the officers that, under the 1884 regulations, were authorized to carry a revolver and, as the toughs turned towards him, he claimed to have drawn his gun and warned: 'I shall shoot the first man who tries to escape.' The press preferred to report this as: 'The first man who moves I will shoot.'[18] A few years later Percy Sillitoe, Chief Constable of Sheffield, established a special squad recruited for their size and toughness, to take on the gangs run by the city's gambling rackets.[19] Gang violence caused an occasional outcry in the press, particularly when there was a major incident, but such incidents were largely confined to the early 1920s. Even so a significant police presence was maintained at race meetings to prevent trouble and keep order, and plenty of minor offending continued. As a young constable in Cambridgeshire at the end of the 1920s, Arthur Almond recalled being on duty at Newmarket Races where ' "dips" would leave dozens of rifled wallets in lavatories and other places of concealment'. He also recalled mounted policemen having money tucked in their boots to turn a blind eye to the various games in which tricksters fleeced naïve punters with various three-card tricks and other games of chance. There were also unsolicited tips of silver coins for the foot police given by successful book-makers as they stuffed rolls of notes in their pockets.[20] But the corruption problem between bookmakers and police was far more serious in working-class districts away from the race courses and where, as a result of the 1906 Street Betting Act, the placing of bets in the street was prohibited.

Even after the exposure and conviction of Sergeant Goddard, the Street Betting Act continued to foster corruption on a variety of levels and with varying degrees of seriousness. Fred Fancourt recalled how bets were taken in a factory area in Birmingham where he had his beat in the early 1930s.

It was well-known that recognised bookmakers had regular pitches to serve the local factory workers. These pitches were consid-ered 'safe' and the only way to deal with the problem [was] for the policeman to stand on the pitch himself . . . In the course of time arrangements were worked out between the bookmaker and the plain-clothes policeman. To give satisfaction to both sides the bookmaker stood up an individual complete with betting slips and money to be taken by the plain-clothes policeman. This would occur at each pitch at regular intervals. In this way the pitch would keep functioning with the least interruption. The 'stooge' would be charged, taken to court the next morning, plead guilty and be fined ten pounds. Whereupon the book-maker would pay up.

Unfortunately, as an innocent young constable deployed in plain clothes Fancourt knew nothing of these arrangements. He spotted a runner, vaulted a fence and arrested him. 'What took place between the [police] and the bookmaker, I never did find out.'[21] A Liverpool Bobby made an even worse error when he nabbed a man called Billy. ' "For God's sake, let me go." I said, "I can't let you go Billy, you know." He said, "I've got all the CID bets in here." "Oh," I said, "don't be daft." "I have, honestly...".' And he had.[22]

Harry Daley described the profits made from bookmakers by all ranks of police during his first posting to Hammersmith in 'F' Division. It was common for any constable on a beat with a bookmaker to receive half-a-crown a day from the bookie for looking the other way.

> Young constables were barred from beats where the bookmakers thrived; it was a matter of bribery and negotiation with the Inspector through his crafty clerk . . .
>
> Collection was all too easy. The bookmaker was usually down an alley or behind a pub. You approached slowly, gazing straight ahead with what you hoped looked like dignified indifference, and wiped up the half-crown from the ledge on which he had placed it before getting out of the way for you to pass. Brewers' draymen, window cleaners, painters and decorators, gossiping women, all suspended their activities for a moment or two to watch the familiar ceremony. It was a low performance. If you think I should have been ashamed of myself, the answer is – I was, but not quite enough. I wish they could have sent the money to me in a plain envelope as I knew they did to my Superintendent – but they did not and I was prepared to collect it.

At Christmas time the superintendent welcomed bookmakers and publicans when they turned up at the police station with hampers and parcels. Daley rarely gives dates, but it appears that the division was cleaned up, and that the superintendent and inspector were removed following the appointment of Sir Philip Game as Commissioner in 1935.[23]

Prostitution presented Bobbies with similar problems of enforcement and also with opportunities for corruption. Uniformed officers had to see a woman importuning a man in order to make an arrest and they also had to prove her inten-tion. Many of the men approached by women, however, did not wish to give evidence in court for fear of the stigma. Beat offi-cers appear often to have been prepared to let the women get on with things, just as long as they did not create any general annoy-ance or nuisance. On occasions there appears to have been an unofficial policy not to make arrests because the suggestion that prostitutes were active sullied a town's or a district's reputation. Nat Turner recalled such a policy in the prosperous seaside resort of Worthing at the end of the 1930s. He and his mates in the West Sussex Police were given 'advice' not to bring prostitutes in: 'if you take them to court, you are not going to get anywhere at all.' In some places a few Bobbies may have taken advantage of the women to satisfy their own desires, as the affair of Helene Adele appears to suggest. Harry Daley was annoyed by allega-tions that Bobbies took bribes from prostitutes and insisted that this had ceased with the exposure of Goddard. In all his time as station sergeant in Vine Street, just off Piccadilly, he insisted that 'no prostitute ever offered a bribe to me or anyone I know'.[24] But implications from later in the century suggest that a degree of corruption remained.

One Job, Many Tasks

There continued to be occasional outbreaks of industrial unrest that led police officers into confrontations with strikers. The most notable of these during the inter-war period was the general strike of 1926. While this was largely a humiliation for the Labour move-ment and the Trades Union Congress, it served to enhance the image of the police among the conservative, respectable classes.

The latter played up the stories of football matches between police and strikers and forgot any less sporting incidents.

Police were also called upon to supervise marches by the unemployed and political demonstrations as groups from the left and the right in Britain aped, with less lethal results, the Communist and Fascist parties of Continental Europe. There were many complaints of police partiality during these demonstrations. Where the police were less than sympathetic to Jewish victims of Sir Oswald Mosley's British Union of Fascists they were probably reflecting the relatively widespread prejudice towards Jews in inter-war Britain. Harry Daley recalled a few young constables in Vine Street and Hammersmith strutting around in black shirts when off-duty and distributing anti-Jewish literature. Officers in Vine Street frequented a neighbouring coffee house run by an elderly Jewish couple but when, during the Blitz, Daley suggested that the terrified couple be permitted to share the police air-raid shelter, a large number of men objected. H.B. Green confessed to being impressed by Mosley, adding: 'It is much easier to like a man who is carrying a Union Jack, who is smart and clean with close-cropped hair, than a man who has shouted an obscene insult at you and spat in your face.' But his attitude changed following Blackshirt violence at their Olympia rally in 1934.[25]

Many Bobbies were suspicious of left-wing orators; when it came to violent clashes they usually found themselves fighting the political left as opposed to the political right. Police officers could be very rough in these confrontations, but their behaviour was not necessarily an indication of political sentiments. Bobbies were often annoyed at losing a day's leave, with no overtime pay or time off in lieu, to police a political demonstration. Violence may have been the result of a mixture of relief and exhilaration when, after a period of standing in a line and taking abuse and occasional missiles, they were directed to clear the ground. It could also be the result of the mixture of fear and adrenalin that flowed in confrontations. Ted Lyscom and two other constables found themselves cut off from other police during the battle of Cable

Street in November 1936 when Mosley's attempt to march the BUF through the East End was stopped by angry crowds. The eldest of the three constables, who had served in the East End for many years, took command:

> We would attack the fifty and fight our way out. I had drawn my truncheon a few times but never actually used it on a human being . . . The older PC had other ideas, 'use your rolled cape' he said. Our police capes were rolled like an umbrella, fastened with a small leather strap, and hung from our belts. They were about three feet long when rolled, and weighed about three pounds . . . The East End copper gave us a demonstration, he charged the crowd, waving his cape and lunging forward. We followed suit and anybody getting in the way was sent flying. The crowd turned and ran and we ran after them . . .[26]

But the rank-and-file Bobbies also often showed sympathy towards hunger marchers and the unemployed. 'My colleagues and I at least had jobs,' recalled H.B. Green when describing the policing of hunger marchers and the way in which police and marchers struck up conversations as they walked side-by-side. Green, a working-class lad brought up by his mother in Huddersfield after his father had died from TB, had joined the Metropolitan Police in 1930. He disliked the order to take the sticks and poles from the marchers' banners. 'I was convinced, as I am sure were my colleagues, that there was not and never had been any threat of violence.'[27]

Most policemen were, like Green, still largely recruited from the working class. Harry Daley, as mentioned earlier, came from a Lowestoft fishing family; he joined the police because he was big, too old for the Royal Navy and could not think of anything else. Fred Fancourt, born in Stamford in Lincolnshire, left school at fourteen and spent the next six years in the workshops of his father's cousin, a motor engineer. He turned to the police when he found himself out of work. Arthur Pickering came from a police family;

his father and both of his grandfathers had served in the Bedfordshire Police. John Rutherfoord was rather different in origin. He went to a minor public school and had dreams of Sandhurst or university until the economic depression hit his family and forced him into an insurance office; for him the police was an opportunity to get out of a dull, miserable office.

Fancourt and Rutherfoord both joined the Birmingham City Police. They shared memories of training under the tyrannical regime of a ferocious inspector named McWalter. They also recalled learning by rote from the *Police Law*, which was used across England and Wales for a quarter of a century, and which had been written by C.C.H. Moriarty, the deputy Chief Constable, and later Chief Constable of Birmingham. Fancourt had to spend his first year in digs, where he even had to share a bed with another recruit. In London, Green and his mate Bert Jarvis did not have to share a bed, but their first landlady made it clear that they were not expected in the house other than for the appointed meals. When their second landlady and her teenage daughter started coming into their room 'to indulge in a bit of playfulness', alarm bells began to ring and the two young Bobbies were relieved to be moved to the section house. Rutherfoord was luckier; he joined in 1934, five years after Fancourt, and was posted to a brand-new section house.

After a few years, and after having their prospective wives vetted by their superiors, both Fancourt and Rutherfoord got married and proceeded, very gradually, to rise through the ranks. Much to the continuing annoyance of the rank and file, however, the post of chief constable, especially in the county forces, was still inclined to go to a former army officer, sometimes with little or no police experience. Attitudes to promotion in London were worsened in 1934 by the scheme of the Commissioner, Lord Trenchard, to establish a Police College at which potential senior officers might be trained and groomed for fast-track promotion. A high percentage of the men selected for the course at the college, set up in the old premises of the London Flying Club at Hendon, were already serving in the Metropolitan Police; but this did not silence the critics and when the scheme was ended in 1939 there were few mourners. Most of the Hendon men did well and rose to senior positions in both London and the provinces. Even thirty years after the college opened, its legacy within the service was striking. Of the 197 men who had attended the courses between 1934 and 1939, sixty-nine were still serving in 1966: they held the top six posts in the Metropolitan Police, twenty-five others were provincial chief constables, and five held posts in HM Inspectorate of Constabulary, including the chief inspector, Eric St Johnston, who had previously commanded in Oxfordshire, County Durham and Lancashire.[28] But Trenchard's young gentlemen were never popular with the aggressively artisan spirit of the rank and file, as is evidenced by a poem published in *Police Review* in 1936.

> Now they're shouting for recruits
> To wear regulation boots,
> To patrol the dirty streets on town beats
> So that the Hendon 'nobs' can get the 'cushy' jobs.
> And snore till ten in the morning.[29]

In the public imagination an aura of romance surrounded the detective even though, in popular literature at least, the archetype of the police detective was commonly the dogged but uninspired Inspector Lestrade of the Sherlock Holmes stories. In the classic country-house murder mysteries of the inter-war period the ordinary police detective remained a dullard compared with the dazzling brilliance of an Hercule Poirot, a Lord Peter Wimsey or a Miss Marple, and he never matched the derring-do of the boy's magazine hero, Sexton Blake. Some Bobbies preferred CID work, not least because of the freedom that it gave them from the monotony of the beat. But neither Fancourt nor Rutherfoord enjoyed it. The former spent time in plain clothes in the centre of the city working the 'Jewellers' Patrol' with a colleague. This duty required the carrying of a loaded pistol in his pocket in case of a raid, though he confessed to never having received any instruction about how to use the gun or under what circumstances he might do so. Fancourt was much happier when he was able to use the skills that he had learned in the motor workshop, driving and tinkering with various police vehicles and, eventually, training others to do so.

While working in the Birmingham traffic department enabled Fancourt to indulge his passion for vehicles, traffic duty involved a range of activities. A glance through any court records pre-dating the creation of the police institution reveals constables, and others, prosecuting individuals for driving dangerously and causing accidents; a cart or carriage poorly handled or with, for example, a faulty wheel or defective harness, could be as lethal as any vehicle powered by an internal combustion engine. Police preoccupation with traffic in Victorian London has already been mentioned; and half a century before Fancourt joined it, the Birmingham Police found itself having to take men off night-time beats to deal with daytime traffic problems.[30] Bottlenecks and busy cross-roads led to the burdensome task of point duty. For wearying hours constables stood at fixed points in towns and cities giving clear hand and arm signals that temporarily halted traffic in one direction and enabled that moving in another to pass. The hours of holding arms up and out straight turned a man's upper limbs into aching lead weights, often aggravated by a hot sun, by freezing temperatures, or by the effects of steady rain on a uniform.

The advent of motor vehicles meant dangers from new rates of speed on the roads. In the early 1930s Parliament dithered about whether a speed limit was enforceable, let alone desirable; and when limits were imposed, and were required to be enforced by the police, the opportunities for friction and confrontation between the police constable and the respectable member of society mushroomed.[31]

While there were concerns about police relations with the general public during the inter-war period and while friction and police high-handedness made good copy for the press, it would be quite wrong to characterize this as either the only form that these relations took or, indeed, as the norm. Harry Daley and H.B. Green described London police stations in the inter-war years as often resembling a mixture of citizen's advice bureau and community centre. Green was hoodwinked by a tearful young woman who came to his station claiming to be a nurse and saying that she needed to get to Brighton to see her sick mother. He organized the usual cup of tea and a collection for her fare. 'Unfortunately, on looking through Police Informations afterwards, I saw that a nurse answering perfectly the description of my nurse was wanted under a warrant for obtaining money in the same way.' On a more cheerful note, he recalled his station being used as a first aid post for a child with convulsions and also for organizing the delivery of a baby.[32] Arthur Almond had similar memories from his service as a beat constable in Portsmouth.

> Everyone in trouble, especially in the slum areas, sought us out
> . . . There's hardly a man in the force of those days who hasn't
> been called in as a midwife a few times in his career! And quite
> a few mothers gave their boys the same Christian name as the
> copper who came to her aid.[33]

But the principal task of the uniformed Bobby of the inter-war years remained that of patrolling a carefully designated beat.

The Inter-War Beat

The Bobby still plodded his beat on foot, looking out for the extraordinary and suspicious but dealing more often with the usual and the mundane. The rigidity of the Victorian period was relaxed in many forces and here the constable was allowed to use his discretion and initiative in precisely how he patrolled his beat. This appears to have been popular with the men and many considered it to be more effective in preventing and detecting crime. The Bobby still was not allowed to gossip with colleagues on neighbouring beats or carrying out other duties, but it was expected that he would get to know the locals and pick up general information from them. In some areas the discipline might be rigorously enforced, while in others it was relatively easygoing.

As a young metropolitan constable in the early 1930s, Arthur Battle had occasion to visit the police station at Cheshunt, on the northern fringe of the Metropolitan Police district. The station was 'very old . . . and primitive in every way'. The station sergeant lived there, kept ferrets and had a garden well-stocked with fruit and vegetables. But the sight that really struck Battle was the night relief as they prepared to set off on their semi-rural beats carrying large, heavy sticks and attended by dogs. Neither sticks nor dogs were permitted in Metropolitan Police orders.

> Each man wore the skirts of his greatcoat pinned away from his knees, like the old-style French infantryman . . . The men were older types with heavy moustaches, and they looked very impressive as they slowly cycled or walked away from the station, with their dogs trotting easily behind, or walking close to heel.[34]

The development of police boxes, with direct telephone links to police stations, meant that the patrolling constable in the larger urban forces became less isolated from his commanders. The boxes also provided a shelter, though not necessarily a warm one, where a man might snatch a sit down and a bite to eat in the middle of the night. 'I was in a box . . . having my supper one night about two o'clock in the morning,' recalled Clifford Jeeves of the Bedford Borough Force, 'and somebody knocked on the door and this woman says: "I'm going to have a baby." Yes, cor, oh dear.' But the beat, especially at night, was generally an uneventful, quiet and often lonely manner of earning a living. In the early silent hours of darkness the streets belonged to the beat officer. To quote Jeeves again:

> I mean, if you was on nights . . . as soon as the cinemas closed at half past ten, we had the streets to ourselves and not a soul

about other than railwaymen, postmen, bakers in the early morning going to work. If you stood at the end of the street, you'd see someone go across the road and you would say to yourself that's so-and-so, and so-and-so . . .

And if the person was unknown, the constable would be after them. Jeeves received a commendation for stopping two such strangers one night and finding the proceeds of a robbery on them. What made the catch particularly sweet was that the men were also wanted by the Metropolitan Police.[35]

Sometimes the younger constables liked to extend the horseplay of the section house on to the beat, especially at night-time, and to play tricks on each other. Bottles might be thrown, or otherwise engineered to break immediately behind a man on patrol. Catapults were fired and black thread arranged tightly to knock off a helmet.[36] There were good beats where, passing a bakery, for example, a man might get a fresh, still-warm sandwich; and there were grim ones, rows and rows of factories or warehouses where every door had to be checked and where few mates were within calling or larking distance. The expansion of suburbs and the static police numbers in the inter-war years meant that the longer, lonelier beat became more and more common.

Arthur Almond liked number 12 beat that covered both sides of Commercial Road in the centre of Portsmouth. In the mornings it rumbled with trams and 'the mighty rush of Dockyard "mateys" on their bikes'. Tobacco and newspaper shops and kiosks opened early, and the newsboys were at strategic points shouting their wares. He could nip into the Guildhall at 7.00 a.m. for breakfast – 'a slice of liver – a few kidneys – a haddock or something similar ... (and it never cost over 6d)'. There were serious traffic problems with the market on Tuesday, Thursday and Saturday mornings, especially if people tried to park cars. The beat was equally busy in the afternoon and evening. When the pubs and theatres emptied there might be trouble, and when an individual tried to leave a restaurant without paying. There were occasional petty thefts: 'sailors would sometimes take glasses and mugs from pubs – Indian pedlars [might have] an item pinched from their packs.' There were prostitutes, drunks and the occasional fight. The Naval Patrols often left the civilian police to get on with it, but on number 12 beat help was always near at hand from the men on numbers 3, 4 and 5 and big men were always chosen for the evening relief. The chief constable 'believed in putting the men with the finest physique where the hooligans could see them! They were the chaps whose appearance on the scene of a brawl was a signal for beating the retreat by the unruly.'

For several years Harry Daley patrolled a beat in Hammersmith where he met the same, sometimes peculiar but quite harmless folk.

I liked the solitary lady who kept pets and had their skins turned into fur coats when they died . . . Another strangely dressed solitary lady greeted me with a smile and stopped to gossip. I was always proud that these people stopped with such confidence in our friendliness . . . I liked the young man who thought he was a number eleven bus . . . Twice a day he shuffled along the regular number eleven route, put on his brakes and changed his gears, issued tickets and stopped at the proper stops . . . Then there was Lousy Henry and the man who enjoyed shitting himself, even in cold weather.[37]

The cold weather, as well as hot sunshine and rain may not have bothered Lousy Henry, but it affected the patrolling Bobby. Fred Fancourt, like many others, remembered the rain, what it did to his boots – 'they will only stand so much wet, and will eventually become saturated' – and his uniform. 'The cape . . . was made of very close and heavy velour material . . . [It] used to come to a level just above the knees and for a time the material would absorb the wet. But there comes a point when the wet begins to just run off on to the knees, legs and feet.' The problems of getting dry if the rain persisted over a period of days were enormous, especially if a man was quartered in digs with a family where only the kitchen fire was available for drying clothes.[38]

In the smaller towns and in the countryside the pattern of beat policing also remained largely unchanged from the system that had developed during the Victorian period. The most significant difference was that, by the inter-war years, bicycles were generally permitted for the longer beats and for running messages when there was no telephone. The bicycle's handlebars provided a place to hang a bag and, according to 'Old Pick', no self-respecting PC went out without a bag in which he might collect some food from the local farmer. There was little serious crime in the countryside and policing was often concerned with sorting out domestic disputes. But there were also specific rural tasks, notably keeping an eye out for animal diseases such as foot and mouth, swine fever and, worst of all, anthrax. In cases of anthrax it fell to the local Bobby to have to destroy the carcasses of the infected animals. Anthrax, in Arthur Pickering's recollection, 'always seemed to pick real good beasts' and that meant digging a very large pit and using 'about a ton of coal'. Shortly before the outbreak of the Second World War PC Nat Turner and a colleague were ordered to go to a farm in West Sussex where thirty-two cattle had been destroyed and to organize the digging of a pit and the burning.[39]

For Arthur Almond, a bright, reasonably well-educated young man from a village a dozen miles north of Cambridge, serving in a rural force seemed like a dead end. He joined the Cambridgeshire Police in September 1928, a couple of months after his twentieth birthday. After ten weeks' training, for which he was sent to Birmingham and the fearsome regime of Inspector McWalter, he was sent to the village of Bourn – 'a pokey little village and lonely'. Almost immediately he exchanged postings with the village policeman of Great Shelton who was rumoured to have taken rather too much interest in the 'blue eyes and fair hair' of his landlady. Almond did not receive his uniform and equipment for two to three weeks and, particularly in comparison with the bustle of Birmingham, he soon found the Cambridgeshire force to be 'antique'. It had no detectives, no cars, no phone, at least for his posting, and showed little interest in the men's welfare. Almond describes some of the 'characters' in his village: his elderly 'maiden lady' landlady, for example, and the village drunk, 'who never gave any more trouble than having to be carried home'. There was also Dick Marsh, the George V's racehorse trainer, who lined up his family and bowed as the royal train passed en route for Sandringham; the train allegedly slowed and the King and Queen acknowledged the bows with a wave. Almond's rural patch also had a vestige of a former age in a parish constable, a mine of anecdotes, who was also the village blacksmith. But while there was the occasional crime to excite his interest, Almond found the general ignorance of his immediate superiors annoying, and feared that there was little chance of getting on in the service if he stayed where he was. In August 1930, after less than two years in Cambridgeshire, he transferred to the City of Portsmouth.[40]

Portsmouth was not Birmingham, but it was a lively and ancient urban centre that had been elevated to city status a few years earlier, in 1925. It had a population of around 300,000, many of whom worked in the Naval Dockyard. There was a military garrison and an enormous, shifting presence of Royal Navy personnel that guaranteed a lively night-life as well as the male and female prostitution that the army and navy generated. The Portsmouth Police consisted of just over 300 men, enough to make it the sixteenth-largest urban force in England and Wales, and bigger than some county forces. It was commanded by an enthusiastic Welshman, Thomas Davies, who had joined the Carmarthen Police in his late teens in 1890, had spent five years in the Hove Police and finally had taken over as Chief Constable in Portsmouth in 1907. Davies was keen to recruit men that were not only physically fit but also well educated. He would, according to Almond, periodically 'ask recruits to spell "parallelogram", "unparalleled" and so on'. Almond thrived in his new environment; he rose to the rank of superintendent and stayed with the Portsmouth force until his retirement in 1959.

But if, during the inter-war years, the beat patrol remained the principal modus operandi of the Bobby, the system, nevertheless, faced a succession of new and major challenges. A freeze on police expenditure during the Depression meant that police numbers could not be increased, while the enormous spread of newly built suburbs greatly extended policemen's beats. And there was that steady growth in the ownership of motor cars, with the resulting conflict between the police and the respectable classes. The problems of expanding suburbs and motor-vehicle ownership were to continue, but their progress was neither steady nor linear and both were to be significantly checked in 1939 by the advent of a new war.

— CHAPTER 9 —

A New War, a New World, 1939–1970

IN 1939 THE police were much better prepared for war than they had been in 1914. Conventional wisdom has it that Britain sought to appease Hitler rather than prepare for war during the 1930s. In 1933, however, a standing committee had been established to consider the role of the police in wartime; its *Police War Instructions* had begun to be circulated in sections from September 1935 and a consolidated set was issued two weeks before the outbreak. Air Raid Precaution training began towards the end of the thirties and police officers were promoted and seconded from their usual duties to take charge of local ARP units. Recognizing the problems that might result from the sudden recall of military reservists from the police, it was decided that no such recall was to occur until three months after the outbreak of hostilities. In addition to the special constables, police reserves had been established, initially from former officers who agreed to come back into service in the eventuality of war. Under pressure from the National Council for Women the Home Office finally agreed in August 1939 to setting up the Women's Auxiliary Police Corps. Young officers, like Ernie Emsley, were only permitted to volunteer for military service from 1941, at the same time that some of the military reservists called up in 1939 were brought back from the battle fronts to pick up their policing careers on the home front. Regular police numbers fell during the war, from 57,000 in 1940 to 43,000 four years later. War reserves, Specials and more women officers helped fill the gaps, but the burdens and stresses on both men and women were severe.

Going to War

Prime Minister Neville Chamberlain's broadcast on Sunday, 3 September 1939, announcing that Britain was once again at war with Germany, was one of those salient events that stuck in people's minds. Many years afterwards people could recall precisely what they were doing when they heard it, or when they heard about it. Arthur Battle had just completed ten years' service in the Metropolitan Police that month. He had been one of the first traffic policemen in the city, first riding a motorcycle and then driving a wireless car. He was stationed in a country district of 'Z' Division at the extreme south-east edge of the Metropolitan Police District.

> I was lying on my back under my old 1928 Austin Seven, busily using the grease gun. I had left the kitchen door open, as we had been told that Mr Chamberlain was to broadcast to the nation at 11 a.m. I think that every radio in the country was switched on.

Hearing the news of war, Battle threw on his uniform, seized his push-bike and hurried to his police station. As he did so the air raid siren sounded. At the station he was one of several officers given a cardboard placard to hang round his neck with the words: 'Air Raid Warning. Take Cover'. Thus attired, the men were instructed to travel the district and broadcast the warning. They dutifully set off to find that everyone had already taken cover. They had not gone far when the 'All Clear' sounded and, feeling rather sheepish, they all returned to the station.[1]

PC Horace Rogers was some sixty miles north of Battle. His experience was very different, but no less vivid. Rogers was born and bred in Wolverhampton, the son of a railwayman and the nephew of a Coventry policeman. As a youth he had thought of being a policeman but, since the Wolverhampton Police only recruited locals if they had been away from the town for three years, he had enlisted in the Grenadier Guards. Towards the end of his three years' army service he had applied to a number of police forces and he was on the waiting lists for vacancies on the Isle of Wight, in Staffordshire and in Surrey. In December 1929, as his battalion prepared for embarkation to Egypt, he and five other guardsmen were invited to sit an examination for the Bedfordshire Police. Three of the six, including Rogers, were successful and, after ten weeks' training in the tough, disciplined environment maintained by Inspector McWalter in Birmingham, Rogers was posted to a rural beat centred on the village of Riscly in north Bedfordshire. Unlike Arthur Almond, he enjoyed serving in a predominantly rural force; he met his wife while performing the mundane duty of checking the pigs and Movement of Animals Register kept by her father, a local farmer. It did not worry Rogers that, when he joined, there was no CID in Bedfordshire. But he was no stick-in-the-mud; he was bright and he seized the opportunities that came his way. He accepted the Chief Constable's idea that the role of detective was the duty of every uniformed man. When the chance was offered, Rogers went to London and obtained the Metropolitan Criminal Investigation Certificate. His aptitude and abilities were quickly recognized and, towards the end of his third year in Bedfordshire, he was marked for promotion and transferred to the force headquarters in the Shire Hall in Bedford. On the morning war was declared Constable Rogers was in the Shire Hall giving a lecture on first aid to members of the special constabulary. His lecture was interrupted and everyone was called through to the general office to hear Chamberlain's broadcast. When the Prime Minister's message ended the Specials were dismissed and sent home, but it was clear that their services would soon be required just as they had been a generation earlier.[2]

Horace Rogers was no longer a reservist, but many other officers were. Nat Turner in West Sussex and Arthur Pickering in

Bedfordshire were both recalled to the colours at the end of the year. Since their police houses were in villages, when they went back into khaki, their wives and children had to move so that another officer could be stationed in their house-cum-police station. Being moved from one police house to another was nothing new and, while these houses were expected to be kept by an officer's wife in a high state of cleanliness and tidiness, the likelihood of a new posting seems sometimes to have discouraged officers and their families from spending money on improvements to what was often shabby accommodation. Station moves were something that men and their wives had to accept as a part of the job, but it did not ease the upset or the disruption for Turner's and Pickering's families, especially when war had already torn the men from their families.

Pickering was with an artillery unit on the south coast when his wife's telegram arrived telling him that she was having to move and that the force had found her somewhere else with a similar rent; his commanding officer immediately gave him compassionate leave to return home to help. He caught the train from the coast to London Bridge; he caught another train to Luton but had to walk the last twelve miles to the police house in the village of Pulloxhill where his wife was packing. Pickering was overwhelmed by the generosity of the neighbours that he had policed in his rough and ready fashion. Two of the village 'terrors' had worked his allotment in the few weeks that he had been away from the community; wood had been delivered for the fire and, when the order had come to quit the house, it seemed that everyone in the village rallied round to help his wife. Pickering took the villagers down to the pub to thank them, and was told off by a local police sergeant for not having reported to the police station immediately on his return – 'and the man who told me off, I hate to say it, but he was one of the best men that ever wore a police uniform'.[3]

Nat Turner was one of the reservists ordered back to the police in 1941, just as younger officers were permitted to volunteer. 'Old Pick' soldiered on and, following D Day, he fought his way across northern Europe rising to the rank of Battery Sergeant Major and winning the Belgian Croix de Guerre.

Bobby at War

The new international conflict revived many of the problems and dangers faced by the police during the First World War. The German bombing campaign against London in 1917 and 1918 had prompted Stanley Baldwin's gloomy prediction that 'the bomber will always get through'. Indeed, bombers did get through. The police and the ARP wardens had to enforce the blackout regulations so that no light helped night-time bombers searching for targets. The blackout gave the police other problems. Thieves took advantage of streets generally darker than many had been for over a hundred years. And even though petrol was rationed and the driving of motor vehicles restricted, vehicles without lights in dark streets meant accidents.

Bombers might not get through with the regularity and destructive effectiveness that had been feared, but this was of little consolation to their victims and to those police officers either who lived in the towns and cities affected, or who were deployed to provide aid in those places. Constable 'Jock' Bell was sent to a bombing incident in Farraday Street, Hull, only to find that it was his own house that had been hit and, worse still, that his wife had been killed. PC Fred Greenstreet, serving in south London, had a similar heart-stopping, agonizing experience in January 1943. An FW190 fighter bomber dropped a bomb that hit Sandhurst Road School in Catford during the lunch hour. Greenstreet had two children at the school; he rushed to the scene with other emergency services to find that his eldest son was among the forty or so children and teachers that had been killed. Further to the west a landmine hit a shelter in Wandsworth killing twenty-seven women and children, and Harry Daley found himself 'holding a handbag, heavy with congealed blood, containing a sailor's address and a note – "If anything happen to me let my son no" [sic].'[4]

As in the previous conflict, there were many more wartime regulations to enforce than simply those relating to the blackout. Chief Inspector Cecil Hewitt of the City of London Police, who wrote a weekly column in the *Police Review* under the pen-name C.H. Rolph, recalled how he found himself focusing invariably on the new orders and regulations for his column.

> [There were] lighting offences and the use of hand torches in the black-out; the smuggling of currency; the use of identity cards; the control of noise; the rationing of petrol, clothing and food; 'curfew' orders in danger zones; looting at bombed premises; alarmist rumour-mongering; road vehicles left unattended (and thus available for German parachute troops); the internment of aliens; the control of maps; the compulsory carrying of gas masks; the presumption of death after air raids; and the huge assortment of officially approved windscreen labels which led an Oxford lady to equip her car with one that said: 'Just Me'.[5]

The enforcement of such regulations often seemed pettifogging and officious to those caught. Some men puffed up with their own importance and with new authority could not resist using it. Arthur Battle recalled confrontations between the Home Guard and the police over showing identity cards. On one occasion a police car from his Division was stopped at bayonet point by members of the Home Guard who demanded to see the identity cards of the police inside. The police refused. The guards detained them. A furious police inspector, known to Battle and his mates as 'Bear's Breath', descended on the guards and demanded to see their identity cards.[6]

Probably, on occasions, some police officers succumbed to the temptation of using wartime regulations to pick on a social superior or someone who had annoyed them. Charles Hanslow admitted to being vindictive in prosecuting a peer of the realm for having a light showing in his rooms at Claridge's Hotel. 'It was a subconscious attitude of revenge for the generally contemptuous attitude to policemen before the war.' A young constable who confronted the member of a European royal family exiled to London during the Nazi occupation of his country was less fortunate. He was 'invited' to join the army.[7]

Police were involved in the pursuit of men who were absent without leave from their units, or who had avoided conscription or deserted. For the families of such men the police could seem unfeeling and oppressive. H.B. Green recalled having to haul men out of lofts, from under beds and even, on one occasion, from up a chimney. One woman from the family of a man apprehended taught her grandchild to abuse Green with 'Fuck the policeman!' Harry Daley described the problems of pursuing refractory conscripts among the Romany community that had settled in Wandsworth.

> As we knocked on the front door we pictured the scene at the back; the leaping over walls, climbing through windows and hiding under other people's beds. The women at the front, employing delaying tactics, were always helpful. 'Do you mean the tall boy, sir, with dark eyes and curly hair?' Yes, we did indeed, for that was the description of every single one of them. 'Try number seventeen, sir.' There were no numbers on the doors, no doors in some cases.

Daley was well aware of the often complex and varied motives for desertion that affected men who would never normally have found themselves being sought by the police, and of the pain felt by families who would never normally have lied to them. These were matters that engendered embarrassment and shame all round.[8]

There were also problems with the men that were with the armed forces, notably when they spilled out from their camps looking for beer, women and song, or when they went on leave and found that things at home were not as they wished. Such problems were complicated by the vast number of service personnel from overseas who, when they had a few drinks inside them, were sometimes inclined to fight with those of another national group over women or any other of a variety of pretexts. But difficulties were not always the results of fights. Nat Turner, a big imposing man himself as befitted a former Grenadier Guardsman, recalled having to subdue a drunken Native American serving with the Canadian Army, who was even bigger. 'He must have been about six feet eight, he certainly was a lot taller than me, and big.' The soldier, for fun, was rearranging some front gardens in Worthing; the iron railings had been taken for the war effort and the soldier had decided to wrench out the brick pillars that had supported them. It took Turner, two other constables and two civilians to overpower the man and take him to the police station. The Canadian Army collected him from the police cells and, subsequently, solved the potential for future problems with the soldier by putting him in the Military Police.

There could be tense moments following the arrest of servicemen as the police waited for the Military Police to arrive. During this time it was not unknown for the arrested men's comrades to consider a rescue. Charles Hanslow recalled about 200 Canadians, several of whom had armed themselves with tools from a nearby road excavation, attempting to rescue fellow soldiers being held in West End Central. Fortunately the cavalry, in the shape of Canadian Military Police, arrived in the nick of time.[9] The Military Police of the different armed forces in the country were uniformly remembered by wartime Bobbies as rough and very free with their batons. But Hanslow also recalled that the headquarters of the US Military Police in Mayfair 'overflowed with coffee and doughnuts, etc, etc, which fact attracted many half starved policemen – like me!'[10]

Large military camps, and large numbers of over-paid, over-sexed and over-here Americans, not to mention Canadians and various European servicemen with romantic names and exotic accents, attracted young women looking for fun as well as women prepared to trade in sexual favours. They also attracted gay men. The latter did not take up much police time; sexual activity between consenting males remained a criminal offence, but a homosexual beaten and robbed by what he thought would be a consenting military partner was not going to complain to the police. The perceived need to protect young women from being led astray, however, was as great as it had been in the previous war. This meant increased work for women police officers and an increase in their numbers, though some chief constables and their watch committees or standing joint committees remained reluctant to employ women and fretted about the corrupting effects on them of exposure to vice. In many instances the new women police found themselves restricted to clerical and administrative tasks, and still resented for intruding into a man's world. As one chief constable put it to another in September 1940: 'We all have quite enough on hand dealing with the Huns without being pestered by females.'[11]

Amidst the bombing, the thousands of servicemen of different nationalities, and the need to enforce wartime regulations, some vestiges of traditional policing continued. Bill Biggs recalled patrolling one night in south London with another constable, Bill Hetherington.

> He and I were walking down the Portman Road, South Norwood . . . and we passed two fellas with something under their arms. Bill, of course, would have let them go by, but I just said: 'Just a minute fellas. What have you got there?' And they had broken into Boots the Chemist at Croydon that had been damaged by a bomb. Climbed up because the windows were covered with plywood and cardboard . . . and stolen scent and stuff, and they were working the pubs . . . So that was a little arrest that Bill and I had that evening. That's the sort of thing you got [in wartime] but there were no smash and grabs or anything because cars were off the road.[12]

The mundane nature of much wartime policing can be glimpsed from a sample of the incidents recorded in the Occurrence Book of Wellington Arch Police Station.[13] The station, one of the smallest in central London, was situated at Hyde Park Corner. In August 1943 there were twenty-four days when all that the station sergeant had to do was record the date, and on the fifteenth of the month the only entry referred to adjusting the clocks in the general office and the communications room. More seriously, there were three incidents of robbery with violence. A man staying at the Park Lane Hotel intervened when he thought he saw two American soldiers attacking a young woman. When this Good Samaritan came to, he found his wallet, driving licence, spectacles and upper set of false, gold-mounted teeth missing. Another man who had enjoyed a big win at the greyhound track was attacked as he left a hotel where he had been celebrating with friends. He lost his wallet with £100 in it. An American soldier was attacked, but lost only his cap and coat. A nurse reported that, while she was lying on the grass in Green Park with another American soldier, her handbag and purse were stolen. On 4 August a man had come into the station saying that he needed to sit down as he felt unwell. He did not want to go to hospital; he claimed that he was suffering from shell-shock. His wife was contacted to fetch him home. A few days later a War Reserve officer working out of the station was called to deal with a man suffering an epileptic fit on the top deck of a bus. A merchant seaman, who confessed to having 'a few drinks', fell over on the pavement, injured his arm, and had to be helped to St George's Hospital. On 11 August a hunt was made for the hoaxer who used the telephone in Hyde Park Corner tube station to call out the fire brigade to the hospital.

The days when there was nothing to write in the Occurrence Book did not mean that officers were not busy patrolling the streets, moving on street sellers and tricksters, directing traffic, resolving minor problems and enforcing wartime restrictions. During the peak of the Blitz, officers appear to have struggled to keep going regardless of their tiredness. But the sickness records for the Metropolitan Police suggest that, as the war continued, physical and mental exhaustion, made worse by declining numbers, was beginning to take its toll. The peak was reached as the conflict ended (see Table 3).

Table 3: Days lost through sickness in the
Metropolitan Police, 1938-1947

Year	Number of days	Percentage rate of sickness
1938	181,326	2.66
1939	183,478	2.71
1940	215,228	3.25
1941	204,732	3.27
1942	192,931	3.32
1943	219,603	4 15
1944	244,667	5.17
1945	345,671	7.52
1946	291,335	6.14
1947	252,608	4.85

(Source: *Report of the Commissioner of Police for the Metropolis for the year 1948*)

Winning the Peace

The war fought by the Battles and Rogers at home and the Pickerings
and Turners abroad ended in victory for their side, but the country
to which the servicemen returned had changed greatly. The centres
and often the suburbs of the great cities were to be littered with
bombsites for years. The rubble was cleared and any unsafe shells
of buildings were demolished; grass and weeds sprouted on the
scarred earth and skeletal remains, but reconstruction took time and
money. The bleak bombsites were the visible manifestation of deeper
injuries. The cost of two world wars had wrecked the British
economy and left a substantial debt. There may have been full
employment at the end of the Second World War, but paying for
the war meant government-imposed austerity, and pay for the
unskilled and semi-skilled working in the public sector was poor.
The police largely remained a semi-skilled, working-class job and,

given the low remuneration throughout the late 1940s and 1950s, there were always vacancies.

Policing remained a tough job. Men continued to be subjected to fierce discipline and the principal task continued to be the often monotonous beat patrol. The toughness helped shape the men's consciousness and the pride that many of them felt in their job. Their uniform was a symbol of this pride and when, from 1948, the high-collared tunic began to be replaced by an open-neck tunic with a shirt and tie, many resented it. Arthur Battle and his mates did not want to 'look like ambulancemen or firemen'. He described men slinking out of the station on their first day in the new uniform, feeling self-conscious and pleased it was raining so that they could conceal the new uniform under their capes. As one of the 'Old School' put it to Battle: 'They'll be making us wear bleeding berets next to go with this lot.'[14]

On the Home Front during the war, with so many shortages, the Black Market spiv seized the opportunities to cash in as the friendly entrepreneur providing anything that was rationed or in short supply. The rationing and the shortages continued in the first years of peace when people looked for a restored sense of security and many hoped to build the new Jerusalem. This was the period when everyone's favourite copper, Dixon of Dock Green, was created, though in his first manifestation in 1950, in the film *The Blue Lamp*, he was PC Dixon of Paddington Green, rather than the fictional Dock Green, and he was shot dead by a young thug robbing a cinema box office. PC Dixon of post-war Britain may represent an image of a Golden Age of British policing but, at the time, there were many who failed to appreciate anything of the sort – not least many police officers themselves. There was no significant pay award after the Second World War as there had been following the 1918 strike and the Desborough Committee. In addition, the national housing stock was in a sorry state, particularly in the big cities where German bombing had been most severe, and this created problems for police officers seeking accommodation, especially those who were married. In September 1946 the Commissioner of the Metropolitan Police described how the housing shortage was forcing the separation of men from their families and costing them money that they could ill afford.

A case in point is that of a married recruit who joined the force in April 1946 and was posted in July 1946. His total emoluments less deductions, amount to £5.0.7d. a week, of which he has to send his family £3.10.0d. to cover their maintenance outside the Metropolitan Police District at a place where he was stationed when in the Navy. His prospects of obtaining accommodation for his family within the MPD in the near future are non-existent. Once in 7 weeks he visits his family, the fare being 24/7d, which he must save out of the 30/- a week which is left to him. The recruit in question shows signs of being a very good police officer, if he decides to stay on in the Force. Many similar cases could be quoted and there is no question that housing is one of our most serious problems.[15]

Tony Armstrong, the son of a Northumberland miner, a staunch Methodist and supporter of the Independent Labour Party, had tried to join the police as a young man on the eve of the war. He had been rejected by the Northumberland Police as being too short; he was 5 feet 8½ inches. The police may appear an odd choice for a man who considered himself a pacifist but, as for thousands of others, the war brought major changes to Armstrong's life. When war was declared in 1939 he registered as a conscientious objector and volunteered for duty with the British Red Cross. He served in Finland during the Russo-Finnish War, in Norway, where he was briefly interned following the British withdrawal, and in North Africa. His experiences with the Red Cross undermined his pacifism and in 1943 he enlisted in the Lancashire Fusiliers. Shortly after getting married he was sent to the Far East where he rose to the rank of captain, serving much of his time in the Military Police. Volunteering for the civilian police was a way of getting demobilized quickly following the Japanese surrender and, in spite of being some two inches shorter than other members of the Northumberland Police, he managed to talk his way into its depleted ranks. But, as in London, there was a shortage of accommodation in his first postings to Wallsend and then to the shipbuilding area of Willington Quay; for several months Armstrong lived with a local family, while his wife lived in Newcastle with her parents.[16]

Armstrong was happy to have got the job that he had wanted, but been refused, before the war. But some men who had gone into the services were often disgruntled to find themselves commanded by men who had stayed at home and who seemed to have been promoted through the application of 'Buggins's turn'. Arthur Pickering may have been a brave man and an able leader of others in the noise and confusion of battle, but he was his own man who spoke his own mind. This may have been acceptable in an army at war, keen to promote men of courage and initiative, but it did not suit rural society where policing remained coloured in Victorian hues and still demanded deference. Back in the Bedfordshire Police, 'Old Pick' never rose above the rank of constable. C.H. Rolph was astounded by the stoicism with which men, some of whom had achieved high rank in the armed forces, 'settled down again to the monotony and juniority of the jobs that had been kept open for them'. But as one such veteran said to him, returning to the rank of constable: 'It's not what you call stoicism, sir, whatever that is; it's just bloody despair. What else can I do?'

John Wainwright, a veteran of Bomber Command, joined the West Riding Police after war service. He described the scene in Mansfield Police Training College when he, together with fifty or so other war veterans, was addressed by a senior officer who had not gone to war, and who clearly lacked Rolph's empathy.

He was not a man with natural panache, and he was stage-centre facing more than half a hundred of us, all sporting war medals. A very lonely Defence Medal ribbon (a gong given to Boy Scouts) was all he had to wear . . . Every man in the room knew why he

. . . held the substantive rank of superintendent . . . Because of
the war. Because of *our* war.[17]

Wainwright walked a series of West Riding beats for nearly twenty
years with the doggedness and stubbornness of 'Old Pick' in
Bedfordshire. He never rose above the rank of constable and
believed that this was because he had refused to perjure himself at
the request of a senior officer. He retired to follow a successful
writing career after the publication of his first police procedural
novel, *Death in a Sleeping City*, in 1965.

The number of attested women police officers had gone from 282
in 1940 to 418 in 1945. The increase continued during the post-
war years, though it was not always easy to reach the numbers of
women designated for the establishment of each force. The requirement that women officers be single and that they resign upon
marriage was dropped, though the pay rates of women officers
remained about 10 per cent lower than those of their male counterparts. Women officers were given greater opportunities for
performing the different kinds of police duty, but many male officers still considered policing to be 'man's work' and were reluctant to see women sworn in and accredited even when they dealt
primarily with women and children.[18]

Overall it is probably fair to say that the position of the woman
officer improved in the generation following the Second World
War; equally that the position of the police wife improved significantly. After the war it became less and less acceptable for an
officer's fiancée to be required to provide references or have her
past investigated before the marriage was authorized. Restrictions
on a wife taking paid work were generally relaxed during the war
and ended shortly afterwards. Even so, in 1946 the Home Office
found itself having to instruct one chief constable that he should
not seek to prohibit the wives of four of his officers from working
as school teachers.[19]

Policing Post-War

Eric Royden was a grammar school boy but when he finished his National Service in 1950 he opted to join the Liverpool City Police.[20] It was a tough force, but a proud force that revelled in its distinct black uniform with the striking silver cap braid worn by inspectors and above. Eric Royden's training was not greatly dissimilar from that of men like Daley and Fancourt who had joined the police a generation earlier. When he came out of training school he was posted to the relatively quiet suburbs to the south of Liverpool where for two weeks he patrolled on foot learning the ropes with an experienced constable. For the next few months he worked his beat on his own. At night he began in the traditional style, making sure that all shops and business premises were securely fastened. 'On one beat that I had one time, there were 590 shops. Just one long row, line of shops, a major road.' He concluded his eight-hour patrol in the same way that he began, by shaking hands with the shop door knobs. There was a 45-minute rest break, timed to the minute; when once he arrived at the station two minutes early by the clock, he was sent outside to wait. After a few months Royden found himself posted to a rather less arduous, but much longer beat through tree-lined housing estates; the size of this beat meant that it had to be covered by bicycle. After two years he was given a spell in the CID, but like Fancourt and Rutherfoord in Birmingham, he disliked it. He reasoned that, since there were fewer ranks in the CID, there was less chance of promotion. In addition, the CID also worked long hours and while long hours meant good overtime pay, this did not suit his aspirations for future home life and bringing up a family. But he was happy to transfer to the city centre in the mid-1950s.

All cities have their unique aspects, and these have implications for the local police. Eric Royden's Liverpool probably had more such aspects than most and, over the next two decades, it was to acquire a new glamour and new notoriety as a centre of music and a linked youth culture. In the 1950s, while its importance was in decline, the city was known first and foremost as a great seaport. The city police in Liverpool had absorbed the dock police in the 1830s and pilferage from the docks became their problem for the next century. As late as the 1950s constables were posted on the dock gates to discourage pilferage and to make periodic checks for the small-scale theft of cargo. On moving to the city centre Royden was posted to a mobile unit – five men in a Land Rover – whose task was to make wider patrols in order to prevent larger dockyard thefts and to pursue those responsible, particularly where groups, rather than individual workers, were involved.

Seaports provide lively attractions and sex workers that cater for seamen between voyages. Liverpool was no exception. In the early 1960s there was a whiff of corruption about sections of the Liverpool Vice Squad and its relationship with clubs and prostitution. Royden had just been promoted to inspector in the city's Traffic Division, a post that he had set his heart on and for which he had worked hard. But he was known by his superiors for his honesty and his strong Christian commitment; they thought him the ideal man to sort out the Vice Squad, and it was not the kind of request that he could turn down. In addition to prostitution, clubs and an increasing problem with drugs, the squad was also required to deal with illicit gambling. In 1961 the problems with street betting had been swept away with the creation of licensed betting offices, but in Liverpool there remained difficulties with large-scale illicit betting among the city's sizeable Chinese community. Again, like most seaports, Liverpool had a high proportion of resident foreign seamen, their families and descendants but, during Royden's service, the biggest cultural divide in the city was sectarian rather than ethnic.

Exactly one hundred years before Eric Royden joined the Liverpool Police a confrontation following the Orange parade of 12 July had ended with shots wounding three people, one fatally. Sporadic flare-ups continued over subsequent decades, usually sparked on the Orange side by some success on the part of the Catholic Church in raising its status within British society or else by an outbreak of violence by Irish nationalists.[21] By the middle of the twentieth century the aggressive Victorian anti-Catholicism in Liverpool had given way to a more secular element within the Orange parades. Shrieking fifes and clattering snare drums still proudly beat out 'The Sash My Father Wore' and 'The Protestant Boys', but anti-Catholicism and anti-Irish sentiment became the front to an otherwise unarticulated expression of working-class identity and community. No one, but no one, was permitted to cross the lines of an Orange parade, and Royden recalled that even police officers who ran across the road to break up trouble on the other side were turned on by furious marchers, some of them clutching bibles to their Orange sashes. From his own Christian perspective, nothing infuriated Eric Royden more than seeing those bibles brandished as tokens of Orange sectarianism.

Orangeism in Liverpool gained a new lease of life during the 1970s with the troubles in Northern Ireland and their spillage over on to the mainland. In the 1960s, however, it was Beatlemania and the music, as opposed to the police understanding of 'Mersey beat', that hit the headlines. The fans' pursuit of 'the Fab four' and other pop idols, together with the need to maintain order outside pop concerts, meant new deployments for the police. This was not especially stressful except, as some veteran officers would complain, for the effects of shrill fan screams on the eardrums and, perhaps also, the throb of the music.

There were other elements of post-war youth culture that harked back to the youth gangs of the nineteenth century and maintained the tradition of pub brawls. Teddy Boy gangs fought in the 1950s. Mods fought Rockers in the 1960s and began meeting for ritual bank holiday confrontations at seaside resorts. Police officers were not targeted in these conflicts, but they were expected to step between the combatants, make arrests and persuade the majority to go home quietly. Clashes between football fans also had a long pedigree, but from the late 1960s these also appeared to be getting worse and requiring more and more police effort to control them.

Politics also brought crowds on to the streets during the 1950s and 1960s. These crowds protested about nuclear weapons, the United States' involvement in Vietnam, immigration, the Apartheid regime in South Africa and a variety of other issues. Sometimes police officers themselves were sympathetic to the demonstrators. They chatted to the crowds as they had done with the unemployed marchers a generation earlier. Sometimes the police orders were ill-considered, and such orders as well as the behaviour of the crowds led to the demonstrations becoming difficult and violent. As during the 1930s, the tempers of Bobbies who were missing a rest day because of the need to police a demonstration added to the potential for trouble. But different forms of crowd control had always been a feature of police work; other changes and problems required shifts in the way that officers performed their duties.

Immediately after the Second World War, Horace Rogers was posted as station sergeant to the small town of Stotfold. His district took in some ten miles of the Great North Road between Baldock, on the Hertfordshire border, and Biggleswade. Motor traffic increased at the end of the war, but Rogers's application for a car allowance was turned down and he found himself having to police the road, to handle accidents and to liaise with the Hertfordshire Police in Hitchin or Letchworth with nothing more than his push bike. Within a few years the impossibility of continuing in this fashion became apparent to his superiors and the Bedfordshire force, like many others, found itself having to create a substantial, specialist traffic division. Traffic policing had begun to bring the police into conflict with respectable members of the public before the war; the growth of personal transport from the 1950s increased such confrontations.

The expansion of suburbs had begun significantly to lengthen beats during the inter-war period. The house-building programmes initiated both for slum clearance and to replace the housing stock destroyed during the war aggravated the problem. One of the most glaring examples of this came with the building of the new town of Kirby on the Lancashire edge of the city of Liverpool. The construction of Kirby began in the 1950s, but while the planners had thought about houses, they had paid little attention to amenities such as shops, churches, pubs, places of amusement and recreation. The town acquired a reputation for crime and vandalism. Moreover, the continuing shortages of police manpower meant that by 1963, when the population had reached 60,000, the Lancashire Police could find only six uniformed officers at any one time to cover the town's eleven beats. Eric St Johnston, who had been one of Trenchard's Hendon protégés in the 1930s and who was then Chief Constable of Lancashire, accordingly reorganized the policing of Kirby. Only the small shopping precinct was to be covered by foot patrols and the rest of the town was divided into five mobile beats for single officers in cars carrying pocket radios so as to be able to communicate, or summon help, whether inside their vehicle or out of it.[22]

Almost immediately the experiment was celebrated in a new television series, *Z Cars*, in which four tough Bobbies were paired in two police cars, working in partnership with an equally tough detective inspector and detective sergeant based in Newtown, part of an unnamed northern city. *Z Cars* brought widespread publicity to St Johnston's reorganization, which heralded the development of 'Unit Beat Policing'. By the end of 1968 it was claimed that this new style of policing covered 60 per cent of the population of England and Wales; it involved patrol cars with uniformed officers working in teams with detective officers and, in theory at least, constantly exchanging and collating information.[23]

But if senior officers, politicians and officials at the Home Office argued that technology was the answer to reducing crime and making policing more interesting for the constables than simply patrolling a foot beat, some of the rougher forms of police behaviour continued unabated. As during the inter-war years these issues, once again, began to be aired in the media. The year after Dixon of Dock Green began his long-running television series, the BBC televised *Tearaway* and then, three years later in 1959, *Who, Me?* These plays were far removed from the world of Dixon. The idea of a non-comedic, working-class, uniformed policeman as a central figure, like Dixon, remained a novelty and the main police characters in both *Tearaway* and *Who, Me?* were detectives. Also in contrast to Dixon, these detectives were ambiguous characters. In *Tearaway* the people of the northern slum in which the play was set appeared almost as nervous of the police as they were of the eponymous local thug. *Who, Me?* was set in a police station, and concerned the interrogation of three suspects over a shop theft. Detective officers were generally complimentary about its accuracy, but some of the civilian audience were concerned by what they saw. These concerns prompted a letter from the director, Gilchrist Calder, that, fifty years later, appears equally disconcerting: 'the people being interrogated in the programme were, if you remember, already criminals with bad records. The methods used would obviously not be used in normal circumstances.'[24] *Who, Me?* followed hard on the heels of a succession of police scandals that echoed concerns about the 'third degree' in the 1920s.

In December 1957 came the scandal of the 'Thurso boy'. A group of boys jeered at two constables of the Caithness Police when they entered a café. One of the constables warned: 'If there's any more cheek, I'll mark you for life.' John Waters accepted the challenge and when he refused to give his name and swore at the officers, he was taken to an alley and chastised. Such behaviour appears still to have been relatively common in rough areas and the local Procurator Fiscal declined to prosecute. The local MP, however, was not prepared to let the matter rest. He took up Waters's case and, after much effort from him, the government agreed to an inquiry that was critical of police behaviour in its report, published in April 1959.

A few weeks before the 'Thurso boy' report an officer was found guilty in Wrexham of assaulting another youth; the youth was described as 'a bully and a hooligan', but it was symptomatic of a change in the courts that this no longer excused police behaviour. Two other cases of assault by police officers, one in Birmingham and the other in London, also made news that April. In July Günter Podola, suspected of shooting a detective sergeant, had to be taken to hospital from Chelsea Police Station where he had been held for several hours without charge and without seeing a solicitor. The following November Parliament debated the payment of £300 by the Commissioner of the Metropolitan Police to settle civil proceedings brought against one of his constables for assault and battery. The offending constable, the critics noted, had not been disciplined.[25] These incidents were the ones that hit the headlines; there were others, tougher than that portrayed in *Who Me?*, that remained behind closed doors.

The detective remained a romantic character and a succession of memoirs, such as those of Robert Fabian and John Gosling, contributed to this.[26] There were successes that stemmed from dogged determination and experience, often combined with careful forensic work. But some results were achieved simply by tough detectives bullying and threatening their suspects. Sir Robert Mark remembered a senior detective in post-war Manchester who greeted suspects with: 'Will you talk or be tanned?' If a suspect refused to talk his head was held in a toilet bowl that was repeatedly flushed until he changed his mind.[27]

In the early 1950s Tony Armstrong was one of three detectives stationed in Whitley Bay. His two colleagues, one a sergeant and the other a constable like himself, were hard drinkers. After a long day they retired to the pub, and if it was after closing time, they woke the publican up and drank through the early hours. Armstrong did not want to join in the drinking bouts, which led to some difficulties in the relationship. The detective sergeant, moreover, had his own way with suspects.

When he got a young man in front of him who was suspected of theft say, or burglary, he just terrified the fellow out of his skin. They sat either side of a very narrow desk . . . He would take his truncheon out of the bottom drawer of his desk and the poor suspect didn't know what was going to happen, and he would hammer the desk with this truncheon and the desk had got weal marks on it, and he'd shout at the top of his voice: 'Tell the truth and shame the devil' . . . The poor fellow was terrified and the information would come . . . And when he went to court he would say: 'And I asked the prisoner certain questions, and he said: "Yes, I did it." '

Armstrong himself confessed to using some dubious tactics for a confession, following the advice of the station caretaker, himself a former policeman. The tactics involved the use of the chargers, kept by the caretaker, that were used to recharge the wet batteries for the lamps that constables carried on their belts during night beats.

There was a couple of youths who were proving to be very difficult and we couldn't get anything out of them, although it was pretty certain that they'd done the jobs they were suspected of, so the old caretaker . . . [who] used to wander in and out during interrogations and lend his advice . . . said: 'I know what we'll do Armstrong ... we'll put them on the lie detector.' I didn't know what he was talking about at all, I'd never seen a lie detector, least of all at Whitley Bay. So we went out into the caretaker's cubby hole where the charger for wet batteries was. And he made these lads hold on to the terminals of the charging equipment and then he put a little charge through and the chaps gave a little jump and he said: 'Now, the detective will ask you the questions.' So I asked the questions and . . . the caretaker was shouting: 'They're telling lies. They're telling lies.' And eventually they admitted the whole thing. They really thought it was some machine to detect lies.[28]

The Sixties: Policing for a New Era

The succession of public scandals, and particularly the incident involving the £300 payout by the Metropolitan Police that prompted questions in Parliament, led directly to a new Royal

Commission on the police. The Commission, chaired by Sir Henry Willink Q.C., the Master of Magdalen College, Cambridge, and a member of Churchill's wartime government, was charged with looking at the constitution of local police authorities, the accountability of police officers, and the relations between the police and the public, particularly with reference to the handling of complaints by the latter against the former. It was also asked to consider how to attract the best men to the police service and retain them.[29]

The Royal Commission presented an interim report on police pay in November 1960. This provided a formula leading to a pay increase that, for some constables, amounted to 40 per cent. The main report, presented in May 1962, heralded major organizational changes. For a hundred years voices in government and the Home Office had been arguing for the amalgamation of the smallest forces with their larger neighbours. A minority report by Dr A.L. Goodhart, Emeritus Professor of Jurisprudence at Oxford, proposed the formation of a national (English and Welsh) police force; but the majority of the Commission recommended the amalgamation only of the smaller forces. Following the majority recommendations successive governments, both Labour and Conservative, brought forward legislation – the Police Act of 1964 and the Local Government Act of 1972 – that resulted in the number of forces outside London being reduced to forty-one.

Horace Rogers retired as an inspector in 1964; his force, Bedfordshire, with just under a thousand officers, was one of the smallest to survive but it experienced a two-year conflict with the even smaller force in Luton which steadfastly resisted amalgamation until compelled by the Home Secretary. In 1967 Eric Royden's Liverpool City Police absorbed that of Bootle; and when the Local Government Act came into force in 1974, Liverpool and Bootle expanded into parts of the neighbouring counties to become the Merseyside Police, around 4,000 strong. Tony Armstrong's Northumberland absorbed Newcastle upon Tyne and Tynemouth in 1969; five years later it amalgamated with parts of Durham, swollen by the acquisition of Gateshead, South Shields and

Sunderland, to form the Northumbria Police. But Armstrong himself was long gone, and in 1974 he became the Chief Constable of Bedfordshire.

Armstrong's career, from pit village to chief constable's office, was not an example of something entirely new. As the careers of John Dunne and Henry Goddard had demonstrated in the nineteenth century, the police had consistently offered some men the opportunity for social advancement. But in the aftermath of the Second World War such opportunities increased significantly. The chief constable recruited from the military, or from a para-military imperial force, disappeared. Sir Joseph Simpson, who became Commissioner of the Metropolitan Police in 1958, was the first to have joined the police as a constable; and while, with his public school and university education, he was hardly typical, all of his successors also began their careers as constables.

The process of change in the generation after the war also meant major changes to the broad structure of the police career. The advocates of Unit Beat Policing maintained that their new system made the job more interesting for the ordinary constable. The system was, in part, the result of changes in society; other changes in the use of public space as well as in offending, meant the growth and expansion of specialist departments. Traffic divisions were an obvious example of this development; the investigation of fraud prompted the creation of a specialist squad in London in 1946; growing use of recreational drugs fostered anti-drugs units; and shortages in manpower led to the formation of the first Special Patrol Group in London in 1965. The SPG was initially designed as a mobile unit to help any division that had a high crime rate or other immediate problems, but within a decade it had acquired many of the characteristics of a mobile anti-riot squad. The use of cars by the public and the expansion of beats, aggravated by shortages of manpower, meant that more and more officers were also put in cars and given larger areas to cover. Isolated police houses began to appear uneconomic and police officers were brought out of the villages and small towns and concentrated in large urban police stations. In some ways this also suited the officers; in an increasingly home-owning society, police officers aspired to be home-owners themselves and few policemen's wives were prepared any longer to work as unpaid police auxiliaries.

Many of the post-war changes happened imperceptibly. Some within the police service embraced the faith in technological advance; a few had doubts. A few probably recognized the cultural reorientation required by the growing insistence on gender and racial equality; the majority, almost certainly did not. The future is rarely predictable. The benefit of hindsight enables the historian to explain the shift from Britain's 'swinging sixties' to the bleaker 1970s and early 1980s. Only a few Cassandras could have predicted the shift, and even they never envisaged soaring crime figures, three-day weeks, governments brought down by industrial militancy, blazing inner-cities and terrorist bombs.

— CHAPTER 10 —

Everything Changes, Everything Stays the Same

It was, perhaps, during the 1970s that Britain's changed position in the world finally came home to the majority of the people living in the country. The British Empire had become the Commonwealth and, rather than British people going out to run the colonies, people from the former colonies were coming to Britain for a new life. Two world wars had created massive debts and Britain's economic position was shaky, with poor products and, in many respects, an overstaffed and overpaid industrial workforce. The changed situation had repercussions for policing.

Within the confines of Britain crime figures were rising inexorably. The increase had begun early in the century but had taken a sharp upward turn towards the end of the 1950s. Crime also became a political football and central to the manifestos of political parties. The police became embroiled in these debates, particularly as an expansion of tasks combined with the new managerialism and the imposition of targets and measures to assess efficiency and effectiveness. They also found themselves more exposed to media criticism. This was in part because of the lack of deference that gathered pace during the 1960s alongside the glamorization of youth culture. But it was also fuelled by an increasing self-awareness among women's groups and among the children of immigrants from the former empire who would no longer tolerate or keep silent about sexist and racist behaviour in any section of society.

The Royal Ulster Constabulary: Policing the Troubled Province

As described in Chapter 7, the police that was considered as a model for many imperial forces in the heyday of empire, the Royal Irish Constabulary, had come to a sorry end in the aftermath of the Anglo-Irish War. The Royal Ulster Constabulary (RUC), created for the statelet of Northern Ireland, continued much of the organization and tradition of its predecessor. Its uniform and badge were similar. Its officers still carried firearms and might live in barracks. It was a centralized force responsible to the Minister of Home Affairs in the Northern Ireland government. Responsibility to a government minister made it similar to London's Metropolitan Police, except for the fact that the minister in Northern Ireland generally took a much greater interest in his province's police than the Home Secretary at Westminster took in the capital's police. This was primarily because the RUC was the police of a polity that felt itself threatened by a larger neighbour and by the potential fifth column of its Catholic minority.[1]

When it was established in 1922 about one fifth of the RUC's personnel was Catholic. By the mid-1930s the proportion of Catholics had fallen to about 17 per cent and by 1970 it was about 11 per cent. The extent to which Catholic officers were isolated by their fellows is difficult to assess. In many ways it seems that there was a broad esprit de corps among the rank and file that commonly ignored the sectarian divide. But there was also a belief, often picked up by the families of Catholic officers, that their religion checked their chances of promotion.

Northern Ireland did not have a serious problem with crime and the RUC's statistics suggested that it was relatively successful in dealing with it. During the inter-war years, like the old RIC before it, the RUC shelved many of its paramilitary trappings. The protection of the border was left to the Ulster Special Constabulary. These part-timers were Protestant to a man. The government of Northern Ireland resisted attempts by the British government at Westminster to develop the Territorial Army, preferring what was, in essence, a sectarian force to guard its frontier and to be ready to support the RUC on the streets in any emergency threatening public order. The system worked, more or less, to the extent that it faced down the violent attempts launched by the Irish Republican Army in 1939 to 1940 and again in the late 1950s. But, during the 1960s a Catholic Civil Rights Movement was established that protested particularly against local government gerrymandering and discrimination in housing allocation. Violent police response served merely to highlight the sectarianism of the Ulster Special Constabulary and a problem of legitimacy for the RUC among Catholics.

The British army was brought on to the streets of Northern Ireland initially to protect Catholics from violent Protestant attacks. The old Specials were disbanded. But soon both the army and the RUC found themselves in conflict with the revitalized Provisional IRA and its offshoots. The ensuing conflict, which continued for more than twenty-five years, left 302 RUC officers dead and thousands wounded. As with the Anglo-Irish War, there were allegations of police involvement in the murders of republican activists, often in league with Protestant paramilitaries. A subsequent investigation, by the Police Ombudsman for Northern Ireland, concluded that there was no effective control of the RUC Special Branch during the troubles and that 'it acquired domination over the rest of the organisation which inhibited some normal policing duties'. Even more serious, Special Branch and detective officers turned a blind eye to terrorist crimes committed by police informants.[2]

When an agreement was reached at the close of the century to end the violence, an Independent Commission on Policing was established under the chairmanship of a former Conservative minister, Chris Patten. The commission was charged with looking into the future of policing in the province. Among its key recommendations was that the RUC be restructured. In particular, the commission recommended that the force's numbers should be reduced from a ratio of one officer to every 140 members of the population to a number closer to that on the mainland, one to

390. It was recommended further that there be positive discrimination to ensure that equal numbers of Catholics and Protestants were recruited over a ten-year period to increase the proportion of Catholics to 30 per cent. It also suggested that the reorganized force be given a new name, the Police Service of Northern Ireland (PSNI). On 4 November 2001 the RUC became PSNI and the first set of newly trained officers took to the streets six months later.

'Pisney', as one proud member of the old RUC put it, 'rhymes with Disney.'[3] But the newly named body set out rapidly to re-establish and maintain a system of patrolling like that of other police institutions in the United Kingdom. It was the first to have complaints and allegations of misconduct referred to an independent police ombudsman. It tried hard to implement the policy of positive discrimination to reduce the Protestant imbalance in its numbers, and at the end of 2006 the percentage of Catholics had risen from under 10 per cent to just over 20 per cent. Even so, press comment claimed that the Catholic numbers were improved by the number of recruits drawn from Polish immigrants, and suspicion still remained in the republican community.[4] PSNI remained the only British police institution in which officers routinely carried firearms, and the murder, by the Continuity IRA, of PC Stephen Carroll in Craigavon in March 2009 showed the continuing danger threatened by a diehard republican rump.

Irish republican activism had spread to the mainland in the 1860s and 1880s. It did so again in 1920 and on the eve and in the early months of the Second World War. But it was the Irish troubles that began in the late 1960s that brought the most sustained and lethal wave of Irish terror to the mainland. The bombing campaign began in the early 1970s most notably with bombs directed at the army in Aldershot. But then, in November 1974, ordinary members of the public were targeted in the Birmingham pub bombing, which left 21 dead and 162 injured. The Provisional IRA's campaign on the mainland ended in 1996 with massive bombs in London's Canary Wharf and at Manchester's Arndale Centre. The casualties were relatively light in the last explosions, but the economic costs ran into millions.

In order to meet the threat a new Anti-Terror Branch was created at New Scotland Yard in 1976. Across the country as a whole police activity against the bombers had mixed results. There were significant arrests; some attacks were prevented; and there was much personal bravery. But there was also disquiet about the way some individuals were targeted and prosecuted. Four people convicted of planting bombs in Guildford and six convicted of the Birmingham bombing were released, on appeal, after serving fifteen years and sixteen years of life sentences respectively. In the first case brought before the Court of Appeal, that of the four found guilty of the Guildford bombing, the entire validity of the convictions disappeared with revelations about the manner in which the police had constructed the accused's confessions.

Conflict in the Middle East brought a different brand of terrorism to Britain, most shockingly with the destruction of an American airliner over the small Scottish town of Lockerbie in December 1988. This, together with the continuing IRA threat, meant that the sight of Bobbies in flak jackets and armed with Heckler & Koch MP5 carbines became a common sight at airports in the closing years of the twentieth century. Moreover, the Good Friday Agreement of 1998 that brought the problems of Northern Ireland to some kind of conclusion did not mean an end to terrorism. The new threat came from extremists claiming to act in the name of Islam. Many of the new terrorists, while their ancestry was in distant parts of the world that had once been part of the empire, were born and bred in Britain.

The Problem of Multiculturalism and Race

For most post-war Bobbies, even at the height of the IRA bombing campaign, the sectarianism that plagued Northern Ireland was not an issue. Much more bewildering and difficult was the emergence of a multicultural society. Most public services in post-war Britain

– hospitals, trains and buses – were fully prepared to recruit Commonwealth immigrants into unskilled or semi-skilled jobs for which labour was hard to find. The police, in spite of their vacancies, resisted. And whatever the need for people to do public sector jobs that many British-born white people rejected, sections of British society were inclined to make the link between immigrant and criminal; worse still, some subscribed to a shallow but appealing notion, drawn from the Victorian idea of the Great Chain of Being, that situated the 'coloured' immigrant at a lower point than themselves on an evolutionary or 'civilized' scale. It has rarely been recognized that this unpleasant side to mid-twentieth-century white British culture coincided with the idealized police image manifested by Dixon of Dock Green. Nor has it been much acknowledged that, while the public might have welcomed the Dixon character and praised the police in various opinion polls and inquiries, it remained difficult to fill police ranks. Equally, few at the time took much notice of the failure to create any Dixon-like policing in imperial possessions beyond the White Dominions. This failure became dramatically apparent from the late 1940s as the colonies demanded independence and as thousands left these colonies for a new life in Britain.

On 6 June 1948 the SS *Empire Windrush* docked in Tilbury with nearly 500 passengers, mainly from Jamaica, eager to work in the Mother Country for which many of them had fought between 1939 and 1945. The arrival came at almost a mid-point between riots and deaths in Accra, the capital of the Gold Coast (now Ghana), during late winter and early spring, and the appointment, on 1 November, of William Johnson, a former Chief Constable of Birmingham and HM Inspector of Constabulary, as the first Colonial Police Adviser. The trouble in Accra indicated serious flaws in colonial policing. Johnson's appointment was indicative of the Colonial Office's recognition that all was not well and that both modernization and a degree of uniformity were required. The choice of a man from the English civil tradition, rather than someone who had enjoyed a career in the empire, suggested also that there was a desire to establish something akin to an idealized English model in the colonies. The move was too little, far too late.

For a variety of reasons and under a variety of pressures, the aftermath of the Second World War saw the gradual reconfiguration, often with unrest and violence, of the British Empire into a commonwealth of independent states. The process of decolonization, and particularly the disorder that accompanied it, fostered paramilitary and political policing, both of which were traditionally excluded from the idealized practice of the Bobby. Throughout the 1950s and 1960s British police officers were seconded to parts of the dissolving empire, sometimes with the intention that they should impart the English model of policing, but sometimes to use their brains as Special Branch detectives or simply to provide a dependable brawn. Karl Marx once commented that history repeats itself, first as tragedy then as farce. The endgame of imperial policing that began with tragedy in Accra in 1948 ended with bathos in Anguilla twenty or so years later when members of the Metropolitan Police Special Patrol Group were put ashore alongside soldiers to subdue a tiny Caribbean island of 5,000 to 6,000 souls seeking independence from the larger neighbouring island of St Kitts.[5]

Norwell Roberts was born in Anguilla and had come to England with his family as a small child. As the solitary black boy in his junior school he met a mixture of curiosity and prejudice and, although he had passed the eleven-plus examination, his mother was advised by his headmistress that he could not go to a grammar school because he still had to learn English ways. At his secondary modern school he still stood out. Some senior boys dropped him on his head to see if his blood was red like theirs; the scar remained prominent on his forehead. The promise of his eleven-plus was not maintained; he left school with only two 'O' levels but managed to get a job as a laboratory technician at one of the University of London's colleges. In 1966, having seen an advertisement in the *Daily Mirror* stating that London needed more policemen, he applied – perhaps mainly out of curiosity because he knew of other black people who had applied and been rejected. Senior officers in the Metropolitan Police were still reluctant to appoint a black officer but, under prompting from the Home Office, they made an exception in his case. He was not the first black officer ever. There appears to have been a black officer serving in Carlisle in the early years of Victoria's reign, and Timothy Cavanagh recalled a Superintendent Branford, appointed to command M Division of the Metropolitan Police during the 1850s, who was 'a half-caste, commonly called in the division (but not when he was present) "the nigger"'. Two officers from minority ethnic communities had been appointed to forces in the West Midlands in 1966. But Roberts was the first black officer appointed in London following the arrival of the *Empire Windrush* almost twenty years earlier.[6]

Norwell Roberts may have been ready for the police, but not many in the police service were ready for him. He was used by the police publicity machine and the Commissioner praised him in the press but, sadly, many of those who should have become his comrades shared the shabby attitudes towards Afro-Caribbean immigrants and their children. Roberts recalled enormous prejudice against him from senior officers as well as fellow constables. Within the first week of his first posting, to Bow Street Police Station, he remembered a sergeant saying to him: 'Look nigger, I'll see to it that you never pass your [two years'] probation.' Each night in the early months of his police career he returned to his section house and wept, because he felt that he had no one to turn to. But Roberts, a physical giant with tremendous grit and determination, stuck it out. He transferred to the CID where he received several commendations for work with the Drugs Squad and also for the arrest of a group of contract killers. After thirty years he retired as a detective sergeant, the first black officer to be decorated with the Queen's Police Medal for Distinguished Service.

Norwell Roberts's grim experiences were shared by other men who joined from the Afro-Caribbean, African and Asian communities that grew during the 1960s and subsequently. Those who survived the training period commonly found that each day on the streets was a struggle for acceptance and recognition. Sometimes they faced difficulties with members of the general public, both black and white; and black officers in black communities were sometimes seen as having joined the 'other side'. But often the difficulties were closer to home and were situated among their own police colleagues.

When, at the close of the 1970s, the Metropolitan Police invited the Policy Studies Institute to undertake an investigation into the force and its relations with the London public, there were just over 100 officers from the city's ethnic minorities in a force of around 25,000. When the investigation finished at the end of 1983 the number of black and Asian officers had nearly doubled, but the researchers painted a bleak picture of racism and racist banter among majority white officers. On occasions this was moderated in the presence of black and Asian colleagues; sometimes it was argued that the comments were helpful for the ethnic minority officers as it was only good fun and helped them to get used to the abuse they would get on the streets. Among the higher ranks there appeared to be a complete lack of awareness of the distress and embarrassment that it caused.[7]

Even after the racist problem had been highlighted, it was extremely difficult to eradicate. The police remained a close-knit community in which loyalty was valued. Loyalty is a worthy virtue, but it can be misdirected. New recruits had to fit in and any junior or probationary constable who publicly voiced criticisms about the attitudes and behaviour of experienced officers was going to face difficulties of acceptance into the community. Similarly orders from above and lectures on 'community relations' could be mocked by those at the sharp end as emanating from an out-of-touch management or from those who had never engaged with real life on the streets. The close-knit community bonded more closely when they found themselves engaged in a succession of vicious inner-city riots across the country during the early 1980s. The experience served to strengthen prejudice against management. Among officers in London one popular story told of the frightened young constable who ran from the fighting in Brixton in April 1981 only to be stopped by a senior officer. 'Calm down, constable, what's your name?' 'And who the fuck are you?' 'I'm Superintendent Smith.' 'Oh, sorry sir, I didn't realize that I ran that far back.'

The frightening experience of having a variety of missiles, including petrol bombs, thrown at them could also cement any suspicions and prejudices that officers had about those they identified as rioters. The majority, but by no means all of the rioters were black youths. The inquiry by Lord Scarman that followed the Brixton riots pointed to the anger of young blacks at being repeatedly stopped, questioned and searched by the police. Yet many, perhaps most police officers seem to have continued to believe that black youths were more likely to be up to no good.

Four-and-a-half years after the riots in Brixton, and the similar disorders in Bristol, Liverpool and Manchester, came still more serious rioting, and tragedy, on the Broadwater Farm Estate in Tottenham. A black youth, Floyd Jarrett, was arrested for having a suspicious tax disc on the car that he was driving. During the police search of his home on the estate his mother, Cynthia Jarrett, died of a heart attack. One story was that a police officer pushed her. Furious crowds besieged Tottenham Police Station. Then on the evening of the following day, Sunday, 14 November 1985, serious rioting erupted on the estate. Immediately officers from different parts of London were brought together, kitted out with the relatively new riot equipment of flameproof overalls and visored, metal helmets, and allocated to small serials of a dozen or so men. Among the men in these ad hoc serials was PC Keith Blakelock, a married man with three children who had joined the police in his mid-thirties some five years before. Blakelock's usual posting was as a home beat officer, essentially an old-style community Bobby, in a peaceful area of Muswell Hill. His ad hoc squad of eleven men, commanded by Sergeant David Pengelly, was directed to assist a group of firemen who were trying to put out a blaze on the first floor of a block of flats, but who had come under attack from the rioters. Pengelly's small serial also came under attack and was forced back. As they turned away from the assault members of the serial became separated and Blakelock fell. Before he could get back on his feet the crowd leapt on him, stabbing and hacking with a variety of weapons. PC Richard Coombes tried to fight his way to help Blakelock, but was knocked unconscious with a blow to the face that smashed his jaw. Pengelly and three or four other officers were more fortunate. They fought their way back to Blakelock, but he was already mortally wounded.

Police officers were furious at the brutal killing of a comrade and shaken by the viciousness of the attacks directed against them; understandably they were determined to find those responsible. Six young men were charged with Blakelock's murder. Three, all juveniles, were released, but the prosecution of Mark Braithwaite, Engin Raghip and Winston Silcott went ahead. All three were convicted, and four years later all three were released after forensic tests suggested that their confessions had been fabricated. Controversy over Winston Silcott continued. He had been on bail for another murder at the time of the riot. He continued to be demonized by sections of the press and, allegedly, some police officers leaked information about him after his release. But many of the black youths on the estate looked upon him as a heroic and victimized figure.[8]

In the midst of these controversies the police and their political masters continued to make attempts to recruit more officers from the ethnic minorities. There were success stories and, gradually, more and more of the senior ranks began to be occupied by officers from these minorities (see Table 4). But by the turn of the millennium the percentage of all ranks drawn from the minorities remained below the percentage of those minorities within the population (see Table 5).

The problem of police attitudes to ethnic minorities was brought to the fore with particular acuity by Sir William Macpherson's inquiry into the botched investigation of the murder of the black teenager Stephen Lawrence. Macpherson's report, published in 1999, took well over a year and came nearly six years after the case that it addressed. Macpherson concluded that, not only had the initial murder investigation been marred by instance after instance of professional incompetence, but also that officers had treated the Lawrence family in a much less caring and sympathetic fashion than might have been the case had they been white. His damning judgement was that the Metropolitan Police was 'institutionally racist'.[9]

Table 4: Minority ethnic representation as a percentage of each rank 1992–2002

Rank	% minority ethnic 1992	% minority ethnic 2002
Constable	1.43	2.9
Sergeant	0.45	2.0
Inspector	0.30	1.6
Chief Inspector	0.06	1.5
Superintendent	0.20	1.8
Assistant Chief Constable	0.00	1.3
Chief Constable	0.00	1.9

(*Source:* Michael Rowe, *Policing, Race and Racism*, Cullompton, Willan, 2004, p. 31)

Table 5: Number of minority ethnic officers and resident population in selected areas, 1999 and 2002

Force	Size in 1999	% of population minority	Number of minority 1999	Number of minority 2002	% of minority 1999	% of minority 2002
Bedfordshire	1050	10.00	36	49	3.4	4.5
Greater Manchester	6890	7.58	166	213	2.4	3.0
Hertfordshire	1706	4.71	20	31	1.2	1.7
Lancashire	3245	5.00	39	59	1.2	1.8
Leicestershire	1974	11.00	88	97	4.5	4.6
Metropolitan Police	26,106	25.00	865	1286	3.3	4.9
Nottinghamshire	2269	3.52	60	72	2.6	3.1
Thames Valley	3789	5.35	80	106	2.1	2.8
West Midlands	7215	16.11	300	369	4.2	4.8
West Yorkshire	5065	9.45	134	152	2.6	3.1

(*Source:* Rowe, *Policing, Race and Racism*, p. 35)

There followed another wave of attempts by senior officers to grapple with the problems. Unfortunately cases continued to be unearthed which revealed the kinds of racial hostility faced by officers like Norwell Roberts a generation before. Virdi Gurpal, a Sikh, was born in Delhi, where his father had served in the police before moving to England. Gurpal had been keen to follow in his father's footsteps and had joined the Metropolitan Police in 1982. In 1997 he was on the executive of the Black Police Officers' Association and was serving as a detective sergeant in Ealing. In December of that year thirteen of the fifteen minority ethnic officers in Ealing, including Gurpal, received racist hate mail through the internal mail. Gurpal was identified as responsible, although the Crown Prosecution Service declined to prosecute. In spite of a solid alibi, he was taken before an internal disciplinary panel where it was alleged that he had sent the letters in revenge for being turned down for promotion. He was convicted and dismissed. He appealed and an employment tribunal, having heard expert witnesses both for Gurpal and the police, concluded that his alibi was watertight, that the computer evidence on which he was convicted was unreliable and that a white officer, who had also been a suspect, had been treated in a completely different fashion. Gurpal was reinstated and awarded compensation.[10]

Gender Equality

Women had been present in the police on a regular basis for much longer than officers from the ethnic minorities. Many of them continued to have difficulties with their male counterparts, not least because of the toughness of the job and the cult of masculinity that this fostered among many of the men. But there were also success stories.

Maureen Scollan was born in 1944, and grew up in the Essex village of Silver End, midway between Braintree and Witham, in the austerity decade following the war. The house next door belonged to the village policeman. Maureen was a big-boned, sturdy girl and family friends told her that she had 'just the figure for a policewoman'. Her mother had served in the ATS for part of the war and urged her to join the army; but, partly because of her affection for her next-door neighbour, Maureen was more interested in joining the police. She applied for the Essex Police cadet scheme when she left school, but was rejected when the medical revealed a heart murmur. She started work as an assistant on the Marconi house magazine and then, after a year, a fascination with local history led her to become an archivist at the Essex County Record Office; but her interest in the police remained. She became a special constable and in 1971, armed with a specialist doctor's assurance that her heart murmur was nothing serious, she applied again to join the Essex Police.[11]

Essex had been one of the last of the county forces to agree to the employment of women officers. In spite of the acknowledged value of women police during the First World War, during the inter-war period successive chief constables had resisted the demands, particularly from women's groups, for their introduction in peacetime. As elsewhere, the exigencies of the Second World War led Essex, once again, to employ women, but largely in auxiliary and administrative roles. On this occasion, however, following central directives at the end of the war, the county force advertised for women to join as constables with full powers. When Maureen Scollan joined more than a quarter of a century later, there remained a sharp distinction between the Women Police Department, with its own separate identity and promotions structure, and the rest of the Essex force. But significant change was imminent. In 1970 Essex appointed a new Superintendent of Police Women, Helen Welburn, who had come from Cheshire with nearly twenty years' service. Helen Welburn had never subscribed to the idea that women officers should just deal with women and children and had notched up a series of firsts in Cheshire. She had been the first woman chair of a Police Federation Branch Board; and, as a detective sergeant, she had been a Special Branch officer. Even before the Sex Discrimination Act of 1975 required that no distinction be made in recruitment and deployment on the grounds of gender, Superintendent Welburn was determined that her officers were to be police officers and not women police officers.

Welburn's ambitions were not to the liking of many male officers who, even after the legislation of 1975, still saw policing as man's work. In particular they insisted that women would be unable to cope with violence on the streets and to fight, shoulder to shoulder, with male officers in a riot. Many experienced women officers were also unhappy about the changes. They had no problem with the separate sphere in which they worked; in many instances they found that the ideas of officers like Helen Welburn, and then the legislation, meant that their own situation changed significantly with some male colleagues. While such things are difficult to measure it appears that, for example, in the police canteen the barrack-room language and the boasts of sexual prowess were no longer suppressed in the hearing of women officers. Most new male officers were teased, but following the equal opportunities legislation, the teasing of women constables often acquired a sharp new sexist edge. Like the new black and Asian officers the women were expected to take it as all part of the community 'fun'. But, again as with the black and Asian officers, the 'fun' could be a smokescreen for scarcely veiled resentment – at times it was nothing more than calculated hostility or sexual harassment. As one woman later explained to two British academics, when she joined in 1972 a woman recruit was 'either a nymphomaniac or a dyke, you couldn't be normal'.[12]

The worst aspects of male harassment and hostility seem to have appeared after the act of 1975. PC Scollan became aware of some of them when she did her initial thirteen weeks of training at Ryton-on-Dunsmore in Warwickshire, and then on her first posting to Basildon, where the inhabitants had a very different attitude to the police from the one that she had grown up with in Silver End. But whatever the attitude of her male colleagues, and of the civil community in which she found herself, Scollan was intent on being a police officer as opposed to a woman police officer and she proceeded to notch up her own succession of firsts in Essex.

In the summer of 1974, without having had a secondment to CID, Scollan went on a CID training course in Wakefield and, while she enjoyed the course and earned considerable credit in the weekly debates, she found herself as one of only five women among ninety-one men. The women agreed that, given what appeared foremost in the majority's minds, 'the three initial letters of the course should be altered from CID to SEX'. Boring lectures were enlivened by sticking notes to colleagues' backs. Typically, one of the other women officers found 'I'm a sexed starved raving nymphomaniac' attached to her back. Double entendres abounded, often at the expense of the women, but when Maureen laughed at one, the storyteller responded by reflecting a double standard: 'I would have thought you could keep your mind above your knickers!' The women were dared by their male colleagues to join them at a strip show. Much drink was consumed, notably in a pub near the training school that was run by an ex-policeman and where drinking continued until 2.30 a.m. Two officers on the course who went into Wakefield town centre were beaten up by bouncers after going into local clubs and being identified as off-duty police from the training school. Criminal proceedings were started and the men attending the course were warned about seeking revenge.[13]

The drinking, the tough exterior and the focus on sex echoed the experience of Tony Armstrong and others in earlier years; it was also picked up in the television series *The Sweeney* that was first broadcast in 1975. But even as Constable Scollan ran the gauntlet of the double entendres and the male partying, the CID culture was coming under close investigation from senior officers. In the Metropolitan Police particularly, from the time of Howard Vincent's reforms in the 1870s, the CID considered itself an elite and had increasingly developed as a force within a force. The real problem, however, was that a few officers had seen opportunities within the job for outdoing the offenders that they were supposed to be pursuing and for becoming a little too close to businessmen whose most profitable entrepreneurial activities were against the law. *The Times* began the process of exposure with a front-page article at the end of November 1969. When Maureen Scollan was doing her CID training in Wakefield, Sir Robert Mark, the Commissioner of the Metropolitan Police, was engaged in a crusade against detective corruption, though it is probably fair to say that it took the passage of time and the regulations of the Police and Criminal Evidence Act of 1984 to tame the old school of 'Will you talk or be tanned?'

Back in Essex Scollan became a motorized beat officer in Chelmsford, providing excellent public relations opportunities for her force. In the summer of 1975 the *Essex Chronicle* sent a reporter – a woman naturally – to spend a shift in 'Whisky One'; 'Whisky' was the word in the phonetic alphabet for 'w' and hence 'woman'. 'It's all in a day's work for eagle-eyed Maureen' trumpeted the headline of a full-page spread describing driving around the north of Chelmsford sorting out traffic problems and minor offences, supervising idle but daring children on school holidays, and reassuring the elderly about suspicious callers. Promotion to sergeant in 1978 and a posting to the training school at Ryton was followed by becoming the first woman in the country to head a territorial unit, again with accompanying PR opportunities. The press, with the enthusiastic support of the police, could draw a parallel between the situation in Essex and a new television series, *Juliet Bravo*, about a woman inspector commanding a small station in Yorkshire.[14] Inspector Scollan concluded her police career in charge of the Halstead division, where vestiges of a bygone England were to be found among the gentry and the local fox-hunt. The Master of a local hunt brought an official complaint after she had ignored his hand claps to get her attention and then had the temerity to insist that he dismount before speaking to her. Her superiors rejected the complaint.

By the beginning of the new millennium women were playing leading roles in the police service. Pauline Clare, the first woman to be appointed as a chief constable, took command of the Lancashire force in 1995. Yet, while women served side-by-side with men and performed the same duties, there were gender preferences in the way that individuals opted for duties. Male officers appear to have preferred leaving women to deal with sexual assaults and women were to be found in greater numbers in Child Protection Units, sometimes disparagingly referred to as 'Cardigan squads'. Between 2002 and 2005 1,133 officers in the Metropolitan Police applied to train as firearms officers; only fifty of these were women. Over the same period eighty-two officers qualified in this role; only one was a woman.[15]

The Beat Goes On

As Maureen Scollan was having her uniform decorated with sergeant's chevrons, in Liverpool, the focus of so much that had been swinging in the sixties, Eric Royden was looking forward to exchanging his superintendent's uniform for a clergyman's dog collar. His son Charlie went through his late teenage years wondering which of his father's careers to follow. In the summer of 1978 Charlie sat his 'A' levels; depending upon the results he had a place to read Theology at Durham University. While he waited for the results he decided to try the police. During his time at the Police Training School at Bruche, near Warrington, his mother told him on the phone that his exam grades were good enough to take up the Durham offer. He decided to stick with the police, at least for a while.

Bruche, like Ryton where Maureen Scollan began instructing as Charlie Royden began training, was a mixed police college. Even so, the regime at Bruche had many of the elements that would have been familiar to Fred Fancourt and Horace Rogers in Birmingham half a century earlier. There were parades and fierce, military-style discipline. Charlie remembered a drill instructor who, one morning, told him he was a 'toe-rag' because his hair was too long, and ordered him to get it cut. The instruction led to three haircuts, one after the other. 'I had to keep going back to him after I'd had my hair cut and in the end I must have been bald or something – you could polish me with a duster!' It was this severity that made him determined to stick with the police; he was not going to be beaten by it. But apart from the harsh discipline and the tough physical training, things had moved on. There was role playing to work through some of the issues that might confront officers on their beats. And there were handy tips about how to persuade a reluctant suspect to move or to get into a police car by twisting their little finger. But after the training came the real world and a canteen culture that advised forgetting about little fingers in preference to a knee in the groin or a blow with something hard and heavy.[16]

Different perspectives can lead even people who are very close to have divergent memories of the same events. Eric Royden saw Charlie as 'a very brave boy' in the way he coped with some hostility and resentment because his father was a senior officer in the same force. Charlie remembered being one of a team of young men dependent upon each other and ready to help each other in time of trouble; though he also admitted that he had to prove himself as someone who could make arrests, would stand for no nonsense and would join in to help a mate in trouble. The only trouble that Charlie remembered from a senior officer came from his sergeant, who had been investigated for corruption by his father and who tried to prevent Charlie's application for the plain-clothes section from going forward.

For the first two years of his police career Charlie Royden walked the beat in the tough centre of Birkenhead. This was not Unit Beat Policing, but in some respects even foot beats had changed by the late seventies. Officers were no longer paraded and marched out of the station to start a patrol; sometimes, if the beat was some way from the central station, constables were driven by car to the start. Officers no longer patrolled exactly the same beat day after day, or night after night. The beats could also be long and far apart. Faced with trouble, officers now called for assistance on a personal radio.

You knew that if you pressed that button down you'd get help within minutes and so there was nothing you ever needed to really be afraid of. You know, if you were facing a gang of 20 lads, you knew you could take them on if you had your radio . . . and you'd have Bobbies there helping you.

Jokes continued to be played, especially on men who were nervous on night duty and who were, according to the general consensus of the group, better suited to sitting in a control room. Like generations of Bobbies before him, Charlie soon got to know where to get breakfast and tea on his patch: 'they said that a decent Bobby was never short of a free cup of tea.' And if it was a prime spot on a special occasion, such as Becher's Brook during the Grand National, it might even be a free glass of champagne or two.

Occasionally constables were given special tasks. As a young, fresh-faced constable, Charlie was instructed to watch out for men 'cottaging' in and around public toilets. He caught one of his former school teachers but he had not the heart to ruin the man's career, so in a reversal of their old roles, he gave the man a strong lecture and sent him on his way. The opportunity for using discretion with offenders had always been available to the beat officer but, by the 1970s, officers were also allowed much more discretion in the way that they patrolled their beats. Many of the problems on those beats, however, remained the old ones: the domestic dispute, the disorderly drunks, the 'suspicious' young men that were stopped on a hunch, sometimes yielding a find of stolen property about their person. The expanding consumer society meant that there were also more and more regulatory offences to check up on, especially with reference to motor vehicles. Everyone had to have a car, but they did not always accept that they could not just park anywhere, that their vehicle had to display a valid tax disc and that they had to have passed a driving test and possess valid insurance. Sometimes the beat patrol was uneventful, but it was rarely predictable.

After two years on the beat, and in spite of his sergeant's attempt to bin his application, Charlie moved into plain clothes and, to maintain his cover and keep up with the fashion, was permitted to have long hair. In the Plain Clothes unit he, together with a woman partner, was given even greater discretion to find his own cases. Specifically, as a pair, they were expected to find and pursue anyone dealing in drugs, pornography and the illicit sex trade. Things had changed significantly in this respect. Only a few years earlier when Eric Royden, as head of the Liverpool Vice Squad, had raided a brothel, he had to have a woman officer present, but she was never allowed to share a car alone with a male officer. Charlie, in contrast, spent his entire working day, or night, driving round with his woman partner.

Emergencies meant separation and even meant that a long-haired, plain-clothes officer could be ordered back into uniform. In the same way that Keith Blakelock was put into riot gear to confront the trouble at Broadwater Farm so, in 1981, Charlie was rushed back into uniform to confront rioters in Toxteth. Flameproof overalls and visored helmets were not available in 1981. The officers at Toxteth, like their contemporaries facing similar crowds in the St Paul's area of Bristol, in Brixton and in Manchester's Moss Side, had the old cork helmet with a strengthened chin-strap and their usual blue uniforms. They were also issued with long Perspex shields. Charlie recalled crouching behind such a shield, feeling like a target for the people throwing bottles, bricks and other missiles. The temptations to lash out at any assailant, and to put the handcuffs on too tightly when an offender was seized, were as strong in the 1980s as they had been a century before, and they were not always resisted.

During the rioting at Manchester the police adopted aggressive mobile tactics which brought the trouble under control fairly quickly; they were subsequently criticized for their aggressive behaviour. The police in Liverpool, like those in Brixton, maintained static, slow-moving cordons that had little effect. Charlie Royden bitterly recalled how, having withstood the missile attacks behind their shields, his cordon was ordered backwards. He and his colleagues retreated, slowly, steadily but reluctantly, along streets whose inhabitants begged the police line to stand firm and protect their property. After the initial clashes Charlie was ordered back into plain clothes and instructed to mix with the turbulent crowds and to identify the local drug dealers that were thought to be organizing outbreaks by use of walkie-talkies. This was risky work. Undercover officers in such situations did not want to be identified to the crowd for who they were; nor, if it came to a clash with the police, did they want to get hit by their own side.

Dixon of Dock Green or Darth Vader?

After five years Charlie Royden left the police to take his degree and to enter the Church. He left while scandals about the behaviour of some detectives dragged on and before still others were unearthed. He left also before the major industrial confrontation of the 1984 to 1985 miners' strike that suggested to many that, more and more, the police were becoming a strong-arm instrument of an oppressive central state. Ordinary policing is something that continues in the background. Scandals and high-profile public order policing have always made headlines and often serve to undermine confidence in the ordinary. Unfortunately, during the 1980s, scandals and public order were rarely out of the headlines.

There was always a problem, especially for detectives, when officers believed that they knew who committed an offence, but lacked the evidence to prove it. This has led to a mindset that considers the ends justify any means. Tony Armstrong and Sir Robert Mark were quoted earlier, describing how confessions were forced from suspects. Mark had to confront the problem of corruption in the CID from the moment that he took over as Commissioner of the Metropolitan Police. But it was the West Midlands Serious Crime Squad whose behaviour caused the most alarm towards the close of the 1980s. The squad, whose origins lay in a special unit established in the old City of Birmingham Police, was set up in 1974.

It appeared to be successful at solving high-profile crimes and getting the perpetrators convicted. But in 1985, following a series of complaints, officers from the Metropolitan Police were directed to investigate the squad. The investigation's report was never made public, but it was known particularly to have criticized the way that interviews were conducted and the length of time that men were permitted to remain as members of the squad. No action seems to have been taken and complaints continued until, in August 1989, the Chief Constable disbanded the squad and a new investigation was launched by the Police Complaints Authority and the West Yorkshire Police. Over the next decade these investigations acknowledged the truth of a large number of complaints, particularly from black and Asian people who had been targeted by members of the squad. Other stories emerged of men being tortured into signing confessions by being brought close to asphyxia having plastic bags held over their heads. One officer was claimed to have boasted that his fist was a 'truth drug'. Excessive overtime had been claimed, usually meeting contacts on licensed premises. As a result of this investigation dozens of cases were quashed; thousands of pounds were paid in compensation and damages. But while some of the officers in the squad were found guilty of disciplinary offences, not one was ever prosecuted in a court of law.[17]

A lot of public order work meant sitting on buses bored, joking, playing cards, reading, talking, eating sandwiches, waiting for something to happen. Jim Whitfield had moved from Liverpool to London in 1966 hoping to make it on the music scene as a saxophonist, alto and tenor. Three years later, about to get married, he felt that he needed a bit more security and joined the Metropolitan Police. During his thirty years' service he was in the front line in the disorders in Brixton and the Notting Hill Carnival. A liberal-minded man, he felt hurt at a clash between the National Front and the Anti-Nazi League while a man goose-stepped in front of the police line with his right arm raised and shouting 'Sieg Heil'. He also noted the disdain with which such police lines appeared to be viewed by some young lawyers, some of whom went on to be ministers in the New Labour government. He struggled with pickets during the News International Dispute and the two-year strike at the Grunwick film processing plant. His abiding image of Grunwick, however, was not the fighting, but being cold, sitting around in a bus and eating 'the standard refreshment . . . a frozen pork pie and a Wagon Wheel biscuit'.[18] Generally there was much more sitting around than fighting, but that never made a good story, did not provide dramatic pictures and, in consequence, was not the activity that appeared in the press or on the television. During the miners' strike of 1984–5 enormous numbers of officers were moved around the country, billeted in mining districts and deployed to enforce peaceful picketing and to protect men who refused to strike or who, through force of circumstance, felt that they had to return to work. The riot shields were brought out again, and so too were the new flameproof overalls and the visored helmets. Some police behaved shabbily during the strike; and some boasted about the considerable sums in overtime that they earned during the days and weeks that they spent deployed in the colliery districts.

The most dramatic confrontation came at Orgreave Coking Plant in South Yorkshire on 18 June 1984. Pickets from the National Union of Mineworkers sought to blockade the plant and prevent a convoy of British Steel lorries from entering and loading up. The miners had successfully deployed this tactic during a strike twelve years earlier when a small force of police had been overwhelmed. There were police officers from ten different forces at Orgreave. Most of them wore the ordinary police uniform, but some men were kitted out in the new riot equipment. Some of these carried long shields to lock together as a wall to withstand missiles. Some carried smaller, round shields and were directed to rush forward into the crowd to break up groups and make arrests. There were, in addition, mounted officers who also wore the new equipment. Reported casualties suggested that there were more police injured than strikers, but the police kept the plant open. In scenes resembling a medieval battle, squads of helmeted, baton-wielding officers enabled the lorries to enter the plant, fill up with coke and leave; and at the end of the day the police still held the field. But the victory did little to enhance the Bobby's image. As one constable put it shortly afterwards: 'Tories tend to be verbally supportive but I think we are in serious danger of being used as a tool. Like we were during the miners' strike. No question, we were "Maggie's boys".'[19]

The flameproof overalls, visored helmets and armour were designed to protect officers during a riot but, in the miners' strike and subsequently, their use has served to dehumanize the Bobby; and some officers have aggravated this process by concealing their identification numbers once they have put on the equipment. Any unique quality that the Bobby may have possessed disappears when he or she is kitted out for a riot. The increasing deployment of firearms similarly wears away at any uniqueness. On 22 July 2007 a firearms unit of the Metropolitan Police confronted a man that they believed to be a suicide bomber on a tube train at Stockwell. Only two weeks earlier central London had been hit by four, simultaneous, suicide bombings and, rather than take any chances the officers killed their target; one officer held him while another fired several shots at point-blank range into the man's head. The method used, the Kratos tactic, had been adopted via informal international consultation as the best means of preventing any suicide bomber from activating a device. Tragically the man that was killed, a Brazilian electrician named Jean Charles de Menezes, was innocent. At the inquest, held more than a year after the incident, the officer who had fired the shots, a man with twenty-five years' police service, broke down while giving evidence.

> Everything I have ever trained for, threat assessment, seeing threats, perceiving threats and acting on threats proved wrong, and I am responsible for the death of an innocent man. That is something I have got to live with for the rest of my life.[20]

This use of the Kratos tactic was an indication of how the British

Bobby was becoming caught up in the globalization of police tactics. The deployment of battlefield assault rifles, specifically the Heckler & Koch G36 which fires standard 5.56 mm NATO ammunition at a muzzle velocity of 3,000 feet per second, is another. Concerns have been raised by both the Independent Police Complaints Commission and the former commander of the Metropolitan Police Firearms Unit about the extent to which this kind of weaponry should be available to police working in civilian areas.[21]

No matter how well trained firearms officers are, accidents can happen, especially when their adrenalin is flowing fast. In January 1983, for example, two armed detectives mistook a young film editor, Stephen Waldorf, for a man wanted for armed robbery. They shot him five times and then pistol-whipped him into unconsciousness. The officers were acquitted of attempted murder but as a result of their actions armed officers were required always to shout their presence, aim for a suspect's torso which provided the largest target, and to reassess the situation after each shot. But guns were still fired by accident. In August 1985, for example, a five-year-old boy was shot dead in his bed in Birmingham as police searched for his father, wanted for armed robbery. A few weeks later Cherry Groce was accidentally shot and paralysed by an armed officer seeking Mrs Groce's son for a firearms offence. The shooting sparked serious trouble among the Afro-Caribbean community in south London. Twenty years later, after anxieties about terrorism had encouraged firearms officers to apprehend terrorist suspects in their lairs and to set off equipped with battlefield rifles and wearing overalls and helmets, 250 officers made a morning swoop on a street in Forest Gate, east London. A gun was fired accidentally, hitting Mohammed Abdul Kahar in the upper chest and shoulder. Again Kahar, a driver-collector for the Royal Mail, was innocent, though he and his brother had been wrongly identified as being involved in an alleged plot to make and to use chemical weapons.[22]

The wounding and arrest of Kahar and his brother were extreme incidents. Partly thanks to Kahar himself, when no charges were brought against him and when subsequent rumours that pornography had been found on his computer were proved to be false, there was no violent response. But the potential for trouble remained in those districts where the majority of the population came from an ethnic minority and where, as across the country as a whole, the majority of police officers were white. Since the early 1980s senior officers, with the differing degrees of commitment to be found among individuals in any large organization, had sought to establish and maintain better community relations by linking with those that they took to be community leaders and with representatives from other agencies working in the districts, such as the Youth Service. Some junior officers also made considerable efforts to engage with and even to learn the language of those that they served. But the moment that friction arose it was all too easy for accusations of racism to be directed at the police, and to be directed back on to the community by police officers. During such incidents the community leaders, in whom the police had invested so much time, often appeared to have no influence among the angry youth. In turn members of the Youth Service, who might have had more influence, found themselves both accused of colluding with the police by those engaged in throwing things at the police and ordered out of the way by police officers engaged in what they understood as the suppression of crime and the arrest of offenders. Equally, police officers could find themselves between British National Party demonstrators and young men from an ethnic minority, or even, as happened in the Lozells district of Birmingham in 2005, between two different ethnic minority groups.[23]

Bodies and Minds on the Line

Most injuries received and inflicted during a riot might be regarded by young police officers as akin to the injuries inflicted in a particularly rough rugby scrum. Occasionally, however, like the firefighter and the paramedic, the Bobby has to deal with the most appalling injuries inflicted upon men, women and children. Since the First World War and the recognition of the condition first known as shell-shock, society has become aware that even tough, fit men can experience mental trauma as a result of physical experience and observation. There was little help for many combatants in the two world wars; they had to get on with it. Similarly there was little help for the Bobbies, and others, who had to deal with the victims of aerial bombardment during the wars, IRA bombings in the 1970s and 1980s, as well as the victims of various accidents, fires and other incidents.

In 1992 Jim Whitfield, now an inspector, moved to take charge of the central district of Heathrow and he met with colleagues he had known during an earlier posting to the district in the mid-1970s. Some of these colleagues had been among the volunteers who had taken part in the body recovery duties following the destruction of Pan Am flight 103 over the small Scottish town of Lockerbie on 21 December 1988. Jim was shocked by the impact that the incident had had on his old colleagues, as well as by the fact that a number of other officers who had volunteered to help at Lockerbie had since retired on health grounds, suffered bouts of stress-related illness and experienced problems in their family relationships. Of his old comrades at Heathrow, one was outwardly confident, but from time to time appeared to suffer stress trauma; another talked repeatedly about Lockerbie as if he could not forget. But then, how could he forget? The volunteers had carried out their duties without specialist clothing; they walked the site on their painful task wearing ordinary tunics and helmets. Most of them returned home on Christmas Eve. No senior officer met them to debrief them; no counselling or specialist support was provided. They were expected to go home to their families, and get on with it.

In 1998, as part of his reponsibilities for training at Heathrow, Jim was asked to re-establish the airport's Body Recovery and Identification Team (BRIT). He enlisted the support of the Met's Occupational Health Unit and called for volunteers for the new team. Sixty or so came forward, but after a presentation by his old colleagues, describing their experiences at Lockerbie, a number of the volunteers withdrew. Shortly after the planning was finalized and after final selection was made of individuals that were thought able to cope with being a member of the Heathrow BRIT, it was decided to appoint similar teams across the entire Metropolitan Police District. Old habits die hard and it was envisaged that such teams would be made up of officers nominated by their superiors. Eventually, however, following a presentation by Jim at New Scotland Yard, the Heathrow selection, training and support system was deployed elsewhere. It is possible that one of the deciding factors was the recognition that if non-Heathrow officers were called to deal with body recovery and, as a result, suffered stress-related problems, then claims for damages could justifiably be brought on the grounds that they had not received the same support as those in the Heathrow BRIT.

The police, like other public bodies, were not exempted from the equal opportunities legislation regarding gender and race. They had, however, been granted exemption from the 1974 Health and Safety at Work Act. But the problems of Bobbies traumatized by their experiences following terrorist attacks and other disasters, together with early retirements and a series of court cases following injuries sustained on duty, led to a reappraisal of the situation. The Police (Health and Safety) Act followed in 1997. This introduced risk assessment into policing, often with comic effect which the media was quick to exploit. In March 2007, for example, the front page of the *Camden New Journal* asked its readers how many police officers it took to change a stopcock. Police and council officials in the London Borough of Camden had visited a council flat occupied by a 66-year-old man who was described by local residents as being mentally and physically frail, and frightened of being taken into care. The council wanted to turn off the stopcock in the man's flat as part of their improvement programme for the entire block. It was alleged that, as police and officials entered the flat, the man produced a claw hammer and threatened to attack them. The police officers did not challenge him, but called for assistance and left. The incident was subsequently resolved when four police vans and four patrol vehicles, with thirty officers (some in full riot gear), attended the scene. The man was arrested for threatening to kill and taken to the police station. Several hours later, and after the stopcock had been dealt with, he was released without charge. The point was well made by some residents, as well as by the local press, that police were never seen in such numbers when a burglary was reported.[24]

Just as three officers (Sergeant Christopher Head, and PCs David Wombwell and Geoffrey Cox) were, without warning, gunned down in Shepherds Bush in 1966 (the origin of the Police Dependants Trust), so it remains the case that not every incident can be risk-assessed: it is impossible to factor danger out of the police officer's job. On 18 November 2005 two probationary officers of the West Riding Police rushed to an incident at the Universal Express Travel Agent in Morley Street, Bradford. Both officers were women; both were shot and in the case of 38-year-old PC Sharon Beshenivsky, looking forward to her daughter's fourth birthday party later that day, her wound was fatal. Almost exactly four years later, on 20 November 2009, PC Bill Barker, a traffic officer with twenty-five years' service in the Cumbria Police, stood on Northridge Bridge in Workington during torrential rain. The bridge appeared unsafe since the rain had brought flooding and the fast-flowing river was undermining the foundations. It was Bill's task to warn motorists of the danger; but the bridge was swept away, and Bill with it. He left a wife and four children. He died the day before his forty-fifth birthday. The same media that mocked modern police-management-speak, health and safety and risk assessment, was fulsome in its eulogies and in its broader praise of the thin blue line, as it had been when other officers were killed in the line of duty.

Looking to the Future

The Conservative Party under Margaret Thatcher appeared sympa-thetic to the police. It had fought the 1979 General Election on a law and order ticket and the Police Federation appeared to back the Tory campaign with a series of advertisements. For reasons of public expenditure control, Jim Callaghan's Labour government had held back half of a large and long-promised pay increase for the police. On the first working day after the election the new Thatcher government implemented the award in full. But while, initially at least, Margaret Thatcher's government probably gave the police more benefits and more leeway than other parts of the public sector, the writing was on the wall. From the mid-1980s into the new millennium, there was a succession of legislative changes, and attempted changes that affected police and policing.

The Police and Criminal Evidence Act of 1984 had a long gestation and considerable concerns were expressed that it would give greater powers of coercion to the police. In the event the act had broadly positive results, though some officers still found ways to side step procedures and to defeat or distort the intended objectives. On the positive and intended side, constables could no longer stop and search an individual in the street without making a report and without having reasonable suspicion; youth, long hair and black skin did not count as 'reasonable suspicion'. On arrival at a police station, suspects had to be informed of their rights and given the opportunity for legal advice. Interviews were to be tape-recorded with a copy provided for the suspect. The creation of the Crown Prosecution Service in the following year reduced police involvement in the process of prosecution and led to the disappearance of police officers conducting criminal prosecutions in the lower courts.

The prospect of short-term contracts and performance-related pay was raised in the early 1990s. These were largely seen off by the end of the decade, partly as a result of fierce rank-and-file hostility. But, like every other branch of the public sector, the police were required to develop new management techniques and, by the turn of the century, they also found themselves increasingly having to work with performance indicators, to meet centrally imposed targets and, at the same time, to develop Crime and

Disorder Reduction Partnerships with local authorities. The aims of such policies were admirable in themselves, but from the 1990s they were coming thick and fast. There were Joint Action Groups (JAGs), Local Area Agreements (LAAs), Local Strategic Partnerships (LPSs) as well as a Drugs Harm Index (DHI), Key Performance Indicators (KPIs), National Indicator Sets (NISs) and many more. Partnerships were occasionally dismissed as 'talking shops', though rarely in public, and woe betide any area commander who did not know his Assessment of Policing and Community Safety (APACS) from his LSP. Some senior officers embraced the new management jargon of the period. This, in turn, fed into the rank and file's suspicions that their leaders were too often too far removed from life on the street – a common joke had it that senior officers went to the Police Staff College at Bramshill to have their brains removed. Use of the jargon also prompted press ridicule similar to that which had been previously directed at Dogberrys. In the spring of 2008, for example, the *Daily Mirror* had fun when the Plain English Campaign drew attention to the Norfolk police renaming their Control Room as 'Citizen Focus Demand' while their neighbours in Suffolk had a Director of Knowledge Architecture and a Head of Citizen Focus. 'Ello, ello, ello . . . I'd like you to accompany me to the customer base for a mission statement,' scoffed the *Mirror*, suggesting that this was 'modern Police speak' for 'You're nicked!'[25]

In the same way that it joked about modern police speak, the press was also highly critical of paperwork that dragged Bobbies away from the beat. In October 2009, for example, the *Daily Telegraph* declared that 'Home Office figures' for 2004–05 and 2007–08 revealed a decline in the amount of officers' time spent patrolling from 15.3 per cent to 13.8 per cent, and a corresponding increase in time spent on paperwork from 18.4 per cent to 21.7 per cent. This meant, according to the front-page headline: 'Bobbies on beat for just 6 hours a week.'[26] Constables have rarely enjoyed the paperwork that has always been a part of the job. Arguably at the beginning of the twenty-first century there is much more of it. Politicians regularly agree with both the critical press and the complaints of the police, and they promise to cut form filling. Yet it was the politicians who required the forms, and often for the very good reason that reports were believed to provide a transparent paper trail and restrict the potential for abuse.

In contemporary Britain there are also powerful forces conspiring to pull the Bobby away from local roots. Transnational crime, which involves drugs, people trafficking and terrorism, requires regional if not national police bodies with international links. Armed terrorists and turf wars between drugs gangs have necessitated an increasing armed response from the police. In certain districts of our big cities (and in major transport centres) it is now commonplace to see armed Bobbies on patrol. At the same time control and policy decisions, once made by local chief constables in discussion with watch committees in towns and standing joint committees (of magistrates and councillors) in counties, are now supervised by visits from HM Inspectors of Constabulary and guided by targets set at the Home Office. Some of what used to be considered as basic police duties have been transferred to private companies or to Community Support Officers (CSOs), who are not sworn as constables like the Bobby. Ordinary police officers worry that much of what might be called soft policing, which enabled them to appear as rooted in the community and as individuals who might be turned to in a moment of need, is being taken over by CSOs and other agencies. The consequence is, they fear, that constables, already thin on the ground, will find themselves interacting with members of the public only at moments of confrontation. Such fears have been compounded by some training and by deployment policies.

Jim Whitfield was worried by the way in which Officer Safety Training (OST) developed. During his thirty-year career he could not recall ever being given the kind of guidance available to traffic wardens on the kind of psychological techniques that can be used to calm down irate members of the public.

A typical OST session would take place twice a year and would include specific technical training in how to wield a long baton; how to apply rigid handcuffs, and the use of CS spray. Officers were always taught to adopt an aggressive pose when confronting members of the public. The standard approach to a crowd of demonstrators was to raise one's baton above the head, to project the other arm with open hand in the direction of the public and to shout the phrase 'Get Back'. No training was ever given at these sessions on methods for reducing tension. On the contrary, every aspect of the training was overtly aggressive.

His observations are borne out by an academic study of OST in a predominantly rural force at the beginning of the new century.[27]

Following the major amalgamations of the 1960s and 1970s, as forces became larger, so most small police stations were closed. At the turn of the century there was a move towards Basic Command Units (BCUs) made up of anything from 100 to 1,000 officers that were designed, in contemporary management speak, as the fundamental policing unit for best value delivery. Each force had, and has, several BCUs but their numbers have been diminishing in the face of the constant pressure for control from the centre.[28] At the same time, and recognizing the need to link with local communities, some forces are opening local 'Cop Shops' in town centres that are far from the big, centralized police stations; they are also providing 'Police Surgeries' in local community centres. Charlie Royden is now the Anglican vicar in an Anglican/Methodist partnership in Bedford; both of his churches, three miles from the town centre, have a regular weekly Police Surgery. But where do we go from here?

The policing of the crowds that assembled to protest during the G 20 Meeting in London in April 2009 was controversial. Sections of the crowd were 'kettled' in confined areas for several hours and unable to move; a newspaper vendor pushed over by a police officer died of a heart attack; a young woman was struck across the face by a police sergeant's open hand. The incidents were all recorded on film taken with mobile phones. The inquiry organized by HM Inspectorate of Constabulary was subtitled *Nurturing the British Model of Policing*. The idea that there was a distinctive model remains strong among senior police officers, politicians and at least some of the public. The report annexed the findings of an IPSOS MORI survey which found that roughly two-thirds of the 1,700 people interviewed had a broadly favourable attitude towards the police, though there was an even split between those who thought that the G 20 events had been policed well (46 per cent) and those that thought the opposite (45 per cent). The starting point of the report was that British policing had differed from its continental neighbours in the way that it dealt with public order, and that British policing was based on consent.[29] But there are problems with such assumptions.

The British Bobby has never enjoyed the consent of all of those that he has been called upon to police, and the evidence deployed in the preceding chapters has shown this. Regretfully, but perhaps not always surprisingly, evidence marshalled by other historians has shown that even in those states that have come to be recognized as dictatorial and oppressive, the police often received both support from, and the consent of, those that they policed.[30] When it comes to crowd control, of course police tactics are important and in themselves can determine whether an incident takes a violent turn; and modern police are faced with their behaviour being under much closer scrutiny than ever before. There were no mobile phones to record police behaviour at Coldbath Fields when PC Culley was killed, none when Superintendent Woollaston's men administered 'chastisement' to an election crowd, and none at scores of other incidents. When British Paramount News showed police lashing out at crowds in Hyde Park in October 1932, the commentary eulogized 'the most humane force in the world' but the pictures could not hide what appeared to be police officers losing control. The response of the Commissioner of the Metropolitan Police to the showing of these images was to withdraw assistance to the film company for filming the Lord Mayor's Show, which effectively meant that the procession could not be filmed. It was also during the 1930s that the British Board of Film Censors prevented the making of a film version of Walter Greenwood's novel *Love on the Dole*; the censors feared it might prompt unrest. The film was eventually made in 1941, when support was needed for the war effort and when dreams were being dreamed of a new Jerusalem in the post-war world. One controversial and, for the time, shocking scene in the film showed a group of workers, sympathetic and tragic characters in the film, being beaten by police using their batons – the first time that such an image had appeared in a British feature film addressing a British subject. In the contemporary world of 24-hour news and, especially, of the amateur film-maker with a mobile phone and access to YouTube, the authorities have none of their old control over media images. Yet, arguably, these new images only reveal what had gone on in the past, unobserved by those not involved.

The control of crowds and the use of the baton by police officers remains a relatively rare occurrence, and it is difficult to know how some incidents escalate. Light-hearted banter between the police and a crowd can turn into pushing and shoving; from there a situation can deteriorate as a result of any number of minor annoyances. Methods of defusing a situation may help, though when a crowd wants to do one thing and the police want it to do something different, the notion of policing by consent becomes wishful thinking.

The deep well of sympathy and support for the modern British police officer owes much to the image of the Bobby, and perhaps central here is the image as presented by PC George Dixon. But, even though he continued through the 1960s, George was a policeman from a different, more deferential age. He always had time for the people on his manor; he was always polite, even to those he arrested. What appears particularly to vex people at the beginning of the twenty-first century, and to get reported in the media, is the police failure to find time for the victims of what might, in the great run of things, be trivial hurts and annoyances, yet which remain very important and very distressing to the victim. Similarly, the media always find time for complaints about delays in response or a lack of courtesy. A teacher protested to *The Times* about being stopped on Westminster Bridge after teaching an evening class. The officer who stopped the man thought he was on to something when the Police National Computer failed to recognize the number plate; though this was after the driver's wife told him that he had misread the plate. A superior officer then reported the plate correctly and, following a peremptory search of the car, the teacher and his wife were told they could go, without any apology or acknowledgement of the error. 'We are an elderly couple (62 and 60 respectively)', the teacher explained, 'who have never had any dealings with the police.'

> To make the whole painful ridiculous matter worse, as we left, the police officer gave us the 'police copy' of the official MPS form on which my name was misspelt, the date was wrong and the officer had not even filled his own name in the appropriate place. To misuse powers is bad enough but to misuse them incompetently is extremely unfortunate.[31]

One unfortunate incident does not suggest that all modern officers behave in such a manner, but an accumulation of such incidents will do little for any notion of policing by consent. Such cases are also news in the sense that man bites dog is news and dog bites man is not. *Adapting to Protest* urged better communication with the media, but this will not assuage any accumulated belief that a lack of respect is being shown towards the public.

The notion of policing by consent was far more complex than modern assumptions appear to suggest. The inhabitants of the Victorian rookeries, of the Edwardian East End, and of a range of streets in rough working-class districts throughout the nineteenth and twentieth centuries did not readily consent to being policed, and they were often ambivalent about the soup kitchens and free clothing distributed by officers like Superintendents Bent and Jervis. A tough policeman, and especially, perhaps, one who taught boxing in a local boys' club, might not necessarily have been popular or have patrolled by consent, but he had earned respect by being as tough as the local hard men. And in a deferential society, like Britain before the Second World War, the toughest Bobby was usually polite to the respectable members of the middle class, people who were also recognized as his social superiors.

The clock cannot be turned back; in particular it cannot be turned back to a society constructed with a vision through rose-tinted spectacles. Many police officers of all ranks are keen to connect with the community they police. Beats in city centres are now much longer than they were a hundred years ago and the costs of putting a regular beat officer on every other main street are prohibitive. Some Bobbies do not aspire to be anything other than a community beat officer, and while such officers may be much thinner on the ground than in the past, they are backed by the new CSOs. The problem here is that for many police officers and members of the public the CSO is not a 'real police officer'. The CSO lacks both the training and the powers of a properly sworn constable – rather like Gabrielle West and her sisters during the First World War. But the CSO is cheaper, not least because he or she does not have the same pension rights. To many Bobbies the CSOs look like policing on the cheap, and hence an attempt to devalue their skills, to dilute and devalue their job. Perhaps some of this resentment is beginning to dissolve as the CSOs become better established and as some individuals use the position as a stepping stone to the rank of constable.

There is another side to the connection with the community: the community must see the police as belonging to them. As noted in Chapter 2, while there may have been unimpeachable aims for the new Metropolitan Police, many London ratepayers in the 1830s disliked having to pay for a body of men over whom, unlike the old watchmen, they had no control. When the London County Council (LCC) was established during the 1880s there were demands for the Metropolitan Police to be brought under its control.

These were resisted on the grounds that the force had imperial responsibilities such as the protection of the royal family, of members of central government and of the Palace of Westminster. Concerns were also expressed about what might happen if control of the police fell into the hands of a socialist majority elected to the LCC. Central government, in the person of the Home Secretary, remained the police authority for the Metropolitan Police until a new system of government, with an elected mayor, was established in 2000. Within a decade a Metropolitan Police Commissioner felt compelled to resign, caught between an uninspiring Labour Home Secretary, a dynamic and purposeful Conservative mayor, and with his own reputation undermined by events such as the shooting of Jean Charles de Menezes. Such resignations always depend on circumstances, individuals and personal relationships, but the potential for future difficulties remains. There is an element here of the centre clashing with the local, though difficulties between ministers, mayors and police chiefs are probably far removed from a locality's hopes and expectations of their local Bobbies.

Borough watch committees and, to a lesser extent, the county standing joint committees could tell their chief constables what they wanted doing; the notion of the senior officer's complete operational independence is another twentieth-century fiction. The watch committee and standing joint committee members might have belonged to local élites, but the borough and county police more clearly belonged to a recognizable locality than the men and women who serve in meaningless conglomerates such as the Thames Valley Police or West Mercia Police. It is difficult for a civil community to identify with anything labelled a BCU, especially as these become bigger and fewer. The local police committees of such forces hardly constitute local involvement, while community liaison teams (even where they get serious community involvement) do not necessarily find that such involvement is keen on, or finds much of local relevance in, some of the policies and targets identified by the Home Office or the Inspectorate. Perhaps the time has come to recognize that the Home Office police forces largely constitute a single national police institution and to endeavour to work out how small local divisions of this institution can develop the kind of tight community links that everyone claims to want. Whenever proposals are made for new amalgamations there are protests from those who would maintain the status quo. Yet in all seriousness, what does the existing situation of forty-three forces in England and Wales, a further eight in Scotland and one in Northern Ireland represent? What system of local structures does it readily parallel? At the beginning of the twenty-first century the way ahead for the police, and how they might marry the demands of central government with the desires of local communities, are not at all clear.

When William Fairbrass and Alfred List set out on their regular patrols they carried a wooden baton to defend themselves and a rattle to summon help. Their job was to walk, at a steady pace, over their designated beats. The system had changed little by the time that George Dixon was first portrayed on his fictional beat. Dixon carried a wooden baton, a set of handcuffs and a whistle to summon help. Today's officer may patrol his or her beat by car. He or she has a longer composite baton, carries handcuffs, possibly some incapacitating spray, wears a stab-proof vest and might even have a head camera. Assistance is requested by means of a personal radio. The contemporary Bobby has fewer fellow officers within easy reach than his predecessor of fifty years ago; this is partly because of the increased size of beats but also the result of the growth of the specialisms demanded by the present-day maintenance of order and the fight against crime.

The contemporary problems surrounding policing will not be solved easily; equally it is more than likely that when one problem is brought under a significant measure of control and containment, another will emerge. Fewer police officers may be left to patrol the streets as more and more are hived off to different specialist squads, but those that remain, and those that serve as detectives or in those specialist squads, will do as they have always done.

Some, whatever their dreams and aspirations, will not be cut out for the job and will be unable to cope with the different pressures. A few will take people's generosity for granted and succumb to the temptation that leads to the receipt of a free tea sliding into the receipt of other things and thence to full-scale corruption. A few might still seek to manufacture a case against those that they 'know' to be guilty. The majority – some better than others but none completely immune to different biases and prejudices – will continue to construct a personal vision of their chosen career from a mixture of training manuals, superiors' instructions, peer comment, pressure and their own experience. Like Robert Grubb, Alexander Hennessy, Gabrielle West, Bob Josling and thousands of others, they will get on with the job and do the best they can.

Appendix: Timeline of main legislative and institutional changes

1735	Westminster Watch Act
1739	Sir Thomas De Veil establishes his Police Office in Bow Street.
1748	Henry Fielding appointed as a Westminster magistrate and moves into Bow Street.
1792	Middlesex Justices Act creates Police Offices on the lines of Bow Street across the metropolis (excluding the City).
1798	Creation of Thames Police principally funded by West India merchants; converted into the Thames Police Office, along the lines of the other London Police Offices, in 1800.
1805	Bow Street Horse and Foot Patrols reorganized.
1814	Peel establishes the Peace Preservation Force (the first 'Peelers') in Ireland.
1822	Bow Street day patrol (the 'Robin Redbreasts') established.
	Irish Constabulary Act
1829	Cheshire Constabulary Act
	Metropolitan Police Act establishes a police system for London (excluding the City).
1833	Lighting and Watching Act authorizes small towns and country parishes to appoint inspectors to levy a local rate for local police without recourse to individual, private Acts of Parliament.
	A similar act is passed for Scotland.

1835	Municipal Corporations Act requires new elected councils in corporate boroughs to appoint watch committees with responsibility for police institutions.
1836–1839	Royal Commission on the best means of establishing a Constabulary Force in the counties of England and Wales; reports early 1839.
1839	Metropolitan Police Act cements the new London force and abolishes the forces of the old Police Offices. City of London Police Act Police Acts for Birmingham, Bolton and Manchester establish forces with commissioners responsible to the Home Secretary. County Police Act enables county magistrates to establish a force for the whole or for part of their county if they so wish. A similar act enabled Commissioners of Supply to establish police in Scottish counties.
1840	County Police Act makes minor amendments to its predecessor of the preceding year.
1842	Police in Birmingham, Bolton and Manchester returned to local control. Parish Constables Act seeks to revive and improve the old system of parochial police for those counties not wishing to implement the legislation of 1839–40.
1847	Towns Police Clauses Act prescribes model provisions for unincorporated towns establishing and maintaining police forces under the 1833 (or other) Improvement Acts.
1856	County and Borough Police Act obliges all counties and boroughs to establish police forces, establishes HM Inspectors of Constabulary charged with annual inspections of all forces. Forces declared 'efficient' by the inspectorate to receive from the Treasury one quarter of their expenses for police clothing and pay.
1857	Similar obligatory legislation is passed for Scotland.
1874	Police (Expenses) Act increases the Treasury grant to one half of the cost of pay and clothing for 'efficient' forces.

1887	Police Disabilities Removal Act permits any police officers qualified under the franchise legislation to vote in parliamentary elections. A similar act passed in 1893 allowed such men to vote in municipal elections.
1888	Local Government Act replaces county police authorities made up solely of magistrates with Standing Joint Committees each comprised of an equal number of magistrates and elected county councillors.
1890	Police Act guarantees among other things the legal right to a pension for every police officer after 25 years' service, or after 15 years if forced to retire on medical grounds.
1906–1908	Royal Commission on the Duties of the Metropolitan Police
1910	Police Forces (Weekly Rest Day) Act authorizes that officers receive one day off in every seven.
1914	Outbreak of war leads to the creation of the first women police patrols.
1918	August: Police strike in London
1919	Desborough Committee appointed to look at Police Pay and Conditions across England. Scotland and Wales. Police Act establishes the Police Federation and a Police Council. The former was to provide police officers below the rank of superintendent with an organization that could bring matters of welfare and efficiency before the police authorities and the Home Secretary; the latter established a consultative body bringing together all ranks of the police service, the Home Office and police authorities to consider matters affecting the institution and its tasks. July: Police strike confined to London, Birmingham and Liverpool, largely in defence of the Police Union (NUPPO), ends in disaster. First Women Officers recruited into the Metropolitan Police.
1928–1929	Royal Commission on Police Powers and Procedure
1960–1962	Royal Commission on the Police (the Willink Commission)

1964	Police Act repealed 61 previous acts in part or in full. Gave Home Secretary new powers to promote police efficiency; established new forms of police authority but largely maintained the idea of local county forces; extended the powers and duties of the Inspectors of Constabulary. The reform led to the absorption of borough forces into their larger, generally county, neighbours.
1972	Local Government Act divides England and Wales into metropolitan and non-metropolitan counties and heralds a new round of amalgamations resulting in a total of 41 police forces outside of London.
1973	Women Police integrated with the rest of the service.
1975	Sex Discrimination Act
1981	Inner-city riots, leading to the Report of Lord Scarman urging a new emphasis on training with cultural and racial awareness components.
1984	Police and Criminal Evidence Act
1994	Police and Magistrates' Court Act introduced new powers for Home Secretary to set national police objectives supported by performance indicators.
1997	Police (Health and Safety) Act Police Act establishes National Criminal Intelligence Service (NCIS) and the National Crime Squad (NCS).
1999	Macpherson Report on the death of Stephen Lawrence Greater London Authority Act reorganising local government in London, including an elected mayor and, establishing the Metropolitan Police Authority as the police authority for the metropolis in place of the Home Secretary.
2001	Royal Ulster Constabulary reconstituted as the Police Service Northern Ireland.
2002	Police Reform Act establishing a national policing plan, Police and Community Support Officers (PCSOs/CSOs) and the Independent Police Complaints Commission (IPCC).
2005	Serious Organised Crime and Police Act establishing the Serious Organised Crime Agency (SOCA) incorporating NCIS and NCS together with investigative branches of the Immigration Service and the Revenue and Customs Service.

Abbreviations in the Notes

BPP British Parliamentary Papers
CBOA Charles Booth Online Archive available at
www.booth.lse.ac.uk
H.O. Home Office Papers in The National Archives, Kew
MEPO Metropolitan Police Papers in The National Archives, Kew
MPHC Metropolitan Police Historical Collection
OBSP Proceedings of the Old Bailey, available online at
www.oldbaileyonline.org
OUPA Open University Police Archive

Notes

Introduction

1   The classic statements about the police being created and developed
    by far-sighted politicians in response to problems of inefficient old-
    style watchmen and constables and of increasing crime and public
    order are to be found in the works of Charles Reith, particularly,
    The Police Idea, Oxford: Oxford University Press, 1938; *British
    Police and the Democratic Ideal*, Oxford: Oxford University Press,
    1943; *The Blind Eye of History*, London: Faber and Faber, 1952.
    David Ascoli, *The Queen's Peace: The Origins and Development of the
    Metropolitan Police 1829–1979*, London: Hamish Hamilton, 1979,
    takes a similar line. T.A. Critchley, *A History of Police in England and
    Wales*, 2nd edn, London: Constable, 1978 is rather more critical
    and subtle. More recent, and rather more critical, studies include
    Clive Emsley, *The English Police: A Political and Social History*, 2nd
    edn, London: Longman, 1996, and David Taylor, *The New Police in
    Nineteenth-Century England*, Manchester: Manchester University
    Press, 1997.
2   *Punch*, Jan–June 1853, p. 181.
3   *Solicitors Journal*, 5 November 1932, pp. 767–8; and see also
    11 October 1930, p. 665 and 27 August 1932, p. 599. The
    'intellectual course' story, probably apocryphal, had been told
    fifteen years earlier in *Justice of the Peace*, LXXXI (10 February
    1917), p. 64.
4   Malcolm Young, *In the Sticks: Cultural Identity in a Rural Police
    Force*, Oxford: Clarendon Press, 1993, pp.128–9, note.

Chapter 1: Policing Georgian Liberty

1   See, for example, T.A. Critchley, *A History of Police in England and Wales*, London: Constable, 1987, pp. 10–11 and 18–19; G.W. Keeton, *Keeping the Peace*, London: Phillamore, 1975, pp. 14–15.

2   W.C. Abbott, ed., *The Writings and Speeches of Oliver Cromwell*, 4 vols, Cambridge, MA: Harvard University Press, 1937–47, iv, p. 407.

3   For these developments see, for example, J.M. Beattie, *Policing and Punishment in London 1660–1750: Urban Crime and the Limits of Terror*, Oxford: Oxford University Press, 2001; Andrew T. Harris, *Policing the City: Crime and Legal Authority in London, 1780–1840*, Columbus, OH: Ohio State University Press, 2004; Elaine A. Reynolds, *Before the Bobbies: The Night Watch and Police Reform in Metropolitan London, 1720–1830*, Basingstoke: Macmillan, 1998.

4   OBSP, t17871212-77; t17790915-4, and t17700425-23.

5   OBSP, t17820703-58.

6   OBSP, t17820911-6; and for other trials at which Hunter gave evidence, see OBSP, t17810711-52; t17810711-54; t17820410-28; t17830910-64; t17830910-72; t17840707-14.

7   Payne, William 1717/18–1782, *Oxford Dictionary of National Biography*, Oxford: Oxford University Press, 2004.

8   Harris, *Policing the City*, p. 20.

9   Tim Hitchcock and Robert Shoemaker, *Tales from the Hanging Court*, London: Hodder Arnold, 2006, p. 336.

10 Gilbert Armitage, *The History of the Bow Street Runners, 1729–1829*, London: Wishart and Co., 1932, is a popular account. The fullest, and most up-to-date history is David John Cox, ' "A Certain Share of Low Cunning": An Analysis of the Work of Bow Street Principal Officers 1792–1839, with Particular Emphasis on Their Provincial Duties', Ph.D, Lancaster University, 2006.

11 Cox, ' "A Certain Share" ', pp. 2–3.

12 Cox, ' "A Certain Share" ', p. 114.

13 Sir Leon Radzinowicz, *A History of English Criminal Law*, Vol. 2. *The Enforcement of the Law*, London: Stevens, 1956, pp. 266–8.

14 Hitchcock and Shoemaker, *Tales from the Hanging Court*, pp. 27–32.

15   Cox, ' "A Certain Share" ', pp. 255–6.

16   Gerald Howson, *Thief-Taker General: The Rise and Fall of Jonathan Wild*, London: Hutchinson, 1970.

17   Ruth Paley, 'Thief-Takers in London in the Age of the McDaniel Gang, c.1745–1754', in Douglas Hay and Francis Snyder, eds, *Policing and Prosecution in Britain, 1750–1850*, Oxford: Clarendon Press, 1989. Two of McDaniel's confederates, James Eagan and James Salmon, died as a result of injuries received when they stood in the pillory. John Berry died in Newgate Prison. McDaniel's own fate is unclear. It has been variously said that he too died in Newgate, that he was sent to India as a soldier and even that he was transported to Jamaica.

18   Henry Fielding, *An Enquiry into the Causes of the Late Increase of Robbers and Related Writings*, ed. Malvin L. Zirker, Oxford: Clarendon Press, 1988, p. 153.

19   John M. Beattie, 'Garrow and the Detectives: Lawyers and Policemen at the Old Bailey in the Late Eighteenth Century', *Crime, histoire et sociétés/Crime, history and societies*, 11, 2 (2007), pp. 5–23.

20   *The Whole Four Trials of the Thief-Takers and their Confederates ... Convicted at Hick's Hall and the Old Bailey, Sept. 1816, of a Horrible Conspiracy to Obtain Blood Money, and of Felony and High Treason*, London, 1816. The trials in which the quoted allegations were made against Vaughan were OBSP, May 1815, trial of Cole, and May 1816, trial of Soames, Cooper and Cooper.

21   Peter King, *Crime, Justice and Discretion in England, 1740–1820*, Oxford: Oxford University Press, 2000, pp. 65–75; Gwenda Morgan and Peter Rushton, *Rogues, Thieves and the Rule of Law: The Problem of Law Enforcement in North-East England, 1718–1800*, London: UCL Press, 1998, p. 38.

22   Lynda Haywood, 'Aspects of Policing in the City of York, 1722–1835', M.A., University of York, 1996.

23   Randall McGowen, 'The Bank of England and the Policing of Forgery, 1797–1821', *Past and Present*, no. 186 (February 2005), pp. 81–116.

24   Mary Thale, ed., *Selections from the Papers of the London Corresponding Society, 1792–1799*, Cambridge: Cambridge University Press, 1983, p. 140.

25   Clive Emsley, 'The Home Office and its Sources of Information
     and Investigation, 1791–1801', *English Historical Review*, XCIV
     (1979), pp. 532–61.
26   H.O. 42.67, John Sargent to John King, 12 May 1803, enclosing
     Francis Lynam's letter and a report by the Treasury Solicitor; H.O.
     43.14.89, John King to Francis Lynam, 8 July 1803.
27   Clive Emsley, 'The Pop-Gun Plot, 1794', in Michael T. Davis, ed.,
     Radicalism and Revolution in Britain, 1775–1848, Basingstoke:
     Macmillan, 2000; A.F. Freemantle, 'The Truth about Oliver the Spy',
     English Historical Review, XLVII (1932), pp. 601–17; John Stanhope,
     The Cato Street Conspiracy, London: Jonathan Cape, 1962.
28   Quoted in Tony Hayter, *The Army and the Crowd in Mid-Georgian
     England*, London: Macmillan, 1978, p. 170.
29   Hayter, *The Army and the Crowd*, pp. 179–80; George Rudé, *Wilkes
     and Liberty: A Social Study of 1763–1774*, Oxford: Clarendon Press,
     1962, chapter 3; Clive Emsley, 'The Military and Popular Disorder
     in England 1790–1801', *Journal of the Society for Army Historical
     Research*, 61 (1983), pp. 10–21 and 96–112.
30   *Morning Chronicle*, 24 August 1829.

Chapter 2: The First Bobbies, 1829–1860

1   The New Police Instructions were printed in full in *The Times*,
     25 September 1829.
2   BPP 1834 (600) XVI, *Select Committee on the Police of the
     Metropolis*, qq. 46 and 105.
3   MPHC, Police Orders, 5 May 1830.
4   H.O. 61.13, Commissioners to Home Secretary, 13 November
     1834.
5   MPHC contains six volumes of newspaper cuttings dating from the
     early 1830s, with the letters from the divisional superintendents
     filed alongside them.
6   'The New Police',
     http://www.nls.uk/broadsides/broadsides.cfm/id/14850; MPHC,
     Police Orders, for talking with servants see 1 November 1830; for
     gossiping, 14 July 1830; for talking with women, 21 April and
     15 June 1830; for concealing numbers, 11 October 1829 and 25
     October 1830.

7   The Critics Group, *Waterloo-Peterloo (English Folk Songs and Broadsides 1780–1830)*, Argo Record Company, 1968.

8   *Weekly Dispatch*, 4 October 1829. The *Weekly Dispatch* was the newspaper most frequently represented among the critical cuttings collected by the commissioners and sent to the superintendents for comment.

9   A Parliamentary Committee inquired into the Calthorpe Street Affair: BPP 1833 (718) XIII, *Report from the Select Committee on the Cold Bath Fields Meeting*. The fullest modern account is to be found in Gavin Thurston, *The Clerkenwell Riot: The Killing of Constable Culley*, London: George Allen and Unwin, 1967.

10 *Times*, 15 (p. 3), 16 (p. 6), 17 (p. 2), 20 (p. 6) and 21 July 1833 (p. 5).

11 F.C. Mather, *Public Order in the Age of the Chartists*, Manchester: Manchester University Press, 1959, p. 105.

12 *The Charter*, 14 July 1839. The paper added: 'We say, and we say it advisedly, that the people were justified *legally* and morally in resisting the police – and that if they had put every one of them to death, no honest jury but *must* have returned a verdict of justifiable homicide.'

13 MPHC, 'The Life and Police Career of William Edwin Fairbrass, 1806–1876', compiled by Sylvia Fairbrass; for the Bow Street case see, inter alia, *Daily News*, 6 May 1848 and *Morning Chronicle*, 6 May 1848; [W.J. O'Brien], 'The Police System of London', *Edinburgh Review*, XCVI (1852), pp. 1–33.

14 *Cobbett's Weekly Political Register*, 17 August 1833.

15 BPP 1833 (627) XIII, *Report from the Select Committee on the Petition of Frederick Young and Others . . . complaining that policemen are employed as spies.*

16 See, inter alia, *Daily News*, 1 May 1850, 12 December 1850, 30 September 1853 (when Jeapes was referred to as 'a detective officer'), *Reynolds's Weekly Newspaper*, 5 May 1850, and *Lloyd's Weekly Newspaper*, 28 August 1853; H.O. 45.6099, Correspondence relating to the involvement of Metropolitan Police Constables being in league with pickpockets, 1855. For the cases involving Jeapes mentioned in the text, see OBSP, t18420131-781, t18470405-946, t18480131-643 and t18500506-969.

17 H.O. 45.6099; *Times*, 23 January (p. 9), 9 February (p. 9) and 12 February 1855 (p. 9); OBSP, t18550409-484.

18   Charles Dickens, 'On Duty with Inspector Field', *Household Words*, 14 June 1851, pp. 265–70.

19   Belton Cobb, *The First Detectives and the Early Career of Richard Mayne, Commissioner of Police*, London: Faber and Faber, 1957; David J. Cox, '"A Certain Share of Low Cunning": An Analysis of the Work of Bow Street Principal Officers 1792–1839, with Particular Emphasis on the Provincial Duties', Ph.D, Lancaster University, 2006, pp. 304–5. Cobb appears to have been unaware of Shackell's transfer to Bow Street and to have assumed that he was a novice at detective work when he applied to work in the Met's Detective Branch. For an example of constables working together, see OBSP, t18340220-83 in which PC Richard Baylis worked alongside James Tilt, an officer in the Worship Street Police Office.

20   Kate Summerscale, *The Suspicions of Mr Whicher: or, the Murder at Road Hill House*, London: Bloomsbury, 2008.

21   BPP 1844 (549) XIV, *Report from the Select Committee on Dog Stealing*, qq. 196 and 429–31.

22   *The Trial of James Thomas, Earl of Cardigan before the Right Honourable the House of Peers, in Full Parliament, for FELONY, on Tuesday the 16th Day of February 1841*, London: Gurney, 1841; OBSP, t18380917-2251 and t18410301-997.

Chapter 3: Country Cousins: Policing outside London, 1839–1860

1   *Bedfordshire Mercury*, 11 April 1840. For Clough's police career see Andrew Francis Richer, *Bedfordshire Police 1840–1990*, Bedford: Paul Hooley, 1990, p. 12.

2   Thomas Woollaston, *Police Experiences and Reminiscences of Official Life*, West Bromwich: Bates, 1884; new edition published by Berkswich History Society, Stafford, 2007.

3   Clive Emsley and Robert D. Storch, 'Prosecution and the Police in England since 1700', *IAHCCJ Bulletin*, 18 (1993), pp. 45–57. The quotation is from BPP, 1854–55 (481) XII, *Select Committee on Public Prosecutors*, q. 2396.

4   David Philips and Robert D. Storch, *Policing Provincial England, 1829–1856: The Politics of Reform*, London: Leicester University Press, 1999, pp. 85–92.

5   BPP, 1852–53 (603) XXXVI, *First Report from the Select Committee on Police*, qq.1004–1113, 1205–1324 and 1929–2044.

6   Henry Goddard, *Memoirs of a Bow Street Runner*, London: Museum Press, 1956.

7   Maureen Janet Scollan, 'Parish Constables versus Police Constables: Policing Early Nineteenth-Century Essex', Ph.D, Open University, 2007, pp. 173–6, 188 and 190; *Bedfordshire Times*, 10 January 1846; Woollaston, *Police Experiences*, pp. 4–6.

8   David J. Cox, ' "A Certain Share of Low Cunning": An Analysis of the Work of Bow Street Principal Officers 1792–1839, with Particular Emphasis on the Provincial Duties', Ph.D, Lancaster University, 2006, pp. 22–3.

9   Bernard Elliot, 'Leicestershire's First Chief Constable – Frederick Goodyer (1839–1876)', *Journal of the Police History Society*, 3 (1988), pp. 95–6.

10 B.J. Davey, *Lawless and Immoral: Policing a Country Town, 1838–1857*, Leicester: Leicester University Press, 1983.

11 John Field, 'Police Power and Community in an English Provincial Town: Portsmouth, 1815–1875', in Victor Bailey, ed., *Policing and Punishment in Nineteenth-Century Britain*, London: Croom Helm, 1981, p. 49; Scollan, 'Parish Constables versus Police Constables', chapter 6; Roger Swift, *Police Reform in Early Victorian York, 1835–1856*, York: Borthwick Paper no. 73, 1988, pp. 8–10.

12 I am grateful to my colleague Chris A. Williams for sharing with me the considerable research that he has done on the life and career of George Bakewell.

13 The Bolton force, the smallest of the three, became little more than an appendage of the Manchester Police when its Chief Constable, Lt. Col. E.A. Angelo, resigned in October 1839. The Manchester Police were commanded by Sir Charles Shaw, another veteran of the Napoleonic Wars who had more recently fought in the intervention in Spain. Stanley H. Palmer, *Police and Protest in England and Ireland, 1780–1850*, Cambridge: Cambridge University Press, 1988, pp. 438–40.

14 Michael Weaver, 'The New Science of Policing: Crime and the Birmingham Police Force, 1839–1842', *Albion*, 26, 2 (1994), pp. 289–308; F.C. Mather, *Public Order in the Age of the Chartists*, Manchester: Manchester University Press, 1959, pp.121–7.

15   Chris A. Williams, 'The Sheffield Democrats' critique of criminal
      justice in the 1850s', in Robert Colls and Richard Rodger, eds.,
      *Cities of Ideas: Civil Society and Urban Governance in Britain
      1800–2000*, Aldershot: Ashgate, 2004, pp. 96–120.

16   John E. Archer, *'By a Flash and a Scare': Arson, Animal Maiming,
      and Poaching in East Anglia 1815–1870*, Oxford: Clarendon Press,
      1990, p. 13; Leslie C. Jacobs, *Constables of Suffolk: A Brief History of
      Policing in the County*, Ipswich: Suffolk Constabulary, 1992, p. 64;
      Clive Emsley, ' "The Thump of Wood on a Swede Turnip":
      Police Violence in Nineteenth-Century England', *Criminal Justice
      History*, 6 (1985), pp. 125–49.

17   H.O. 45.6811, Chairman of Cheshire Police Committee to Lewis,
      20 December 1859; Chief Constable of Cumberland and
      Westmoreland to Lewis, 23 December 1859; Chief Constable of
      Kent to Waddington (Under Secretary of State), 13 January 1860;
      McHardy to Waddington, 16 August 1860.

18   Anonymous [Thomas Hall], *The Life, Adventures, and Opinions of a
      Liverpool Policeman and his Contemporaries*, Part One, Liverpool,
      1841, pp. 249–54.

19   Clive Emsley, *The English Police: A Political and Social History*,
      2nd edn, London: Longman, 1996, pp. 45–6 and 49–54.

Chapter 4: Further Afield: A United Kingdom, an Empire and Two Models

1   David Martin Smale, 'The Development of the New Police in the
      Scottish Borders c.1840–1890', Ph.D, Open University, 2008,
      especially chapter 4.

2   Edinburgh City Archives, Edinburgh Police: Minute Book of
      Watching Committee, 16 April 1839–16 June 1844, ff. 172–3.

3   David G. Barrie, *Police in the Age of Improvement: Police Development
      and the Civic Tradition in Scotland, 1775–1865*, Cullompton: Willan
      Publishing, 2008; John McGowan, 'The Emergence of Modern
      Civil Police in Scotland: A Case Study of the Police and Systems of
      Police in Edinburghshire,
      1800–1833', Ph.D, Open University, 1996, especially chapter 2.
      Most of the following paragraphs draw on Barrie's book.

4   See, for example, Duncan Grant, *The Thin Blue Line: The Story of*

the City of Glasgow Police, London: Long, 1973, and Hamish Irvine, *The Diced Cap*, Aberdeen: City of Aberdeen Corporation, 1972.

5   Edinburgh City Archives, Edinburgh Police: Minute Book of the General Commissioners, 6 July 1812–4 October 1819, ff. 126–7, 165 and 371–6.

6   For the Peace Preservation Force and the beginnings of the Irish Constabulary, see Galen Broeker, *Rural Disorder and Police Reform in Ireland, 1812–1836*, London: Routledge, 1970, and Stanley H. Palmer, *Police and Protest in England and Ireland, 1780–1850*, Cambridge: Cambridge University Press, 1988.

7   Elizabeth Malcolm, *The Irish Policeman 1822–1922: A Life*, Dublin: Four Courts Press, 2006; Gary Owens, 'The Carrickshock Incident, 1831: Social Memory and an Irish *cause célèbre*', *Cultural and Social History*, 1, 1 (2004), pp. 36–64.

8   Palmer, *Police and Protest*, pp. 403–5; Brian Griffin, *The Bulkies: Police and Crime in Belfast, 1800–1865*, Dublin: Irish Academic Press, 1997, p. 24,

9   B.C. Jerrard, 'The Gloucestershire Police in the 19th Century', M.Litt., University of Bristol, 1977, pp. 61–2, 70 and 78; David Philips, *Crime and Authority in Victorian England*, London: Croom Helm, 1977, pp. 65, 73 and 76.

10   Gwyn A. Williams, *The Merthyr Rising*, London: Croom Helm, 1978; David J.V. Jones, *Rebecca's Children: A Study of Rural Society, Crime and Protest*, Oxford: Clarendon Press, 1989; Richard W. Ireland, ' "A Second Ireland"? Crime and Popular Culture in Nineteenth-Century Wales', in Richard McMahon, ed., *Crime, Law and Popular Culture in Europe, 1500–1900*, Cullompton: Willan Publishing, 2008.

11   David Philips, *William Augustus Miles (1796–1851): Crime, Policing and Moral Entrepreneurship in England and Australia*, Department of History, University of Melbourne, 2001, quotations at pp. 139 and 159.

12   Richard S. Hill, *Policing the Colonial Frontier: The Theory and Practice of Coercive Social and Racial Control in New Zealand, 1767–1867*, Wellington, NZ: V.R. Ward, Government Printer, 1986, especially, pp. 122–3, 131–4 and 148–9.

13   Robert Haldane, *The People's Force: A History of the Victoria Police*,

2nd edn, Melbourne: Melbourne University Press, 1995, especially pp. 20–36, 48–9 and 57.

14   Haldane, *People's Force*, chapter 3; John McQuilton, 'Police in Rural Victoria: A Regional Example', in Mark Finnane, ed., *Policing in Australia: Historical Perspectives*, Kensington, NSW: New South Wales University Press, 1987; W. Ross Johnston, *The Long Blue Line: A History of the Queensland Police*, Brisbane: Boolarong Publications, 1992, pp. 25–6.

15   The figure of 14 RIC men is given in Lorne and Caroline Brown, *An Unauthorized History of the RCMP*, Toronto: Jasper Lorimer, 1978, p. 14. See also R.C. MacLeod, *The NWMP and Law Enforcement 1873–1905*, Toronto; University of Toronto Press, 1976, chapter 6.

16   S.W Horrall, 'Sir John A. Macdonald and the Mounted Police Force for the Northwest Territories', *Canadian Historical Review*, 53, 2 (1972), pp. 179–200; Sir Joseph Pope, ed., *Correspondence of Sir John Macdonald*, Toronto: Oxford University Press, 1921, p. 128.

17   David Neal, *The Rule of Law in a Penal Colony: Law and Power in Early New South Wales*, Cambridge: Cambridge University Press, 1991, pp. 150–4.

18   Richard Hawkins, 'The "Irish Model" and the Empire: A Case for Reassessment', in David M. Anderson and David Killingray, eds, *Policing the Empire: Government, Authority and Control, 1830–1940*, Manchester: Manchester University Press, 1991, makes a powerful case that there was no real 'Irish Model'.

19   Georgina Sinclair, *At the End of the Line: Colonial Policing and the Imperial Endgame, 1945–80*, Manchester: Manchester University Press, 2006, pp. 24–30.

20   Clive Emsley, *Gendarmes and the State in Nineteenth-Century Europe*, Oxford: Oxford University Press, 1999.

21   *New York Times*, 9 December 1857. See also, Wilbur R. Miller, *Cops and Bobbies: Police Authority in New York and London, 1830-1870*, 2nd edn, Columbus, OH: Ohio State University Press, 1999.

Chapter 5: 'An Institution Rather than a Man': The Victorian Police Officer, 1860–1880

1   [A. Wynter], 'The Police and Thieves', *Quarterly Review*, XCIX (1856), pp. 160–200; at p. 171.

2   Hennessy's Notebook is in the MPHC; there is a copy in the OUPA.

3   MPHC, *Report on the Condition of the Metropolitan Police Stations, 14 April 1881*; MPHC, MS Property Register, pre-1890.

4   Charles Tempest Clarkson and J. Hall Richardson, *Police!*, London: Field and Tuer, 1889, p. 141.

5   Timothy Cavanagh, *Scotland Yard Past and Present: Experiences of Thirty-Seven Years*, London: Chatto and Windus, 1893, pp. 36–45; Tom Divall, *Scoundrels and Scallywags (And Some Honest Men)*, London: Ernest Benn, 1929, p. 24.

6   Booth Online B354, pp. 68–77.

7   Between 1869 and 1887 the Annual Reports of the Metropolitan Police Commissioner, submitted to Parliament and printed as Parliamentary Papers, contained reports from the divisional superintendents. The references here are taken from the reports from the Superintendent of 'E' Division.

8   Cavanagh, *Scotland Yard*, pp. 22–3.

9   Cavanagh, *Scotland Yard*, p. 28.

10   'Custos', *The Police Force of the Metropolis in 1868*, London: Ridgway, 1868, p. 13.

11   Cavanagh, *Scotland Yard*, pp. 24–7.

12   OBSP, 18621124-36. For garrotting see Jennifer Davis, 'The London Garrotting Panic of 1862, A Moral Panic and the Creation of a Criminal Class in Mid-Victorian England', in V.A.C. Gatrell, Bruce Lenman and Geoffrey Parker, eds, *Crime and the Law: The Social History of Crime in Western Europe since 1500*, London: Europa, 1980; Rob Sindall, *Street Violence in the Nineteenth Century: Media Panic or Real Danger?*, Leicester: Leicester University Press, 1990.

13   *Police Service Advertiser*, 17 February, 10 and 31 March 1866; *Parlty Debates*, 16 February 1866, col. 597; see also 8 March, cols. 1737–47.

14   'Reports from the Superintendent of E Division'.

15   OBSP, t18610819-683 and t18661022-939.

16 OBSP, t18561124-87; *Times*, 28 January 1857, p. 11.

17 Custos, *Police Force*, pp. 8–9.

18 Paul Lawrence, ' "Scoundrels and scallywags, and some honest men . . ." Memoirs and the Self-Image of French and English Policemen c.1870–1939', in Barry Godfrey, Clive Emsley and Graeme Dunstall, eds, *Comparative Histories of Crime*, Cullompton: Willan Publishing, 2003; Haia Shpayer-Makov, 'Explaining the Rise and Success of Detective Memoirs in Britian', in Clive Emsley and Haia Shpayer-Makov, eds, *Police Detectives in History, 1750–1950*, Aldershot: Ashgate, 2006. The books by the three officers mentioned are Andrew Lansdowne, *A Life's Reminiscences at Scotland Yard*, London: Leadenhall Press, 1890; John George Littlechild, *The Reminiscences of Inspector Littlechild*, London: Leadenhall Press, 1894; Benjamin Leeson, *Lost London*, London: Stanley Paul, 1934.

19 BPP, 1867 (14) XXXVI, *Report of Her Majesty's Inspectors of Constabulary for 1865–66*, p. 20.

20 Copies of PC Jackson's diaries are in the OUPA.

21 BPP, 1874 (1) XXVIII, *Report of Her Majesty's Inspectors of Constabulary for 1872–73*, p. 25.

22 Jerome Caminada, *Twenty-Five Years of Detective Life*, Manchester: John Heywood, 1895. Parts of the book were republished with an introduction by Peter Riley, Prism Books, Warrington, 1982 and 1985. The page references are from the 1982 edition; in this instance pp. 22–3.

23 Caminada, *Twenty-Five Years*, pp. 62, 66 and 69.

24 Caminada, *Twenty-Five Years*, p. 19.

25 See, for example, *Manchester Times*, 28 February 1874, 18 April 1874, 23 October 1875, 23 March 1878 and 7 February 1880 for Caminada appearing in court with suspected pickpockets that he had observed and arrested.

26 *Reynolds's Newspaper*, 26 December 1875, p. 3.

27 Andrew Davies, *The Gangs of Manchester. The Story of the Scuttlers: Britain's First Youth Cult*, Preston: Milo Books, 2008, pp. 232–3 and 302–3.

28 Clive Emsley and Mark Clapson, 'Recruiting the English Policeman c.1840–1940', *Policing and Society*, 3 (1994), pp. 269–86; Haia Shpayer-Makov, *The Making of a Policeman: A Social History of a*

Labour Force in Metropolitan London, 1829–1840, Aldershot: Ashgate, 2002, chapters 1 and 2.

Chapter 6: Hard Men and Harder Coppers: Bobby on the Front Line, 1860–1914

1   BPP, 1875 (352) XIII, *Select Committee on Police Superannuation Funds*, q. 1614.

2   Frederick Engels, *The Condition of the Working Class in England in 1844*, London: George Allen and Unwin, 1952, p. 53; Alexis de Tocqueville, *Journeys to England and Ireland*, New York: Anchor Books, 1968, p. 96.

3   Jerome Caminada, *Twenty-Five Years of Detective Life*, 1982 edn, Warrington: Prism Books, p. 7.

4   Andrew Davies, *The Gangs of Manchester: The Story of the Scuttlers: Britain's First Youth Cult*, Preston: Milo Books, 2008.

5   Superintendent [James] Bent, *Criminal Life: Reminiscences of Forty-Two Years as a Police Officer*, London: J. Heywood, 1891; Richard Jervis, *Lancashire's Crime and Criminals*, Southport: J.J. Riley, 1908.

6   Clive Emsley, *Hard Men: Violence in England since 1750*, London: Hambledon, 2005, especially chapter 8.

7   David Taylor, *Policing the Victorian Town: The Development of the Police in Middlesbrough c.1840–1914*, Basingstoke: Palgrave Macmillan, 2002, pp. 84–94.

8   *Birmingham Daily Gazette*, 11 May 1867.

9   *Birmingham Daily Post*, 8, 25, 26 and 29 March 1875.

10 CBOA, Booth B346, pp. 31–3.

11 Tom Divall, *Scoundrels and Scallywags (And Some Honest Men)*, London: Ernest Benn, 1929, pp. 12–17; OUPA, 'The Memoirs of Chief Inspector John Monk, 1859–1946', p. 29.

12 See, for example, Hugh R.P. Gamon, *The London Police Court: Today and Tomorrow*, London: Dent, 1907, pp. 26–7.

13 *Birmingham Daily Post*, 15 August 1862; *Liverpool Mercury*, 28 August 1862; Bent, *Criminal Life*, pp. 75–80.

14 BPP, *Report on Disturbances at Rotherhithe on June 11th 1912, and Complaints against the Conduct of the Police in connection therewith*, 1912, Cmd. 6367; *Southwark and Bermondsey Recorder*, 14 June 1912.

15 John E. Archer, 'Poaching Gangs and Violence: The Urban-Rural Divide in Nineteenth-Century Lancashire', *British Journal of Criminology*, 39, 1 (1999), pp. 25–38; H. Kenneth Birch, *The History of Policing in North Wales*, Pwllheli: Gwalch, 2008, p. 163.

16 L. Perry Curtis, Jr., *Jack the Ripper and the London Press*, New Haven and London: Yale University Press, 2001; Kate Summerscale, *The Suspicions of Mr Whicher: or, The Murder at Road Hill House*, London: Bloomsbury, 2008, p. 223.

17 *Birmingham Daily Post*, 26 March 1875.

18 *Police Guardian*, 25 January 1884.

19 Quoted in Wilbur R. Miller, *Cops and Bobbies: Police Authority in New York and London, 1830–1870*, 2nd edn, Columbus, OH: Ohio State University Press, 1999, pp. 126–7.

20 'Ask a P'liceman', words E.W. Rogers, music A.E. Durandeau. My thanks to Ed Hayward and his unrivalled knowledge of the Music Hall for information on this song.

21 Clive Emsley, ' "The Thump of Wood on a Swede Turnip": Police Violence in Nineteenth-Century England', *Criminal Justice History*, 6 (1985), pp. 125–49; Robert W. Gould and Michael J. Waldren, *London's Armed Police*, London: Arms and Armour Press, 1986, chapters 2 and 3.

22 H.O. 45.9700.A50158, Correspondence re. revolvers for Herts Police, 1891; MEPO 2:163, Correspondence etc. re. arming, 1883–7, Report from P Division, Farnborough Station, 18 February 1887.

23 Justin Wasserman and Edwin Jaggard, 'Electoral Violence in Mid-Nineteenth-Century England and Wales', *Historical Research*, 80, no. 207 (2007), pp. 124–55.

24 Thomas Woollaston, *Police Experiences and Reminiscences of Official Life*, West Bromwich: J. Bates, 1884, pp. 190–9.

25 *Times*, 24 March 1870.

26 *Daily News*, 1 December 1885; *Derby Mercury*, 2 December 1885; *Hull Packet*, 4 December 1885; *Times*, 9, 15 and 17 December 1885 and 13 January 1886.

27 *Report of the Departmental Committee on the Duties of the Police with Respect to the Preservation of Order at Public Meetings*, Cmd. 4674, London, 1909, q. 573.

28 Brian Harrison, 'The Act of Militancy: Violence and the

Suffragettes 1904–1914', in Brian Harrison, ed., *Peaceable Kingdom: Stability and Change in Modern Britain*, Oxford: Clarendon Press, 1982; quotation at p. 63.

29 Fran Abrams, *Freedom's Cause: Lives of the Suffragettes*, London: Profile Books, 2003, p. 148.

30 Bernard Porter, *The Origins of the Vigilant State: The London Metropolitan Police Special Branch Before the First World War*, London: Weidenfeld and Nicolson, 1987.

31 Angus McLaren, *A Prescription for Murder: The Victorian Serial Killings of Dr Thomas Neill Cream*, Chicago: University of Chicago Press, 1993, pp. 107–10; *Reynolds's News*, 19 December 1880; *Newcastle Courant*, 31 December 1880; *Times*, 14 December 1881.

32 George Dilnot, *Trial of the Detectives*, London: Bles, 1928.

33 *John Bull*, 26 March 1949, pp. 16–17.

34 MPHC, Inspector Richard Tanner, 'Prisoners' Apprehension Notebook'; OBSP t18641024-920.

35 Taylor, *Policing the Victorian Town*, pp. 47–8.

36 Edwin Chadwick, 'On the Consolidation of Police Force and the Prevention of Crime', *Fraser's Magazine*, LXXVII (1868), pp. 1–18; at p. 16.

37 Bob Dobson, *Policing in Lancashire 1839–1989*, Blackpool: Landy Publishing, 1989, p. 36; Jervis, *Lancashire's Crime and Criminals*, p. 77.

38 'The Memoirs of . . . Monk', pp. 18–19 and 42; *Times*, 11 July 1868, p. 11; *Report on Disturbances at Rotherhithe*, p. 5.

39 *Police Review*, 28 December 1900, p. 614, and 1 May 1908, pp. 210 and 215.

40 Clive Emsley, *The English Police: A Political and Social History*, 2nd edn, London: Longman, 1996, pp. 95–9.

41 *Police Service Advertiser*, 26 January 1867; *Police Review*, 2 January 1893, p. 1.

42 *Police Review*, 9 January 1893, p. 16.

43 *Police Service Advertiser*, 26 January and 25 May 1867.

44 *Police Review*, 26 January (pp. 45–46), 2 February (p. 54) and 16 March 1894 (pp. 127–8).

45 *Police Service Advertiser*, 13 and 27 April 1867.

46 *Police Review*, 19 June 1908, p. 295.

47 See, inter alia, Gerald W. Reynolds and Anthony Judge, *The Night*

the Police Went on Strike, London: Weidenfeld and Nicolson, 1968, chapter 2; V.L. Allen, 'The National Union of Police and Prison Officers', *Economic History Review*, 11 (1958–9), pp. 133–43.

Chapter 7: War, Women and Wages: Policing the Home Front, 1914–1918

1   *Mr Punch's History of the Great War*, London: Cassell, 1919, p. 1; *Times*, 27 July 1914, p. 6.

2   Information on the origins of the women police is drawn primarily from Philippa Levine, ' "Walking the Streets in a Way No Decent Woman Should": Women Police in World War I', *Journal of Modern History*, 66 (1994), pp. 34–78; Joan Lock, *The British Policewoman: Her Story*, London: Robert Hale, 1979; and R.M. Douglas, *Feminist Freikorps: The British Voluntary Women Police, 1914–1940*, Westport, CT: Praeger, 1999.

3   Imperial War Museum, Dept. of Manuscripts 77/156/1, Journals of Miss G.M. West; Dept of Sound Records 8890/02/01-02, Interview with Miss G.M. West.

4   Levine, ' "Walking the Streets" ', p. 64; Lilian Gladys King, 'Among the Beavers', my thanks to Maureen Scollan for showing me a copy of this typescript.

5   Quoted in Douglas, *Feminist Freikorps*, pp. 51–52.

6   Lilian Wyles, *A Woman at Scotland Yard*, London: Faber and Faber, 1952, p. 28.

7   Ronald Seth, *The Specials: The Story of the Special Constabulary*, London: Victor Gollancz, 1961, chapters 6 and 7.

8   *Times*, 19 and 20 June 1919; for the general problem of disorder see David Englander, 'Police and Public Order in Britain 1914–1918', in Clive Emsley and Barbara Weinberger, eds, *Policing Western Europe: Politics, Professionalism and Public Order, 1850–1940*, New York: Greenwood Press, 1991.

9   Information on the police strikes is drawn largely from Gerald W. Reynolds and Anthony Judge, *The Night the Police Went on Strike*, London: Weidenfeld and Nicolson, 1968; for the important provincial contrasts see, in particular, Joanne Klein, 'Blue-Collar Job, Blue-Collar Career: Policemen's Perplexing Struggle for a Voice in Birmingham, Liverpool and Manchester, 1900–1919',

Crime, histoire et sociétés/Crime, history and societies, 6, 1 (2002), pp. 5–29.

10   BPP, *Report of the Committee on the Police Service of England, Wales and Scotland, Evidence*, 1920, Cmd. 874, XXII, 573, qq. 1847, 1854, 2397 and 2401.

11   BPP, *Report ... on the Police Service*, qq. 2345 and 2365.

12   BPP, *Report of the Mackenzie Committee*, 1924, Cmd. 2297.

13   There is scarcely an edition of *The Bull's Eye* that does not mention militarization; for criticism of Hall-Dalwood, see 1920, nos. 5 (p. 7) and 9 (p. 1); for the 'M.P.' poem, see no. 11; for criticism of the Emergency Powers Act, see no. 7 (p. 4); for concerns about militarization and the Irish experience, see 1921, nos. 2 (p. 1) and 3 (pp. 1–3).

14   Elizabeth Malcolm, *The Irish Policeman, 1822–1922: A Life*, Dublin: Four Courts Press, 2006, pp. 199–200. The following paragraphs draw principally on Malcolm and Donal J. O'Sullivan, *The Irish Constabularies, 1822–1922: A Century of Policing in Ireland*, Dingle, Co. Kerry: Brandon, 1999.

15   Patrick Shea, *Voices and the Sound of Drums: An Irish Autobiography*, Belfast: Blackstaff Press, 1981.

16   O'Sullivan, *Irish Constabularies*, pp. 375–80.

Chapter 8: Good Cop, Bad Cop: Bobby Between the Wars, 1919–1939

1   For the Goddard affair see Clive Emsley, 'Sergeant Goddard: The Story of a Rotten Apple, or a Diseased Orchard?', in Amy Gilman Srebnick and René Lévy, eds, *Crime and Cultures: An Historical Perspective*, Aldershot: Ashgate, 2005.

2   OUPA, Charles J. Hanslow, 'Police Service Memories', p. 11.

3   *Times*, 12 July 1924, p. 12, and 6 June 1931, p. 9.

4   *People*, 18 March 1928, p. 10.

5   MEPO 10/9, Case of Sir Almeric Fitzroy.

6   BPP, *Report of an Inquiry held by the Right Hon. J.F.P. Rawlinson KC MP, into the arrest of Major R.O. Sheppard*, 1924–5, Cmd. 2497, XV, 1049; *Times*, 31 May 1928, p. 11, and for the Miss Adele story see the popular press throughout August and September, and e.g. *Times* 6, 10, 13, 23 and 30 August and 12, 13 and 15 September.

I am grateful to John Carter Wood for sight of his research into the case of Helene Adele; her full name was never released to the press or the public.

7   Lilian Wyles, *A Woman at Scotland Yard*, London: Faber and Faber, 1952, pp. 184–203; Joan Lock, *The British Policewoman: Her Story*, London: Robert Hale, pp. 57–72; see also, BPP, *Report of the Tribunal . . . in Regard to the Interrogation of Miss Savidge by the Police*, 1928, Cmd. 3147, XII, 87.

8   Louise A. Jackson, *Women Police: Gender, Welfare and Surveillance in the Twentieth Century*, Manchester: Manchester University Press, 2006, pp. 186–7.

9   BPP, *Report of the Royal Commission on Police Powers and Procedure*, London, Cmd. 3297.

10   Jackson, *Women Police*, pp. 49 and 58–9; R.M. Douglas, *Feminist Freikorps; The British Voluntary Women Police, 1914–1940*, Westport, CT: Praeger, 1999, pp. 18, 20 and 73–4; Louise Jackson, ' "Lady Cops" and "Decoy Doras": Gender, Surveillance and the Construction of Urban Knowledge 1919–59', *London Journal*, 27, 1 (2002), pp. 63–83; at pp. 65–8.

11   Harry Daley, *This Small Cloud: A Personal Memoir*, London: Weidenfeld and Nicolson, 1986, p. 112.

12   *Justice of the Peace*, 27 June 1927, p. 489.

13   Jerry White, *The Worst Street in North London: Campbell Bunk Islington Between the Wars*, London: Routledge and Kegan Paul, 1986, p. 115.

14   OUPA, Edward Lyscom, 'London Policeman', pp. 35–6.

15   OUPA, H.B. Green, 'A Policeman's Tale', p. 43.

16   Mike Brogden, *On the Mersey Beat: Policing Liverpool Between the Wars*, Oxford: Oxford University Press, 1991, pp. 97 and 109.

17   OUPA, Interview with Arthur Pickering (1987).

18   MEPO 3/346, The Epsom Hold-Up.

19   Sir Percy Sillitoe, *Cloak Without Dagger*, London: Cassell and Co., 1955, pp. 63–7.

20   Clive Emsley, ed., 'The Recollections of a Provincial Policeman: Arthur Ernest Almond', *Journal of the Police History Society*, 3 (1988), pp. 53–66; at p. 58.

21   OUPA, 'The Police Service of George Frederick Fancourt, Birmingham City Police, 1929–1960', pp. 5–6.

22   Brogden, *On the Mersey Beat*, p. 120.

23   Daley, *This Small Cloud*, pp. 94–5; and for the clean-up, see pp. 108–9.

24   OUPA, Interview with Nat Turner (1987); Daley, *This Small Cloud*, pp. 149–51; Brogden, *On the Mersey Beat*, pp. 124–8.

25   Daley, *This Small Cloud*, pp. 172–4; Green, 'A Policeman's Tale', p. 35.

26   Lyscom, 'London Policeman', p. 92; see also, MPHC, Arthur Battle, 'This job's not like it used to be', p. 52; Victor Meek, *Cops and Robbers*, London: Duckworth, 1962, p. 18.

27   Green, 'A Policeman's Tale', p. 19.

28   David S. Wall, *The Chief Constables of England and Wales: The socio-legal history of a criminal justice elite*, Aldershot; Ashgate, 1998, pp. 213–20.

29   Quoted in Brogden, *On the Mersey Beat*, pp. 80–1.

30   C.A. Vince, *History of the Corporation of Birmingham, vol. III (1885-1899)*, Birmingham Corporation, 1902, p. 219.

31   Clive Emsley, ' "Mother, What *did* Policemen do when there weren't any motors?" The Law, the Police and the Regulation of Motor Traffic in England, 1900–1939', *Historical Journal*, 36, 2 (1993), pp. 357–81.

32   Green, 'A Policeman's Tale', pp. 31 and 42.

33   Emsley, ed., 'The Recollections of a Provincial Policeman', p. 65.

34   Battle, 'This job's not like it used to be', p. 30.

35   OUPA, Interview with Clifford Jeeves (1987).

36   John Bunker, *From Rattle to Radio*, Studley, Warks: Brewin Books, 1988, chapter 4; Clive Emsley, *The English Police: A Political and Social History*, 2nd edn, London: Longman, 1996, p. 209.

37   Emsley, ed., 'The Recollections of a Provincial Policeman', pp. 59–61; Daley, *This Small Cloud*, pp. 114–15.

38   OUPA, 'Police Service of . . . Fancourt', pp. 4–5.

39   OUPA, Interview with Pickering; Interview with Turner.

40   Emsley, ed., 'The Recollections of a Provincial Policeman', passim.

Chapter 9: A New War, a New World, 1939–1970

1   MPHC, Arthur Battle, 'This job's not like it used to be', pp. 75–6.

2   OUPA, Interview with Horace Rogers (1987).

3   OUPA, Interview with Arthur Pickering (1987).

4   A.A. Clarke, *The Policemen of Hull*, Beverley: Hutton Press, 1992,
     p. 114; *London Police Pensioner*, 121 (June, 2006), p. 13, 122
     (September, 2006), pp. 5–6 and 123 (December, 2006), pp. 2–3;
     Harry Daley, *This Small Cloud: A Personal Memoir*, London:
     Weidenfeld and Nicolson, 1986, p. 183.

5   C.H. Rolph, *Living Twice,* London: Victor Gollancz, 1974, p. 163.

6   Battle, 'This job's not like it used to be', pp. 79–80.

7   OUPA, Charles J. Hanslow, 'Police Service Memories', pp. 30–1.

8   OUPA, H.B. Green, 'A Policeman's Tale', p. 57; Daley, *This Small
     Cloud*, pp. 187 and 196–7.

9   OUPA, Interview with Nat Turner (1987); Hanslow, 'Police
     Service Memories', p. 25.

10   Hanslow, 'Police Service Memories', pp. 33–4; Green, 'A
     Policeman's Tale', p. 79.

11   Roy Ingleton, *The Gentlemen at War: Policing Britain 1939–45*,
     Maidstone: Cranborne Publications, 1994, chapter 7; the letter
     from the Chief Constable of Hampshire to the Chief Constable of
     Essex, 6 September 1940, is quoted in Maureen Scollan, 'Women
     in the Police Service', which won third prize in the Queen's Police
     Gold Medal Essay Competition, 1975. (Copy in OUPA.)

12   OUPA, Interview with William Biggs (2007).

13   MPHC, Wellington Arch Occurrence Book.

14   Battle, 'This job's not like it used to be', pp. 109–10.

15   H.O. 45.24155, file 681165/26, Report by Sir Harold Scott,
     10 September 1946.

16   OUPA, Interview with Arthur Pickering (1987); OUPA, Interview
     with Anthony Armstrong (1988); Andrew Francis Richer,
     Bedfordshire Police 1840–1990, Bedford: Paul Hooley, 1990,
     pp. 197–8.

17   Rolph, *Living Twice*, p. 137; John Wainwright, *Wainwright's Beat:
     Twenty Years with the West Yorkshire Police Force*, London: Macmillan,
     1987, p. 5. Sir Robert Mark, who went on to become
     Commissioner of the Metropolitan Police, painted a similar picture
     of men returning from the war to the police in his autobiography,
     In the Office of Constable, London: Collins, 1978, pp. 48–9.

18   Barbara Weinberger, *The Best Police in the World: An Oral History of*

English Policing from the 1930s to the 1960s, Aldershot: Scolar Press, 1995, pp. 98–102.

19   OUPA, Sir Arthur L. Dixon, 'The Emergency Work of the Police Forces in the Second World War', unpublished (1963), pp. 166–7.

20   OUPA, Interview with Eric Royden (2008).

21   Frank Neal, *Sectarian Violence: The Liverpool Experience, 1819 to 1914*, Manchester: Manchester University Press, 1988, especially chapter 5.

22   Eric St Johnston, *One Policeman's Story*, London: Barry Rose, 1978, pp. 167–9.

23   T.A. Critchley, *A History of Police in England and Wales*, revised edn, London: Constable, 1978. Critchley had been a senior member of the Police Department at the Home Office during the 1960s.

24   Quoted in Susan Sydney-Smith, *Beyond Dixon of Dock Green: Early British Police Series*, London: I.B. Tauris, 2002, p. 136.

25   See, for example, Weinberger, *The Best Police in the World*, pp. 198–9.

26   Robert Fabian, *Fabian of the Yard*, London: Naldrett Press, 1950; John Gosling, *The Ghost Squad*, London: W.H. Allen, 1959.

27   Mark, *In the Office of Constable*, pp. 58–9.

28   Interview with Armstrong.

29   Weinberger, *The Best Police in the World*, pp. 197–9; T.A. Critchley, *A History of Police in England and Wales*, revised edn, London: Constable, 1978, pp. 273–5.

Chapter 10: Everything Changes, Everything Stays the Same

1   For the RUC see, inter alia, Graham Ellison and Jim Smyth, *The Crowned Harp: Policing Northern Ireland*, London: Pluto Press, 2000; Chris Ryder, *The RUC: A Force Under Fire*, London: Methuen, 1989.

2   *Statement by the Police Ombudsman for Northern Ireland on her investigation into the circumstances surrounding the death of Raymond McCord Junior and other Matters, 22 January 2007*, pp. 143–4.

3   Private conversation, June 2002.

4   See, inter alia, *Belfast Times*, 16 October 2006, p. 6; *Irish News*,
     11 January 2007, p. 1; and, *Times*, 12 January 2007, p. 3.

[??? Missing .pdf pages of notes]

5   Georgina Sinclair, At the End of the Line: Colonial Policing and
     the Imperial Endgame 1945–80, Manchester: Manchester
     University Press, 2006.

6   An article in the Independent, 20 October 2006, reports the story
     of John Kent, known as 'Black Kent', who served in Carlisle from
     1837 to 1844. Timothy Cavanagh, Scotland Yard Past and Present:
     Experiences of Thirty-Seven Years, London: Chatto and Windus,
     1893, p. 50. Michael Rowe, Policing, Race and Racism,
     Cullompton: Willan, 2004, p. 23, notes that Mohamed Yusuf Daar
     joined the Coventry City Police and Ralph Ramadhar (Britain's
     first 'West Indian' policeman) joined the Birmingham City Police a
     few weeks apart in 1966. For Norwell Roberts, see James
     Whitfield, Unhappy Dialogue: The Metropolitan Police and Black
     Londoners in Post-War Britain, Cullompton: Willan, 2004. I am
     grateful to Jim Whitfield and to Norwell Roberts for permission to
     use their taped interview of 2 April 2002; it forms the basis of
     these paragraphs. I am also grateful to Norwell Roberts for sight of
     some of his newspaper cuttings about his career.

7   David J. Smith and Jeremy Gray, Police and People in London,
     Aldershot: Gower, 1985, pp. 423–6. This is an edited version of
     the 4-volume report by the Policy Studies Institute. See also, Ian
     Loader and Aog·n Mulcahy, Policing and the Condition of
     England: Memory, Politics and Culture, Oxford: Oxford University
     Press, 2003, pp. 218–22.

8   See, for example, Observer, 12 January 2004; 'Who killed PC
     Blakelock?', BBC 2, 2 March 2004.

9   Sir William Macpherson, The Stephen Lawrence Inquiry – Report,
     Cm. 4262-I, 1999.

10   See, inter alia,
     http://computerevidence.co.uk/Cases/Virdi/MPA/Submission.htm;
     http://www.redhotcurry.com/archive/news/2005/gurpal_virdi.htm

11   OUPA, Interview with Maureen Scollan (2008); OUPA Scollan
     Papers.

12   Loader and Mulcahy, Policing and the Condition of England,
     2003, p. 215; see also Barbara Weinberger, The Best Police in the

World: An Oral History of English Policing from the 1930s to the 1960s, Aldershot: Scolar Press, 1995, pp. 98–102.

13   OUPA, Scollan Papers, five letters to her parents JulyñSeptember 1974.

14   Essex Chronicle, 1 August 1975; East Anglian Daily Times, 31 December 1984; Evening Gazette, 31 December 1984.

15   Times, 3 April 2008. For women officers in general at the close of the twentieth century, see Louise Westmarland, Gender and Policing, Cullompton: Willan, 2001.

16   OUPA, Interview with Charles Royden (2008)

17   See, inter alia, Independent, 1 November 1999.

18   Based on talking to Dr Whitfield over several years while he was a research fellow at the Open University, and on a personal communication, drafted at my request in October 2009.

19   Roger Graeff, Talking Blues: The Police in their Own Words, London: Collins Harvill, 1989, p. 74.

20   Guardian, 25 October 2008.

21   My thanks to Professor P.A. Waddington for information on this point and also on the Kratos tactic. See also, Police Review, 28 August 2009, p. 15 and 4 September 2009, p. 16; http://www.ipcc.gov.uk/sycamore_report.pdf

22   See, inter alia, Evening Standard, 2 June 2006; Independent, 3 June 2006; Guardian, 25 November 2006 and 3 November 2007; Times, 3 November 2007.

23   See, for example, Janet Bujra and Jenny Pearce, 'Police on the line: between control and correctness in multi-ethnic contexts of urban unrest', and Mike King, 'From rumour to riot: the 2005 Lozells disorders', both in David Waddington, Fabien Jobard and Mike King, eds. Rioting in the UK and France: A Comparative Analysis, Cullompton: Willan, 2009.

24   Camden New Journal, 15 March 2007, pp. 1–2.

25   Daily Mirror, 14 April 2008.

26   Daily Telegraph, 3 October 2009.

27   Personal communication, 22 October 2009; John W. Buttle, 'A Constructive Critique of the Officer Safety Programme Used in England and Wales', Policing & Society, 17, 2 (2007) pp.164–81

28   Many of the concerns about confrontations with the public, the closing of local police stations and the increasing size of BCUs were

expressed at a seminar on 'The Purpose of Policing' held at the QEII Conference Centre by the Police Federation on 12 January 2008.

29   Adapting to Protest: Nurturing the British Model of Policing, published 25 November 2009, available at http://inspectorates.homeoffice.gov.uk.hmic/docs/ap/G20-final-report.pdf

30   See, for example, Robert Gellately, Backing Hitler: Consent and Coercion in Nzi Germany, Oxford: Oxford University Press, 2001.

31   Times, 28 November 2009, p. 27.

Index